I0728496

The Accidental Heretic

Jo O'Neill

First published in Great Britain in 2026 by Ambergris Publishing

Copyright © 2025 Jo O'Neill

The right of Jo O'Neill to be identified as the author of this work has been asserted by them in accordance with the Copyright, Design and Patents Act 1988.

All rights reserved. No part of this publication may be reproduced, transmitted, or stored in a retrieval system, in any form or by any means, without permission in writing from the publisher, except for brief quotations in reviews or critical articles.

This is a work of fiction inspired by historical events. While some characters, places and incidents are drawn from historical records, others are products of the author's imagination. In all cases dialogue, interior thoughts, and motives are fictionalised. Any resemblance to persons living or dead, outside the historical context, is coincidental.

ISBN 978-1-9193558-0-1

Contents

Prologue - Valencia, March 1756

He was always 'Don Antonio'.

If you please. Like they'd never met a nobleman before. Like he didn't sweat through his linen for a soldier's wage like the rest of them.

There he sat, a foot slung over his thigh, an arm draped over his knee; his crate might have been upholstered in soft leather, his space a well-cut coat.

'Don Antonio has an idea,' Matheo had said.

Some idea. Nine soldiers summoned to a cellar, packed like condemned pigs, claiming territory as men will, with bodies and noise.

'This someone's idea of a billet?'

'Who are we hiding from?

'Oi, my *foot*! Fat oaf.'

'Smells like the devil's armpit in here.'

'That's Felipe's soap.'

'I said armpit, not arse.'

Hoots at that last one. Guffaws. A palm clouted a shoulder, a fist a knee. A beat behind as usual, Barbieri didn't join in. A vinegarish belch frothed up his throat; he blew it out the side of his mouth.

As for Matheo, their sargento, he leaned, arms folded, head tilted where the ceiling began its arch, working a whittled toothpick between his teeth. Barbieri had seen him like this before; his patience a wall against which their banter would crumble. Soon enough, only the candles dared break the silence, their wicks spitting and hissing in time with the men's leaping shadows. Then and only then, without hurry, Matheo plucked the toothpick free, tested its end against his thumb, and spoke.

'Someone's been stealing from us.'

A fact, not an accusation, not yet. Barbieri fixed his gaze on the crease at the top of Matheo's nose.

'First, a few garments. Might have been lost. But now, money.' Matheo narrowed his eyes. 'This I cannot overlook.'

'Quite right,' growled Pedro.

'About time,' added Felipe.

Matheo had them now – chins up, listening. The edge of Barbieri's crate dug into the backs of his thighs. He shifted.

'Don Antonio has a way to reveal the thief,' said Matheo.

Course he does.

And as one, the men turned to Antonio. They trusted him, their cabo, more than soldiers ought after barely a year in the sección. They listened to him, sought his judgement, tested their opinions against his. Don *Puto* Antonio.

Now Antonio regarded each man in turn, idly thumbing the ring on his little finger, its milky quartz stone appearing and vanishing like the moon in its phases. Did Barbieri imagine it, or did his cabo look at him just a little longer? He tried not to blink, and the corner of his left eye began to twitch. The face of innocence, he realised, eludes the man who affects it.

Ramirez, reddish-blonde hair, arms thick as ham hocks, broke the silence. 'Are we to swear an oath?'

'A thief is as like to swear as steal. Fetch a bowl of water.'

Antonio instructed no one in particular, yet Felipe – the youngest, and closest to the door – stood at once and left the group.

While they waited, Antonio muttered something to Miguel, who got up and rolled a barrel into the centre of their circle then set it upright. It settled with a thud. The men straightened. Barbieri's bowels grumbled.

'This isn't a test,' muttered Pedro. 'It's a curse. I've seen this kind of thing in Cadiz. One fellow came out bleeding from his ears.'

'What were you singing?' asked Luca.

'Vafanculo,' said Pedro.

'Not bad,' said Gianni. 'It's Va-fan-*cul*-o. Capisci? Say it like you mean it.'

'Ca*pis*ci this,' Pedro thrust his thumb into his fist – no mistaking *that* insult.

The silence cracked again. Like boys they were, comparing profanities in Spanish and Italian. Voices stirred into a low rumble, gathering, building…

Matheo straightened, folded his arms and narrowed his eyes. A small shift. A warning. Clear enough. The noise stopped.

Seconds dragged. The cellar pressed in. Its fug clotted in Barbieri's throat and nostrils – damp stone, fumes from the barrels, rodent shit, and too many unwashed men. A slow drip marked time, and now that he noticed it, he couldn't *un*notice: a rusted wine tap, maybe, or an overfilled gutter outside. His guts folded over. He belched up a huge silent bubble of bile.

Then Felipe reappeared, taking such care not to spill from his bowl, he walked like he clutched a book between his knees.

'Set it down.' Antonio jerked his chin at the barrel.

Felipe did as bid, then took a step back, just one, poised for another instruction.

'The test is simple.' In the dim light, Antonio's dark eyes appeared black. 'This water will show us the thief, by way of a mark.'

An intake of breath. Sideways glances. Frowns – only from the Spanish, Barbieri noticed. All Luca and Gianni seemed to mind was the interruption to their drinking.

'What unholy magic is this?' asked Felipe.

'*Thou shalt not steal*,' said Matheo. 'Nothing unholy about it.'

'It needs darkness,' said Antonio. 'Gather round.' He winked. 'We don't need Miguel stumbling around with the candles out.'

Was that supposed to be funny? More to the point, were they really doing this? Pedro crossed himself, Felipe likewise. Miguel chewed the inside of his cheek. Gianni and Luca sniggered. But each man took their position, and not a single one objected. Barbieri slid behind Esteban; the serious Castilian wore anonymity like a cloak – one worth sharing.

Matheo extinguished all but one candle, which he carried to the entranceway. Against the light of the passage outside, he faded to a shape, and as he pulled the door closed, a ghoul, his features glimmering against the flame below his chin.

'Hold your right hands over the cup. When I call your name. Dip your finger just for a moment.'

Matheo snuffed out his flame, and Antonio began his solemn reciting – his voice low, echoing, accompanied by lapping water.

Barbieri passed on his turn. Nothing, not his cabo, not his camaradas, not even his own mother – God rest her – could induce him to place his finger in that water.

After the last man had been called and Matheo had opened the door, they gathered in the light, the guilty and the innocent, checking their hands, mumbling and muttering.

Barbieri shifted from foot to foot. Why did they wait? Why didn't *Don* Antonio speak? Had his precious plan not worked? Enough. He jabbed his finger into the air, high for all to see. 'There is no mark on me.'

When silence falls fast, it can be loud as thunder. All eyes shifted towards him. Gianni lifted his eyebrows, Ramirez scowled, Pedro shook his head.

Then, as if responding to an unspoken command, all the men raised their right hands together. Every single one bore a mark, a grey index finger.

Barbieri scrambled to understand. He turned to Antonio. To Matheo. Back to Antonio. Neither spoke. They didn't need to. Antonio's gaze shifted. Barbieri followed it, to his own hand, the only clean one. He snatched his arm down, cheeks aflame.

'Our thief.' Antonio didn't proclaim the words. Worse, he sighed them.

Barbieri stumbled backwards, shaking his head, waggling his finger. 'No. No. Naught but a trick. A deceit.' But all the time his thoughts bumped and tumbled, and one fell out: How?

'Jorge Barbieri.' His name, Matheo's voice, sharp against the walls. 'You've betrayed your own sección, and that is a grave thing. I could hand you over to the civil authorities as a thief.'

He swallowed jagged air. He knew the penalty, they all did – crowd control at La Plaza del Mercado was a regular duty – public flogging: a horror and a spectacle.

'Sargento,' Antonio said, 'he didn't steal from me, so perhaps it's not my place –' He looked at Miguel, then Pedro. '– would restitution suffice?'

'It's all I need,' said Miguel, shooting a filthy look at Barbieri.

'I won't turn on a camarada,' said Pedro. 'Even an arsehole.'

Barbieri stared at the dirt floor and imagined crawling beneath it; nothing could be worse than this.

Not true. There was something worse. Antonio pleading for him. Being indebted to a trickster and a… He searched the faces of his comrades, but none looked as shocked as they ought. How had they not seen? 'A trick of the devil.' The words spilled from his mouth unbidden, and with them came certainty.

But Antonio barely reacted. Perhaps a flicker, a widening of his eyes, before he smoothed his features into their usual mask. Such calm was bile in Barbieri's mouth; he spat it onto the ground. 'Sorcerer,' he said.

They gave him nothing but silence and raised eyebrows; Gianni and Ramirez exchanged a glance and rolled their eyes. *Rolled their eyes.*

'You would do well to remember that I've not determined your punishment,' Matheo said. 'Contrition will serve you better than accusation.'

Barbieri shook his head, then caught himself. They were in no mood to listen. Not now, in any case.

'You'll be confined to your quarters while I decide,' Matheo said. 'Pedro and Miguel will escort you so that you may return what's theirs. I suggest you reflect.'

Barbieri trudged from the cellar, the two soldiers flanking him, five pairs of eyes burning into the back of his neck.

Antonio's presence snagged him as he passed. Unbearably close, impossible to ignore, that sureness, that look of… what was it? Pity?

Barbieri leaned into his face and hissed a last insult.

'Heretic.'

Part One - Sic Fiat

So Let It Be Done

Articles of Faith for Conduct of Activities of the Inquisition of Spain. Issued by Tomás Torquemada to the General Assembly of Inquisidors, Seville, 1474.

Article VII
As the crime of heresy is a very heinous one, it is desired that the reconciled may realise by the penances imposed upon them how gravely they have offended and sinned against Our Lord Jesus Christ.

Article XI
If any heretic or apostate who shall have been arrested upon information laid against him should say that he desires reconciliation and confess all his faults, and what is known to him of the faults of others, the Inquisidors shall admit him to reconciliation subject to perpetual imprisonment as by law prescribed.

Article XV
If the said crime of heresy or apostasy is half proven – *semiplenamente provado* – the Inquisidors may put the accused to torture, and if under torture he should confess his sin, he must ratify his confession within three days. If he revokes his confession, the Inquisidors must presume guilt and order that he should publicly abjure his error; or they may repeat the torture.

The Game of the Goose

Don Antonio Albrono turned and began another length of the Puente de Serranos – his sixteenth that morning – blinking away sweat, welcoming the tightness building in his chest. He took long, determined strides, grinding the stone beneath his boots, yet still last night kept pace. Barbieri might as well walk with him, jabbing his finger, accusing.

Most days, Antonio preferred a quiet patrol, but today he sought out incidents, anything to keep from brooding. Breaking up tradesmen fighting over a pitch, moving on a hawker, confiscating tobacco hidden under a cartload of potatoes… he'd even made a chore of giving that old fellow directions – escorting him all the way to the end of the bridge in case he didn't see for himself the crenelated tower lunging at the sky like it wanted to punch a hole in it.

Sometimes he thought of life as a board game he'd played as a child: *The Game of the Goose*. A lucky throw of a die and he'd advance. An unlucky one and he'd meet a hazard, knocking him backwards. So far he'd known more hazards than geese: a father disgraced, a failed military career in Vienna, a botched mission in Spain. It was enough to make a man doubt himself. He'd even managed to lose the love of his life, Luisa – hadn't seen *that* coming. But to dwell on hurt would be to recognise it, and that he wouldn't do. As long as a man can take one step, he can take another. At least he'd avoided the dreaded imprisonment or death squares. He was still in the game.

It was warm. Too warm for March in Valencia. Better to be on the bridge, with the salty breeze sweeping from the Port along the Rio Turia, than enduring the crush of bodies and stagnant air within the city walls. Even so, the sun was ruthless, warming the felt of his hat and plastering his clothes to his skin.

At the centre he took a moment to enjoy the shade under the statue of Padre Jofre. Fitting that the stoic monk tipped his face heavenward; even he wasn't above begging the sun to relent.

His camarada approached from the opposite direction, loping with a practised cadence. Not an easy skill to master – packing the gangly stride of his long limbs into the tidy rhythm of a foot soldier – but master it he had. Miguel's face glowed red, and he puffed harder than a fit man ought. Crowding into the same shadow as Antonio, he dabbed at his face with a handkerchief.

'I owe you,' Miguel said. 'My stolen reales were in Barbieri's quarters. In his stockings.'

'All of them?' Antonio asked.

'Most, a few short.' Miguel brushed rats' tails of damp hair sideways across his forehead.

'Glad I could help.'

They should move on, Antonio knew it, but the traffic had thinned – no harm taking a moment.

'We should have stopped under San Pascual.' Miguel jerked his chin towards one of the other statues. 'A wider saint.'

Antonio followed his gesture. 'That who it is? You know more than I.'

'Sí, beheaded in Granada.'

A stone martyr. The serene countenance, the hands clasped around his rosary. Just a friar, yet he'd offended. 'Why?'

'Ah, that I don't know.' Said Miguel. 'I only repeat what Matheo told me when first he showed me this patrol.' He grinned. A shift – sudden, innocent, and profoundly irritating. It lit his whole face with glee. 'Barbieri! You really made a fool of him.'

God's teeth. Here it came again, the image or memory – whatever; the thing waiting behind his eyelids, shaped like Barbieri with eyes like fury, spitting its accusation: *Heretic.*

That word. It lingered like a stench of rotted flesh. Not just from last night, but from two years before: *Don Albrono, your grandfather, Alessandro, was a heretic. Convicted by the Inquisition in Seville in 1704.* A fifty-two years old verdict, yet fresh as yesterday. Like determined fingers, that verdict had reached further than he could have imagined. Thinking about it, that verdict had brought him here, to Valencia, to this bridge, today.

He wouldn't think about it.

A man in a black physician's coat led a horse carrying a saddlebag. Two officials in wigs and embroidered waistcoats strode behind, debating or arguing – one gesturing with broad arm movements. In the back of a dawdling horse-drawn calesa, a fellow barked out a laugh, the woman by his side fanned herself and turned her face away. The bridge was filling once more.

Still, Miguel wouldn't let it drop. 'Where did you learn your tricks?'

'Vienna –' An approaching youth caught Antonio's eye. Strange that he wore an ornate waistcoat over a coarse greying shirt. '– a friend, the son of a conjurer, taught me.' The lad slowed when he reached the physician with the horse, matching his pace. 'There is no magic, just a quick hand.' He wore nothing on his feet. 'And observation.'

A shout split the air: 'Ayuda! Ayuda!' A girl sprinted out from under the Torres de Serranos, skirts flapping. Every few steps she glanced back over her shoulder, all elbows and flying hair.

Folk got out of her way, straining to see her pursuer. Miguel stepped forward to intercept him. Antonio was not about to take his eyes off the barefoot lad, and when the distracted girl ran headlong into the black-coated man's path, colliding with his mare, he was ready.

The horse reared, whinnying and snorting, foam flying, hooves scraping stone. He knew what he was about, the physician; he barked commands, wrestled with the bridle, and soon had his horse under control. But the effort clearly took all his concentration. He paid no mind to the lad reaching for the saddlebag.

That, Antonio supposed, was the point. Before the would-be-thief's fingers so much as grazed the handle of the bag, Antonio caught his wrist. 'I wouldn't do that, amigo.'

He was younger than Antonio had first thought, no more than twelve. He and the girl shared the same light brown hair and freckled complexion. Hermanos, twins perhaps. A clever idea, and the execution had been not half bad. He grabbed the girl's wrist with his other hand, and pulled them both to the side of the bridge. 'Now, what shall I do with you?'

'We did nothing wrong.' The girl twisted her arm, her skin hot against Antonio's palm. He loosened his grip just a fraction. The boy stared indifferently at the ground.

'I've caught your brother here in the act.' Antonio crouched, fixing them with a stare that held as long as it needed to, moving between the girl's scowl and the boy's pink-cheeked silence until they returned his gaze. Then he stood and opened his hand. 'Out of here and don't let me catch you again.'

They stared, first at their freed hands, then at Antonio.

'Well? Do you *want* me to turn you in?'

The girl snatched her brother's arm and yanked him away.

Antonio followed their retreat – bare black soles, narrow shoulders, growing smaller, then disappearing into the crowd.

Miguel wasn't impressed. 'You let them go?'

Antonio said nothing.

'They tried to rob that physician.' Miguel jerked his thumb at the black-coated man, now walking on, one hand on his horse's reins, the other brushing down his coat.

'But they didn't. Besides, it saves us a report.'

Miguel shook his head, still watching the man with the horse. 'I suppose so.'

'It's getting busy,' said Antonio. 'We should move.'

They turned to go their separate ways, but Antonio hadn't taken a first step before an elbow jabbed him in the ribs.

'Heretic. Ha!' Miguel said. 'Good job we like you.' Then he was away, off into the crowd with a stride so loose it taunted Antonio's own stiffened limbs.

Antonio made the sign of the cross – forehead to sternum, shoulder to shoulder – and resumed patrolling the bridge

A Man of Status

The saddlebag would have been a sorry loss, bulging as it was, not only with medical supplies but with payments from the morning's wealthy clients. Doctor Lorenzo Balleza had spotted the lad, marked his side-eye at the bag, and been ready to box his ears. Then that poor girl crashed into his horse. A soldier had swept them both away, efficient as you like – a well-trained man, rare indeed – and that, clearly, was that.

He brushed down his sleeves and wriggled his shoulders to unstick his shirt. He'd worked up a sweat, what with his long walk, the fuss with the horse, and the unseasonal heat. He could remove his coat, but no, a man such as he did not parade in shirtsleeves like a common labourer. Besides, he couldn't stop again; it wouldn't do to miss the start of his meeting.

He had a favourite way of passing time when walking or in idle moments. Narrating his future biography:

> *Not only was Doctor Balleza a physician of such renown that Valencia's elite vied for his services; he was also the youngest man ever to hold the title of Confessor to the Holy Office's secret prison…*

He managed a single breath of the cooler air under the Torres de Serranos, and all too soon stepped back into an even more stifling heat, among crowds of city dwellers and travellers. Even his long-suffering mare began to pant. He muttered entreaties while leading her around piles of steaming manure, past the ammoniacal channels of damp at the street's edges. He pushed through until the racket and stink of the poor district softened into birdsong and jasmine, drifting from courtyards hiding behind grand facades. The wealthiest district – a place he imagined he would live one day:

> *He maintained a fine home, not for himself, but in order to provide for the comfort of his visitors, among whom were numbered royalty, and those who occupied the highest offices in both church and government…*

Still leafing through the imagined pages of his biography, Lorenzo arrived at the gardens fronting El Monasterio de San Francisco. He handed off his horse without glancing at the monk who took it, and stepped past the entrance, heels ringing on stone. So familiar was he with the hallway that, once inside, he began walking before his eyes had adjusted to the darkness, reaching the Tribunal's meeting chamber with minutes to spare.

An immense crucifix greeted him, bigger than life-sized, meticulously detailed, set upon a whitewashed wall. Though Lorenzo must have seen it a hundred times, it still caught his breath. He could almost feel the weight of flesh dragging from those nails, and, of their own volition, his fingers curled into his palm.

Sunlight streamed through plain glazed windows set high in the wall to his left, lighting the surface of the long rectory table, and its lone occupant, midway along its length: Don Ignacio Ortes de la Peña, Primer Inquisidor of Valencia.

Ortes didn't rise when Lorenzo entered. He rose for no one. Instead, he performed the Inquisidor's accepted greeting – a kind of half-lift of the shoulders, a slight straightening of his spine, setting the terms. Lorenzo bowed his head, acknowledging them.

A young Dominican friar entered, bearing a tray, tankards rattling, jug sloshing, water pooling around its base. Lorenzo's temples throbbed with a thirst headache, but he wouldn't drink before the meeting started. He did not have long to wait; a jostling in the doorway announced the rest of the delegates.

First came Doctor Pedro Montez. A slight man in breeches and waistcoat, with white hair and whiskers combed downwards from a precise parting along the centre of his head. The whiteness of his fashionable silk stock highlighted the grey of the over-washed shirt beneath it and Lorenzo wondered – uncharitably, he knew – if the secretary had dressed in darkness.

Behind Doctor Montez came Don Antonio Inviola, Segundo Inquisidor. He swept into the room, ignoring everyone but his superior, whom he greeted with a nod, before rounding the table to sit beside him.

'Ortes.'

'Inviola.'

Side by side, they made near-mirror images: identical black robes, deep-set eyes and sunken cheeks. Lorenzo differentiated them by their hair – Don Ortes's thick and black, peppered with grey, Don Inviola's pure white, brushed down over his forehead in the old clerical style.

Friar Francisco breezed in, beaming. Lorenzo stiffened, as he always did when faced with the Mercedian monk's exuberance, his shoulder-patting and arm-clutching. The two Inquisidors glanced at the arrival and resumed muttering together.

Last came Friar Augustin, a stooped Franciscan with hair so sparse his tonsure managed itself. With no time left for greetings, he lowered himself into a seat.

The main order of business, after Doctor Montez had run through the standing items, was Freemasonry. A lodge – the '*Gran Logia,*' no less – had been meeting near the western gate for eight months before the Inquisition got wind and inserted one of their spies. To Lorenzo's mind, anyone breaking the Pope's ban didn't warrant mercy, and, frankly, anyone capable of such stubborn stupidity deserved the full force of the law.

'Señor Balleza,' Ortes said. Not *Doctor,* Lorenzo noted. 'I understand that you now have three confessions from the four we arrested last week.'

Those black teeth. Lorenzo dragged his eyes away, and let silence hang at the misuse of his title, just a beat, before replying. 'Yes. Recorded and signed. There is no doubt now that the society met for eight months, and we now know their meeting places – mostly around the Torres de Quart. Furthermore, all three confessed to other practices, specifically: superstitious readings and invoking uncatholic powers.'

'Buena. So, we have three saved souls, we proceed to trial and sentencing.' Ortes continued. 'What of the other?'

'Catalina Margueles. We have depositions testifying that she spoke during the meetings,' said Lorenzo, 'but she claims she only served refreshments. She is stubborn.'

'Or you are not doing your job,' snapped Ortes.

Lorenzo chewed back his reply.

Ortes clasped his hands together on the table. 'If she will not confess, we have the level of proof that Article Fifteen requires.' He said it with the indifference of one placing a lunch order.

Friar Francisco flinched. A minuscule movement, a blink and a tucking of his chin. But the Inquisidor's head swivelled towards him like a compass needle swinging north.

'You have something to say, Friar?'

Although he flushed, the friar held his ground. 'It is most likely a *de levi* sin. Let me first speak with her. It has happened before that the accused do not understand how they have offended. If I were to explain that all we require is public abjuration –'

Inviola cut him off. 'You would decide gravity before the trial?'

Lorenzo, with ever an eye on procedure, nodded. Valid point.

'Nonetheless,' said Francisco, 'we should give her every chance, given what's at stake.'

'Her immortal soul is at stake.' Ortes squinted at the friar, his eyes glistening from inside their folded sockets like wet pebbles in a handkerchief.

Despite the two Inquisidors glaring at him, and the others shrinking in their seats, Francisco persisted. 'Of course, I only ask leave to speak with her before we resort to torture. A woman –'

'Friar!' Ortes slammed his fist sideways on the table. A fleck of spittle flew from his mouth, and Lorenzo did not have the nerve to track its landing, in case the Inquisidor followed his gaze. He smelled it though.

'What matter mortal concerns when souls are in peril?' Ortes continued. 'We deliberated for four months before their arrest. Four *months* in which these Masons have been free to poison others. They have a disease of the soul; if you do not have the stomach for the cure, then step aside.'

If Lorenzo were to remove his scalpel from his physician's bag, he might carve a slice of the air, so thick had it become. The others had all dropped their chins. The grain of the wood before them was, it seemed, infinitely fascinating. Ortes turned towards the crucifix and closed his eyes, muttering a prayer. When he turned back, his scowl had dropped – not quite to serenity but as close as Lorenzo had seen him manage.

'Inviola and Augustin, visit the defendant, show her the rack. Warn her where obstinacy will take her. Doctor Balleza, examine her to confirm fitness.' Ortes settled his gaze on each man in turn. 'Courage brothers. Do not fail our Lord.'

Lorenzo's pulse quickened. His first Inquisitorial torture as attending physician. Few men gained that status.

Bacalao and Bobal

Two weeks after the incident in the cellar, Antonio had all but forgotten Barbieri's accusation – so he told himself. Rigorous duties, long hours, and speculation about the looming war in Europe left little room for reflection, and that served him well. Thinking was over-prized. He had clothes on his back, boots on his feet, and dry lodgings. And he never wanted for food. If anything, these days there was too much of it.

'Bacalao again.' He prodded at his fish.

'Want some help?' Gianni grinned through a hunk of chewed bread – his own plate polished clean with it.

'Here.' He slid his plate to the big Milanese. This far into Lent, everything stank of boiled fish: the walls of the citadel, its benches, even his clothes.

Felipe, beside him, looked up. 'You should eat what's in front of you; some are not so lucky.'

Across the table, Miguel teased out a silken bone, placed it on the side of his plate, then shovelled up an enormous lump of fish. He looked up mid-chew; lips smeared with oily brine. 'Felipe has a point. What's wrong with you, Antonio? Thinking too hard about the war?'

'Thinking too hard about your table manners,' he fired back.

Gianni swiped bread around Antonio's plate and popped the sodden mess into his mouth. 'Quiet tonight, Alfonso.'

Gianni was right; Ramirez hadn't said a word. He pushed his food around with his spoon, first gathering it into one pile, then dismantling it, only to start another on the opposite side of the plate. 'Early start tomorrow,' he said. 'Are you on the bridge?'

'Port,' said Gianni.

A chair scraped, loud enough to hurt. 'Oi, throwing food during Lent!' A man in the dark uniform of an alguacil – a constable of the city – glared down at another table. 'May God forgive you.'

He stalked off, satchel swinging. More of them had joined the garrison over the past couple of weeks. Matheo had told him they'd be demobilizing soon, though the rest weren't to know yet. As if they couldn't work it out. Extra numbers had arrived to manage the changeover, just like Seville and Cartagena before that, and with the temporary swell had come the order to find alternative lodgings.

'Sanctimonious bastard,' Miguel muttered.

'He has a point though,' said Felipe. 'Did we even say Grace?'

With the edge of a fingernail, Gianni hooked something out from between his teeth and wiped it on his sleeve. 'I'll be sure to add it to my prayers tonight. Now if you'll excuse me, I've a señorita waiting.'

A walk before bed, then perhaps he'd write to Luisa; it had been a while. Antonio wove through the tables in the wake of Gianni's broad back. But he didn't make it to the door, because Matheo stepped into his path.

'Cabo.'

'Sargento.'

'A word.' Matheo swung his chin toward a vacant table, and moved without checking he followed. Not that he needed to. With one forearm on the table, Matheo sat half facing him, half watching the comings and goings around them. 'Tomorrow,' he said. 'A prisoner release. Catalina Margueles. They sentenced her to exile. You'll take her to the city boundaries.' He interrupted his watch of the room to fix Antonio with a look, eyes narrowed, searching.

That scrutiny, more than the command, had Antonio's stomach sinking to his boots. It didn't bode well. His fingers found his brass ring, turned it. Cool metal, warm skin.

Matheo's gaze flicked to the ring and back. 'Ramirez will be there. They want Spanish nationals. Men who've sworn loyalty to the Inquisition.' He let that settle. 'But we're a man down. And you're Cabo. Keep your mouth shut and they won't know.'

Antonio flattened his hands on the table. 'Understood.' A soldier obeyed orders.

Outside at last, he walked downhill toward the unfinished port, passing labourers trudging in the opposite direction. He doubted they'd ever finish the job. Whenever they made progress, a storm would come, or an ocean swell, washing away the new-laid banks before permanent construction could begin. He began toying with words and phrases for his letter, but his mind was too occupied with tomorrow's task. Better to get to bed early. Then again, sleep would probably elude him. Catalina Margueles. What had she done to warrant exile?

Did someone call him? He paused mid-stride; half turned. No, just the wind.

'Antonio!' It came again, floating over bustle and voices. But it was a common enough name. Still, he glanced over his shoulder. Only the backs of men, and their shadows. He walked on.

'Antonio!' Louder this time.

The voice tugged at his memory. That tone, that accent… unmistakeable. He recognised the moment before he saw: the short-legged scuttle, those shoe buckles polished so well they blinked even in the dim evening light, and that pristine grey wig.

It couldn't be.

It couldn't be anyone else.

'Enzo?'

'Ciao, Antonio!'

His feet set off before his mind caught up. '*Enzo*!' He reached his friend, and crushed him against his chest, even as the Genoan protested.

'My jacket!'

Jacket be damned, he hugged him again, kissed both cheeks, squeezed tighter. Enzo submitted, liberating an arm to slap his back.

'What are you doing here?' Antonio hardly noticed he'd slipped into Italian.

'Cercando te.' Enzo tugged his waistcoat straight.

Looking for him. Of course. Searching is what Enzo did. 'Why?'

'Unfinished business.'

'There I was thinking you missed me.'

'Of course I missed you.' Enzo grinned. 'It was come here and see what trouble you've landed yourself in, or stay and look after more of your Uncle Luigi's conveyancing.'

'It's you that gets me into trouble, old friend; I've had only peace since you left. Let's get a drink.'

Antonio led Enzo into a low-ceilinged tavern, *La Bodega*. During Lent – La Cuaresma – citizens stayed with their families, so they had the place to themselves. The landlord must have taken the opportunity for a deep clean, because lye-soap lingered, sharp enough to make their eyes water, and the oak table and floorboards had a bruised, recently scrubbed look. He hadn't got around to fixing the three iron chandeliers hanging crooked from the beams; most of their candles had already burned out, and the rest sputtered against the gloom. But nothing could dim Antonio's delight. What was it, a year, since he'd last seen Enzo? No, more. He gestured to the landlord, and soon they were toasting their reunion over a jug of red wine.

'I almost didn't recognise you with your hair so short,' said Enzo.

Antonio rubbed his palm over his cropped scalp. 'Practical. Where are you staying? You found somewhere, no?'

'Near here. *El Mesón del Sol.* It's clean and cheap; more comfortable than most.' Enzo sniffed his drink. 'What wine is this?'

'It's local, Bobal, I think. I prefer it to the bad ale here.'

'I forgot, and ordered cerveza when I arrived. Not sure what was floating on it, only hoped it was grain.'

'In Genoa I missed Austrian beer, in Spain I miss Genoan beer,' Antonio said. 'Perhaps we only appreciate what we don't have.'

'I don't imagine you'll ever miss Spanish beer.' The two men clinked their cups again.

As much as Antonio enjoyed the simple fact of his company, Enzo wouldn't have made this journey, searched him out – and it wouldn't have been an easy search – to talk about beer. He tapped his ring against his mug: an ellipsis, a suspension. 'What brings you here, Enzo?'

His friend's smile dropped. 'As I said, unfinished business.' He leaned forward and lowered his voice, even though the landlord stood on the far side of the bar, cleaning and arranging mugs on a shelf. 'Your Uncle Luigi, he insists your grandfather died in the faith. It makes no sense.'

His heart sank. Of course, what other *unfinished business* would Enzo have meant? He forced a smile, though he suspected he didn't do a very good job of it. 'You always were thorough.'

'His own *father*,' Enzo said. 'Surely, he would have known if he'd been branded a heretic. Then, when you didn't come home… did you discover something in Seville after I left?'

'Nothing to tell you,' Antonio said. 'I only stayed because… well, Spain is as good as anywhere. It would have been wrong to impose on Lucretia any longer, and soldiering is what I know, so I enlisted.'

'So I heard. It's how I found you.' Enzo looked at Antonio's sleeve. 'No rank?'

Typical Enzo bluntness. Antonio took a mouthful of wine; more acid than fruit. His father had been a major general. But since La Famiglia disowned him, anything Antonio accomplished would have to be on his own merit. Enzo could work that out for himself, so he left the question hanging, and worked at a piece of wax on the table with his thumbnail.

'You gave up the cause.'

Now Antonio laughed, a genuine chuckle from deep in his gut. 'Enzo. I am the Lord of Lost Causes.'

'If your grandfather committed no crime… maybe you needn't be.'

Antonio studied his friend for a long moment, then tilted his cup against the candlelight. Red dregs pooled at the bottom. They could have been blood clots. He set it down with a thud.

'Some things are best left alone.'

Vanity and Penance

Don Fausto de Alenya paced. He'd come ten minutes ahead of his meeting, for the peace of it. Ten minutes for himself; an indulgence for a man with his heavy responsibilities. Ten minutes in this place of peace, by repute the greatest space in Barcelona – certainly the most powerful. He tipped his head back to enjoy the stone arches hooped above. Few would say they drew solace in the Grand Hall of the Palau Reial Major – indeed most cowered here. But then few received their calling from God Himself.

With its vast dimensions and austere lines, the hall had been built for grandeur, and put to use for terror. Despite its size, the air inside lay heavy, perhaps with phantoms of the past – those sentenced here to banishment, imprisonment, the galleys, or to be *handed over to the secular authorities* for the sternest sentence, because the Church did not shed blood.

Three quick taps. One more. Fausto ignored them – he was no doorman. Soon enough, hinges creaked, the door shifted one crack at a time, and Señor Enrique García López, Post Office escribiente – and handpicked agent of the Postmaster General himself – crept in, just as the bell from the nearby cathedral tolled eleven. Exactly on time, as always.

Fausto knew he cut an imposing figure because he made sure of it. He had spent years crafting his appearance to reflect his dual roles: layering the cassock of the Primer Inquisidor with the purple-trimmed mozzetta and the purple silk sash of the Vicar General. The gold embroidery on his cape, for anyone who cared to look closely enough, dripped with symbolism: sacred hearts and angels, griffins and crowns, the sword and the olive branch – faith, city, and Inquisition intertwined. Yet, grand as those adornments were, nothing detracted from the magnificence of the pectoral crucifix that swung against his chest from its heavy gold chain – a masterpiece of intricate gold and silver filigree, studded with rubies as crimson as Christ's wounds.

He met the clerk halfway across the floor. 'Buenas noches, Señor García.' He held out his ring.

'Su Excelencia.' The clerk bowed his head and pressed his lips to the golden insignia.

Fausto patted his shoulder as he rose. 'How is your boy? Recovered, I hope?' He cupped the clerk's elbow and guided him to the table.

'Much better. We are so grateful for your prayers.'

Fausto inclined his head. 'It is a hard thing, to sit beside a sickbed, helpless. A father should not outlive his son.'

'And by our Lord's grace, that test was never laid upon me,' said Garcia.

'God is great in His mercy.' Fausto crossed himself.

'Amen.'

Garcia unclipped his satchel.

'Anything unusual?' asked Fausto.

Señor García handed over a pile of letters. 'Not that I noticed. Are there any new names for us this week?'

'No.' Fausto tested the stack's weight, must be about a dozen. 'The existing list stands.' Might as well keep Garcia's job simple. He began rifling, and absently turned away. Half a minute must have passed before he remembered his visitor hovered. Of course, he hadn't dismissed him.

'Gracias, Señor García, that will be all.'

'I bid you a good night, Su –'

'God bless. And my warmest regards to Matilde.'

Fausto watched García's retreat until the doors closed again. Then he gathered the intercepted letters and carried them back to his quarters – a suite of rooms furnished with a bed made to accommodate his height.

Sitting beneath the glow of candles, he snapped seals and scanned pages. The same coded messages – meetings disguised as *betrothal parties, soirees, observances...* as if he couldn't see through a ruse; as if he fell off the back of a hay wagon. The risks these men took... heartbreaking it was, the way the devil took their reason.

And this one. *Valencia.* The paper shifted in his hand as though seeking its own escape. That script, with its swirls and flourishes, a hand as familiar as his own – prettier though, self-indulgent, like the man himself. Don Antonio Albrono.

The letter, as usual, was for Luisa Navas.

La Ciudadela de Valencia,
19 de febrero del año 1756

Mi vida, Luisa,

I have been thinking too much about a certain orange grove. I suppose that is not a proper way to begin a letter, but I cannot put aside the happiest time in my life.

In Seville, I spoke with Lucretia about the peculiar sense I had when I first saw you, that I had known you all my life. You would like my half-cousin, Luisa. You are similar in so many ways. Both of you perceive people beyond the superficial; you both possess uncommon strength of character; and you both have the intellect to outwit me (that can be vexing). But I digress. I told Lucretia that the feeling must have been a trick of my mind, because reason cannot support such a fanciful notion. She lectured upon the wisdom of the heart, and whilst it defies logic, I have to recognise the empirical truth in it. Perhaps that feeling was my heart's way of telling me I had been waiting for you, that fate brought me to Spain to love you.

I have just read over those words, and I am laughing at myself. Never would I have imagined myself writing love letters. Look what you have done to me, Luisa.

Shall I revert to more mundane content? I could tell you I repaired a tear in my camisa earlier today. That it has been unseasonably hot, and Alfonso Ramirez took ill for lack of water. The most notable news is that mi sargento, Matheo, thinks there is a thief in our sección. If he is right – and there is merit in the rumour – then that is most disappointing. What happened to honour among camaradas?
Amore mio, do you remember I once told you I want you to be the happiest woman that ever lived? I meant every word. A reply would fill me with joy, although I expect none. I write for the peculiar joy I find in penning your name.
Te quiero, Luisa.
Suyo en cuerpo y alma.
Antonio

Fausto swept over the lines with eyes like swinging lanterns, illuminating each word. *A reply would fill me with joy.* Of course it would. Let him hope. Albrono was a wolf sniffing after a lamb, but he hadn't reckoned on the shepherd, armed with God's righteousness.

To him, Luisa remained the child who once perched on his knee and called him *Uncle*, her breath sweet as violets as she pushed his hair from his face. If he closed his eyes, he could still feel her warm, slight body against his. She'd grown into a woman so fine she stopped men in their tracks; had them fumbling for words. Not Don Fausto de Alenya. He was proud of his restraint in that regard. At the same time, he recognised the sin in such pride.

He called to his attending friar.

'Juan!'

Like an apparition, the boy emerged from the shadows beyond the door. Fausto nodded to the switch propped against the wall. Penance. The boy's jaw tightened. Wordlessly, Fausto removed his mozzetta and crucifix, laid them on the bed, and stripped to his waist. He knelt, robes pooling about his knees, facing the cross on his wall, hands clasped, eyes closed.

Juan knew what to do. The blows came. The first three took his breath. The next three unleashed tremors. He clamped his teeth for the next three. He offered the pain up for his sins, and to show his mettle. The next strike sent him lurching forwards, panting, palms striking the floor. Juan faltered.

Fausto hauled in a breath and forced himself upright. He looked back over his shoulder.

Juan's chest heaved. Sweat beaded his top lip, and he wiped it on his sleeve. His hand – the one holding the cane – hung limp by his side. His eyes were misted; he scrubbed at them with the heel of his free hand. Fausto nodded. *Continue.* Juan swallowed.

The last two strikes split his skin, warmth trickling from a shoulder-blade and a flank to spread and soak into the robes bunched at the waist. That's when pain crossed the threshold into rapture.

Catalina

The *Cárcel del Santa Oficio* might have been any municipal building – square, functional, shuttered against light and prying. When the sun rose high enough, the walls would be pale, almost pink. For now, it squatted in shadow, hiding its unsavoury business.

Antonio trudged to his task. He still tasted Bobal on his breath, his scalp itched under his hat, and his eyes felt hot and raw from lack of sleep. But none of those things mattered. Not really. Not as much as the thought that had taken root when he left the citadel, and sprouted branches with each step: The Holy Office of the Inquisition must have its reasons for choosing dawn for such work.

Ramirez had already arrived. He stood beside the door with his feet planted, staring unfocused at a spot on the wall opposite, like he'd been assigned sentry duty.

'You've done this before, Alfonso?' asked Antonio.

They both looked up at the prison's vast door.

'Sí.'

That clipped reply said it all. On any normal day it would be harder to get him to shut up than speak. And he'd been off his food yesterday.

Antonio thumped the door with the side of his fist. They waited. Silent.

The door yawned open, spilling the prison's foul breath into their faces. Footsteps clumped, gruff voices grew louder, and Antonio straightened his back, drawing in composure.

He needed it.

Catalina Margueles hung like a marioneta unstrung, yet the guards pushed her forward as if she might stroll into the morning sun. Antonio lunged, caught her, and his breath froze in his throat.

Her face drooped. Hair that might once have been glossy hung in ropes around sunken cheeks. Skin that would have been delicate gleamed greasy, yellow, and mottled. Ash-stained lips. Bruised eyes. Her dark woollen overdress fared better than the parts he could see of the shift beneath – stiff with yellow-brown sweat. Both shrouded a frame so emaciated that her bones seemed poised to break through skin. And the smell. It was a thing of its own. Antonio chose her dignity rather than acknowledge it, bowing his head as if in prayer, breathing through his mouth.

Though they held her upright, one on each side, her joints folded with every step. Ramirez looked back at the guards.

'¿Qué pasó?'

One shrugged.

'¿El potro?' asked Ramirez.

'Un poco,' said the other.

Un poco. That was alright then. They only racked her *a little.*

Antonio bit back his retort and turned his attention to their charge. Not a woman but a shell. What right? What god did they serve? He scooped her up and hastened through the prison gate, with her head bouncing against his chest.

Ramirez trailed. 'Our orders are to take her outside the city.'

His jaw was clenched too hard for a reply, even if he had words.

'Puente de Serranos. We can get her across the bridge and away before people wake.' Ramirez caught up, then jogged backwards, facing him. 'Antonio, yes? The bridge is that way.'

He tightened his grip on the woman lying weightless in his arms and spoke through clamped teeth. 'She will die, Alfonso.'

'Our orders, Antonio.'

'Fuck our orders!'

'Where are you going?'

The question stopped him in his tracks. The woman's arms dangled limp as rags; her eyes stared ahead, at nothing, at his left armpit.

He exhaled. 'I don't know.'

Ramirez threaded his hands at the nape of his neck and drew his elbows together, eyes darting between Antonio and Catalina.

Antonio softened his tone. 'Let's at least get her something to eat and let her rest awhile. She's not garbage to dispose of.'

Ramirez opened his mouth, then snapped it shut. A swallow rolled down his neck. He shifted his gaze once more to the woman, and this time it lingered there.

'I know a place.'

He led the way, clearing the route. They had to duck into a side-alley to avoid a baker's assistant arriving in time to load his ovens, but the early hour was their friend, because they encountered no one else.

It was a hayloft tucked away in the maze of streets behind the citadel. Surely destined to be demolished soon – a marvel the building had not already collapsed – with rotted and warped timbers, it stayed upright by leaning against its neighbours. Inside among fallen beams and tiles, they found a threadbare blanket and straw, clean and dry – small mercies. Antonio didn't bother to ask how his camarada knew of it. They laid out a makeshift bed, and he gathered hay, bunching it up under one end into a pillow, after a fashion.

'Señora… Señorita? Catalina, mírame, look at me.' Antonio leaned in to see her better. Her pupils shrank. Good. Focus. 'Can you speak?'

Nothing.

His throat thickened. 'Find her some bread, and something to drink.'

Ramirez slipped out without a word, leaving Antonio alone with her.

'You're safe now, Catalina. Nobody is going to hurt you, Catalina.' He had an idea that repeating her name might help. He picked up her hand and cradled it with his own. It lay cold and moist against his skin, putting him in mind of a fish laid out on a counter. Though she ignored him, he talked, letting words tumble, all the while chafing warmth into her hands. 'Do you have family? Can I fetch someone? What can I do for you? They won't touch you again. I promise. Catalina, I'm so sorry this has happened to you –'

She reared into a sitting position, inhaling a shriek, fingers clawed so he had to grab her wrists to protect his face.

'Shhh. Catalina. Está bien. Shhh. Tranquila. You are safe.'

She collapsed against his chest, and he held her; stroked her hair.

When Ramirez returned with bread and milk, Antonio tipped the leather pouch to her lips – she swallowed a portion; the rest slipped down her chin and soaked the neck of her shift. As for the bread, she blinked as though she didn't know what it was for. He might as well have been offering her a roof tile.

'What now, Antonio?' Ramirez whispered. 'She cannot stay here. We still have orders.' He faced him square, but his boots pointed at the door.

'Let's make sure she's strong enough to survive,' Antonio said.

She sagged onto the blanket, eyes rolling back, head lolling to one side.

'I'll take responsibility.'

A Suitable Match

Two hours of torment. For two hours Luisa had been trapped in her private suite on the hotel's top floor, at the mercy of Marta and her infernal curling irons. Two hours being perfumed and polished like a porcelain Madonna, preparing for the Delmau soiree – one of Barcelona's most anticipated affairs. Of course they'd been invited; her mother's great talent had always been putting the Spinelli name to good use. Indeed, she'd named the hotel – La Posada del Marqués – purely so she might drop her brother's title – El Marqués de Bellvís – whenever conversation came around to the choice. Which of course was often.

'Monsieur Dupont's carriage, remind Gabriel,' Luisa said.

'Twice you've told me that, see –' Marta waved her hand at Luisa's table book. '– it's on the list. I marked it. Which means I did it.'

'And Señor Mendoza is coming to clean the chandeliers.' Her idea, what with most of the guests going to the soiree, and Señor Valcárcel opting to dine in his room.

'Also on the list,' Marta said.

'The payment is – oi!'

Marta yanked at the laces as though declaring war on her ribs. 'In the pouch, in your desk, top drawer, study. Really Luisa, we can manage for one evening. Gabriel is a perfectly capable under-manager, and I a perfectly capable maid.'

'I know, I know. A fine torturer too,' said Luisa.

She did know. She over-worried. But she hadn't built the finest hotel in Barcelona – so she'd been told – by not allowing it to consume her: mixing with guests, planning meals, keeping ahead of trends, filing accounts, even washing plates and laundry if the staff took ill… from the moment she awoke to the second she laid her head upon the pillow, and sometimes even after. Going out for a night bordered on irresponsible. Positioned as they were, in the centre of La Ribera overlooking the port, it was inconceivable that a disembarking passenger or two wouldn't come seeking supper or a room. And unthinkable that they should close for an evening. But declining the invitation would be even more unthinkable – being seen in the right places was part of being hotel manager.

'Señorita, if you don't stop frowning you will get lines,' Marta interrupted her thoughts. 'Gabriel has everything in hand; your only business is with your dress. Hold still.' She pulled, hard, a relentless methodical cinching, climbing Luisa's spine.

'Now see,' Luisa protested. 'I cannot move. Look how these stays catch at my sleeves; I won't spend the evening with my arms trapped.'

'Are you planning on waving them around? That will be quite the spectacle.'

'No, but I will need to lift my fork.' Luisa wriggled.

'At this rate, you won't *need* to lift your fork. You won't be in time for postres.' She tugged at the cords once again, this time loosening. 'Ttsch, you were less trouble when you were a child.'

'I didn't have to wear these stupid long corsets when I was a child. I cannot breathe.'

Marta shrugged. 'Breathing is over-prized. Look what they do for your breasts.'

'I'm not a side of meat. Now, let's get these awful panniers on. ¡Voto a Dios! No woman is shaped this way.'

'That's for a husband to discover on your wedding night; until then, you need to attract one.'

Marta too. Bad enough that her mother's entire life revolved around one objective – a husband for Luisa – without Marta joining the campaign.

Her skirts pooled on the ground. Marta stood beside them, waiting for her to step in.

Azure, of all colours. It had to be.

'*Blue is your colour,*' he'd said that night, leaning against the balustrade, one foot lazy over the other. Two years since that night, a year since his last letter. Antonio had no right to take space in her mind, let alone her heart. He'd left her. Was probably with another woman at this very moment, telling her how well she wore green. She stepped into the dress.

An hour later, and still Marta buzzed around, adjusting hair, pushing in a comb, and trying to persuade her to wear more jewellery.

'Enough. It's too vulgar.'

'It's impossible to be too vulgar these days.'

Luisa held out a hand. 'My gloves and fan. And gracias, Marta.' She kissed her cheek and pulled on gloves made in the same silk as her dress.

'Have a wonderful evening,' said Marta, stepping back finally, and folding her arms.

Although she doubted her mother would be ready on time, Luisa moved as fast as her gown allowed. Not that it mattered. Timekeeping wasn't a priority in Barcelona society; in fact, being 'on time' would probably insult their host. Sure enough, when she entered the salon downstairs, her mother still had not appeared, which meant keeping company with her father while they waited.

'Good evening, Papa.'

He sat in an armchair, reading trade reports through his new wire-framed glasses. 'Luisa.'

'Are the numbers good?'

'No. A run on silk prices,' he said, his eyes never leaving his paper.

Silence swelled, and Luisa tapped her folded abanico on her palm as if the action would dislodge an idea, something to talk about. 'Are your spectacles of benefit?'

'Sí.' He rustled his papers.

The light caught lines etched around his mouth. He'd aged into his frowns, and his hair had become more white than grey. When did that happen? She opened her mouth to speak again, but closed it when he shifted in his chair, fingers on his brow. Shutting her out.

It was hard to remember a time when her relationship with her father hadn't been frosty. Not strictly true. His brusqueness and oppressive rules had always disappointed her, to say nothing of his temper, but the real fracture had been over Antonio, that day two years ago, in Bellvís.

Where was Mama? As if hearing her unspoken plea, her mother swept into the room with such energy that the air arrived first: a cloud of rosewater ushering in a singsong voice. 'Well, husband, do I make you proud?'

She wore the French style well. Pink roses blossomed here and there over the full height of her powdered wig, while proud bows sprouted wherever Luisa looked, as if Mama had doused herself in sugar water and strolled through the ribbon aisle of a haberdashery. Luisa stifled a giggle; at least she could relax now. To think she had worried about being over-dressed.

'Mama, you look stunning,' she said, and she meant it. Whilst her fashion choices were not to Luisa's taste, Maria Navas y Spinelli carried her years better than most women ten years younger.

On the other hand, her mother found nothing to compliment in Luisa's efforts. 'You should let me advise you.' She studied her from the feet up, finishing at the top. 'Rafael Delmau won't notice you, with hair more suited to a maid than a lady.'

'I like it natural; it's comfortable this way,' said Luisa, reaching for the back of her moño to make sure it had not come loose. She ignored the mention of Señor Delmau. Mother's latest target in her quest for *a suitable match.*

'We do not choose comfort over beauty. Although I truly don't know how my neck will hold the weight of this wig.' She pushed out her bottom lip and turned to her husband. 'I hope you appreciate my sacrifice.'

'You look fine, wife.'

Luisa caught the flicker, the moment her mother's mask slipped, a glimpse of anguish, gone as fast as it appeared.

'Mama is a vision. Is she not? Papa.' She waited, her silence a challenge.

He lowered his paper, folded it, once then again, and rose from his chair, dropping it into the dent left by his backside. Then he stuck out an elbow for his wife, and La Familia Navas set off into the evening.

The affair had been circled in the diaries of Barcelona society for at least six months and, if Luisa's first impressions proved correct, would live up to expectations. From the silver-embossed wallpaper to the floral towers, everywhere she looked revealed a feature or a curiosity. Even the drinks and canapes were served by dancing nymphs and sprites, somehow managing to hold trays aloft while weaving between skirts as wide as furniture. The air smelled of orange blossom; a chamber ensemble played Catalan compositions, and gossip flowed as freely as the fruit cup and Rancio wine.

Luisa spotted her friend across the room and drifted toward her, nodding at business acquaintances and family friends as she passed. She and Marguerite had grown up together, sharing tutors while their fathers shared business interests. Now, as so often at these gatherings, they hovered on the periphery, catching up and entertaining each other with commentary on fellow guests, and, of course, their host.

'Did you speak to him? In the entrance line?'

'Who?' Luisa knew exactly who.

'Rafael Delmau.' Marguerite whispered, angling her fan like a makeshift confessional. 'He looked right into my eyes.'

Luisa sighed. 'Probably checking his own reflection. Must we behave as if he's the only man in Barcelona?'

'He's the only man who fills a suit like that.'

'I'm not about to swoon for a man whose greatest asset is his tailor.'

'Where do you think he disappears to for months on end? I hear he's in the market for a wife now. You –'

'Not interested.' Luisa cut her off, snapping her fan shut.

'But look at him.'

He stood clustered with three young women. They laughed and fluttered, fiddling with their hair. In their shimmering pastel silks, they might have been a tray of sherbets. *Choose me!* All polished boots and square jaw he was: athletic, dark-haired, his smile reaching everywhere at once.

'If only I were single,' Marguerite muttered.

'If only you had shame,' Luisa replied.

'*You're* available,' said Marguerite, arching a brow. 'You might be just his type.'

'He's not mine.'

'How do you know?'

'I don't, I just –'

'Well then.' Marguerite shoulder-shoved her.

To Luisa's relief, they were interrupted by the master-of-occasion announcing dinner. Yet it was a case of out of the frying pan, and into the fire. Her mother had wielded her influence with the seating plan, which placed her at the centre, opposite the man of the hour, Rafael.

With his elderly father, Ramon, largely withdrawn from public life, Rafael had become the de facto head of the Delmau family. Accomplished and respected, he'd elevated their standing in

Barcelona through clever real estate investments. Little wonder, thought Luisa, that her parents were so keen to push her under his nose. Perhaps ten years older than her, he surely wouldn't be single too much longer.

Determined not to be part of a livestock market, Luisa assessed the table, considering how she might blend in. She stood no chance; she barely made it through legumes before Mama's voice skewered her.

'Of course she's too modest to admit it, but my daughter is an accomplished pianist.'

Luisa had no choice but to look up and meet their gazes.

Close up, Señor Delmau had a pleasant aspect: coffee eyes, no wig, hair swept into a thick queue. Other than a few smile-lines at the outer corners of his eyes, he might have passed for thirty. He held himself with ease, yet also with a reserve she hadn't noticed earlier. And now he peered into her eyes, with a curiosity that unnerved her.

'Maybe you'll play for me one day?'

'Mama flatters me. If mediocrity were a tune, I'd excel at it.'

Her mother's eyes flared – horror and murder vying for primacy. Luisa set her fish knife straight and gestured for more wine.

'I understand you oversee affairs at La Posada del Marqués.' Señor Delmau's voice, low and confident, cut across her efforts to appear oblivious.

Her mother jumped in. 'Oh well, she helps out.' Translation: *Don't let him think you do anything so vulgar as work.*

'Yes,' said Luisa. 'I love my work.' She threw the words down as a challenge. Had he echoed her mother's attitude, that would have been the end of it.

'It shows,' he said. 'I hear it's excellent.'

The hum of conversation receded. Luisa looked down at her plate, touched her chin, dropped her hands to her lap, swallowed. When she looked back, his eyes hadn't moved.

Well then.

Further down the table, beyond flashing cutlery and gold-edged plates, Marguerite watched over the rim of her glass. She took a sip, then placed her glass down and lifted one side of her mouth in a slow, and entirely inappropriate smile.

'I wonder if we might share a dance later?' said Rafael Delmau.

Despite herself, and all her convictions, and everything she'd said, and despite Marguerite smirking like a cat that found a barrel of buttermilk, she nodded. She would after all like to get to know him better.

A Letter to Luisa

El Mesón del Sol, Valencia
11 de abril del año 1756

Mi vida, Luisa,
As you will see from my address, I have taken new lodgings. I would not have found it had it not been for an old friend. Do you remember Enzo? He well remembers you. After all, you once saved his life. How astonishing that he tracked me down. Though I suppose it is his talent.
Our landlord, Señor Matheu, is a decent fellow, but very dour. A God-fearing man. I have ever wondered if God appreciates being served in misery. Did not Jesus Himself turn water into wine? Gianni says he will wrest a smile from him before we leave here, and there is entertainment watching him try.
I make light, but my heart has never been heavier. I have had to perform a duty that left me wondering about the good in man. I understood in the abstract how cruel we can be. I think I put it from my mind, so I was unprepared. I haven't been sleeping. But worse, I cannot summon you. I can describe each feature: the softness of your hair, the colour of your eyes, yet I can no longer feel or see them. This is a terror to me. For I do not know that I can lose you twice.
Perhaps if I put right some of the wrongs I have witnessed, God will see fit to restore my memories. Forgive my riddles, amore mio. Perhaps this is not a good time to write a letter. But then, did we not promise honesty always?
Te quiero, Luisa.
Suyo en cuerpo y alma,
Antonio

Domingo de Ramos

Thanks to a word from Enzo, Antonio and some of his camaradas had moved into El Mesón del Sol – a two-storied inn folded around a courtyard, with clean rooms and thick wool mattresses. Its price would have been beyond army coffers, had not the clever lawyer negotiated half-rates for full occupancy. A fine landing.

This evening, in honour of *Domingo de Ramos* – Palm Sunday – their stern-faced landlord, Señor Matheu, had arranged a communal supper of Lenten rice, cooked over a firepit. They shared a table with two ink-blotted scriveners from the tax office – Joaquim and Jose, and two alguacils – Alba and Sanchez. As chance would have it, Alba was the alguacil from the refectory. He ate like a man performing penance and left his wine to collect midges. By contrast, his young colleague Sanchez threw back glass upon glass, and by his fourth was the funniest man in Spain.

At a separate table, directly in Antonio's line of vision, sat three women. Two of them mother and daughter most likely; painted from the same palette, with matching chaquetillas. They muttered together, foreheads almost touching.

'Terrible.' The younger dropped her spoon. 'I cannot touch it.'

The mother hushed her – a whisper loud enough to carry outside. 'They'll hear.'

A sniff. 'Let them.'

Antonio looked at his plate. This '*terrible*' food tasted better than anything he'd eaten in weeks: hot and fresh from the pot, not re-heated so many times it had turned to sludge.

'Luisa. Stop staring at that soldier.'

He jerked his head up, a reflex, the sort that mocks. The woman in question – a maid by her clothes – bore no resemblance to *his* Luisa. She had none of the colour, none of the composure, and she flushed like a child caught thieving. Still, she held his gaze. Antonio nodded and returned to his plate.

'Oi, our cabo has an admirer.' Gianni said.

Antonio scraped at his rice.

'...Don Antonio here, the scourge of thieves. They tremble before him.'

The words drifted over the table, from Luca, gesturing with his spoon in case anyone doubted who he meant.

'Oh?' said one of the scriveners, Joaquim, hair the colour of old pewter, white flecks collecting at the corners of his mouth.

'I don't recall making a man tremble, Luca,' Antonio said. 'What are we talking about?'

Joaqim tapped his chest, where a purse might have nestled. 'Someone stole from me in the crowd today. Not much, a few maravedís. Your friend says you can smell out a thief.'

Gianni winked at Antonio. 'Only the most privileged among us have witnessed it.'

'Then we are indeed honoured,' Joaquim said. 'Let me pour you some more wine. I once tried my hand at the magic arts myself.'

'Not magic,' said Antonio. 'A quick hand. I learnt in Vienna.'

'Of course. Not magic.'

'I thought you were Genoese?' Gianni said.

'Sí, but I grew up in Vienna.'

'That explains your ugly accent.' Gianni grinned.

Antonio punched his shoulder.

'So, are you going to tell me how you caught your thief?' Joaquim appeared beside him, looming too close, and tipped the wine jug with one hand. It spilled – of course it did – some made Antonio's mug, some splashed on the table, the rest dribbled over his own fingers. He licked his thumb, smacking his lips next to Antonio's ear.

'No. Our business, not table-talk,' said Antonio – for the benefit of his camaradas, not this stranger sniffing round them.

Luca launched in regardless, his accent coloured by the streets of Naples, playing to laughs and gasps as he told of innocent fingers turning grey.

Antonio took the opportunity to drop a hunk of bread onto the linen he'd unfolded on his lap; the spoon followed, vanishing full of rice behind the lip of the table.

'Magic is unholy, Señor Albrono,' said Señor Matheu, holding aloft a fresh jug of wine, scanning the table for space to set it down. 'It cannot be done unless by a league with the devil. It's –'

'Thieving is unholy,' Matheo said. '*Don* Albrono –' He let the title hang. '– put an end to it in my sección.'

Antonio let another morsel slide past the table's edge. A hunk of fish. Its warmth seeped through the cloth.

'A man has a right to his hard-earned wages,' Miguel said.

'Amen,' said Luca.

The other scrivener, Jose, rose and left – quiet as a phantom, without even a *goodnight.* Antonio watched him vanish into the shadows beyond the gate. Perhaps he too could leave now without attracting notice. He gathered his parcel into a ball and smuggled it sideways across his lap, into his satchel. A few moments more.

Silence settled and thickened until, true to form, Gianni broke it. 'If nobody wants the last bit of rice…'

The usual sounds of mealtime resumed: scratching spoons, pouring wine, clinking cups, chatter – muted at first, then swelling to its previous hum.

'I hear it's Barcelona next,' Luca said, directing his comment at Matheo.

'You know more than I.'

The same dance every time: Matheo would keep the order to himself; every man in the sección would test him, right up to the moment they marched out.

'That'll finish the coast,' said Gianni. 'Seville, Almeria, Cartagena, Valencia, Barcelona. We'll soon run out of Spain.'

'That the system, Sargento? Miguel said. 'Always moving northeast?'

Matheo didn't look up. 'The *system* is following orders, and not talking about them in public.'

The fire popped and crackled.

'So, Barcelona it is,' muttered Miguel

The men snickered.

All except Antonio. More than likely, in Barcelona, he'd have to accept, once and for all, that Luisa had rejected him. It might be for the best. Despair can be fed. Unlike hope, which always comes back for scraps.

'Perhaps your return is meant to be,' Enzo murmured in Italian. 'A second chance to understand the anomaly.'

Antonio barely suppressed a groan. He opened his mouth to cut Enzo off, but a voice in his ear interrupted him.

'Don Albrono.' Breath digesting fish and wine warmed his cheek. Joaquim Gil's face floated barely a thumb-length away. 'Will you share your magic?' He flashed teeth stained pink with wine. 'I'll pay you for a charm.'

Antonio leaned away. 'Charm?'

'To bring me luck, at pilota.'

A ballgame. A fraudster seeking advantage. 'I can't help you.' Antonio stood, an abrupt movement, deliberately so. *End of conversation.* He nodded to the assembled diners. 'Con permiso, Señoras y Señores, I have letters to write.'

He paused at the gate, listening with his back. Then turned, seeking indifference.

He found it, mostly. The wine had got the better of Sanchez; he dozed with his face propped on his hands, while Alba shook his shoulder, trying to rouse him. The ladies chatted. Señor Matheu cleared plates. Enzo listened to Miguel recounting a tale, his bottom lip thrust out as if about to correct a detail. The others laughed at some Gianni quip. Matheo looked at Antonio and gave him a single nod.

One other watched: Joaquim, the old scrivener. Eyelids at half-mast, working his mouth. Antonio didn't acknowledge him. He turned and slipped through the gate, clicking it shut behind him.

The Confessor and the Spy

Several weeks after Catalina's Article Fifteen interrogation, Lorenzo had all but forgotten her. When she did come to mind, it was in the abstract; a thing that happened, a job done. He went about his work – physician in the morning, confessor in the afternoon – just as he'd done for ten months now. He'd settled into it well, though he couldn't say he enjoyed it. What he liked was the honour, the awe of it. Much of the time, the work involved separating people with grudges from credible deponents, and this afternoon offered more of the same.

The first waited outside. So eager was he to spill his intelligence, he'd been loitering in the corridor when Lorenzo arrived; he'd grabbed at his sleeve. Lorenzo knew him, a paid spy, the kind of bellaco who treated the Holy Office as nothing more than a means to line his pockets. Yet such men had their uses.

'What is the sin this time, Doctor Montez?'

The secretary adjusted his glasses and peered at his paper. 'A soldier of the garrison, who is also a nobleman. Heresy by means of necromancy.'

Lorenzo's ears pricked up. The Holy Office existed on noble wealth, and rewarded those who brought it in.

'His name?'

'Don Antonio Albrono.'

Lorenzo didn't allow his features to move; he stared at the tuft of hair between Montez's eyebrows. The secretary had just dropped one of Europe's most illustrious names – nobility going back centuries: heads of state, cardinals, commanders-in-chief…

'Of the Genoa Albronos?'

'Well, it's a funny thing –'

His smile only vexed Lorenzo; *a funny thing* didn't interest him.

'– the deponent thinks Don Albrono is from Naples. *I* believe he is mistaken. I have looked into it. I checked registers from that city and –'

It occurred to Lorenzo that if he drummed his fingers faster on the table, Montez might take the hint and speak faster. But nothing would deter him from uttering every word on his mind, in his normal nasal drone, at the cadence of one reciting an inventory to a man hard of hearing.

'– there is no *Don Antonio Albrono from Naples.*' Montez took a breath. 'Don Antonio Albrono is the nephew of Luigi Albrono, head of the Genoan family of that name. The accused is indeed of noble birth.' Montez beamed.

'Thank you,' Lorenzo said. 'A *yes* would have sufficed.'

Montez cast his eyes down at his papers, a flush rising above his white whiskers.

'Is there merit to this claim?'

Now the secretary couldn't speak fast enough. 'Yes, My Lord Confessor. The deponent is one of the more reliable spies. Shall I show him in and call the session to order?'

'Yes,' Lorenzo relented a little. 'Gracias, Doctor Montez.'

Lorenzo walked to his chosen spot, where the high window's light elongated his shadow. Commanding, imposing:

> *Doctor Balleza suited his authority well, for few of us are born with the resilience to carry the burden of representing not just the Holy Office of Valencia, not even that of Spain, but of the entire Catholic Church…*

He held his silence as the deponent shuffled in, head bowed, turning his hat in his hands, eager to claim his fee for placing Don Antonio Albrono's life in the hands of the Inquisition.

A Fool to Believe This

The Thursday before Easter found Antonio, on his rest day, in the Mercado en la Plaza Redonda. Folk crowded the fish and meat stands on the western edge, jostling for the best cuts. Antonio wove through them, batting away flies too intoxicated by the brine-blood cocktail to settle.

This was why he hated shopping.

Away from those godawful meat stalls, the air sweetened. Scents of oranges, anise, and chocolate blended with those of the baked goods. If he could but ignore the tang of the sweaty throng – to which he was sure he contributed – this experience might not be too unpleasant.

He cut through the bread stands – a miracle those pyramids didn't collapse; one knock would do it. They smelled good, wonderful, setting his guts growling. But Isabel at the mesón fed him well. He'd keep his coin for those things Catalina needed.

A woman with rough skin and hair spilling out of her mobcap turned and crashed into him, spilling her basket onto the cobbles. Antonio ducked to collect an orange that had begun its rolling escape, then grabbed the onions cascading behind. When he stood again and tried to return them to her basket, he was thanked with a scowl and an accusation.

'¡Bellaco!' *Scoundrel.*

This. This was why he hated shopping.

He knew what he was looking for: a clean shift. Catalina needed to feel human again. Hiding away in that hayloft, reminded every day of the grime of her incarceration; how was she to recover? He'd already bought her a cake of lye and a wooden comb; this exercise was all about stretching his reales. He reckoned he could spare two and still have some left to send her on her way. But now, standing before the stall, the cheapest seemed beyond his purse.

'Five reales? You jest!'

'Señor, if you knew how long it took my good wife to stitch these, you would feel ashamed to pay only five reales.'

'With no disrespect to your good wife, sir –' Antonio rubbed the fabric between thumb and forefinger, testing it, then snatched his hand back. A man fingering an item of women's underwear in public… '– I know for a fact I can have one made for two reales plus the cost of the linen.' A worthy effort, but he knew no such thing. Still, he plunged on. 'Three reales.'

The tendero laughed outright. 'Five, Señor. That's the price.'

Too much. It would leave Catalina so little cash. He turned away.

'¡Señor!'

The tendero held out a hand, signalling him to wait while he served another customer, one who actually had money, by the look of her fine hat – a *bergère* with feathers and a wide brim casting shade down to her chin.

The stallholder finished his sale, then faced Antonio. 'Four reales, final offer.'

It wasn't especially fine linen, coarsely stitched at that. What did he know? He had nothing to weigh against, and too few reales in his purse to waste. He caught the eye of an approaching woman; she looked like she'd bought a few shifts in her time and had the no-nonsense air of someone who wouldn't overpay.

'Is four reales a fair price for a shift?'

She took a look at him and must have decided he had a pleasant enough aspect, for she answered with a firm nod. 'You could shop around, but your wife might catch cold waiting, all for the sake of a few maravedí.'

He grinned, and her face broke into a beam with him.

Turning to the tendero, he said, 'I'll take it.'

He left the market lighter, despite his purchases. He would head for his quarters, assemble the package for Catalina, and still have a couple of hours to spare. Pray he'd done enough, she couldn't hide forever, but still, she was so frail.

A man stepped into his path, and with Antonio's thoughts elsewhere, it took him a moment to place him. The scrivener from the mesón.

If asked to describe Joaquim Gil, he would have used a single word. Grey. From the grey camisa in which he'd likely slept, to the grey breeches over which it hung, baggy and misshapen at the knees. Unruly grey hairs dotted the grey skin of the cavernous chest exposed by the open shirt. Even the long, greasy hair hanging in ropes past his shoulders – grey.

'Don Albrono. What a surprise!'

'Indeed. Señor Gil.'

'I was thinking about you, and here you are. It must be fate.'

'Or we both live here.' Antonio didn't bother to adopt a friendly face. He didn't like the old fraudster and wasn't about to socialise with him, especially not when he had somewhere to be.

'Want to know what I was thinking about?'

'No,' said Antonio, stepping past him.

The scrivener kept pace – thick-skinned didn't begin to describe him. 'The charm we spoke of.'

'We?' said Antonio.

'I can pay you.'

Timely, but no, Antonio walked faster. So did Joaquim.

'A silver dollar.'

His feet planted themselves before his mind caught up. *A silver dollar.* He had to at least listen.

Joaquim smiled, and the tip of his tongue appeared on his lower lip, then retreated into the darkness behind.

A charm. A silver dollar. Catalina. He thumbed the ring on his little finger; worth so little, just brass and a milky quartz stone, but his mother's. Still, better a silver dollar than a trinket. Catalina could pay for a month's lodgings with a silver dollar.

But the dishonesty of it. A line once crossed…

But would it be so bad to get one past a fraudster?

Catalina's face swam before him. Not the hollowed-out version he knew, but glowing with health, smiling in her sleep, hair spread on a clean white pillow.

He touched the ring again.

Joaquim tugged Antonio's elbow. 'Come to my house,' he said, ushering him down a side alley.

Should Have Understood

For all his hesitation out there in the street, he'd never doubted he would take the scrivener's bargain. Not really. And now, kneeling beside Catalina on the blanket, he knew he'd made the right decision. She had a chance. For the first time her cheeks held colour, and fragments of the woman she'd been emerged in the straight line of her back, in the clarity of her gaze.

'This is for you.' One by one he transferred items from his satchel to a linen bag: the rolled-up shift, bread, fruit, cheese, the soap… 'So that you may bathe.'

'Must I leave?' Her eyes darted: his face, the doorway, back to him.

'Sí, it's not safe here. Besides –' He forced a smile. '– you deserve a softer bed.'

She drew in a breath and nodded.

A linen bag. Barely any weight; its sides caved inwards as she gathered it up. Had he not collected more than this? He delved into his satchel again. Bread and soap. She needed a new heart, or at least a mended one, not a block of *cheese*. Frantic now, he rummaged for more.

She touched his hand. Livid scars encircled her wrists, skin raised and puckered at their edges. Though he had seen them before, now, in this moment, he couldn't drag his eyes away.

'Señor, gracias.'

He swallowed.

'My friend, Enzo, will be here soon.' His voice was rough. He cleared his throat. 'He'll take you to Almassera. Once you're there, he'll help you find lodgings, and when you're stronger, you'll be able to find work there, or move on to Meliana if that suits you better.'

To think would be to break. He kept moving. Taking a cloth purse from around his neck, he tipped its contents onto the blanket. 'It's not much, but, a start.'

Two reales, a few maravedís, and there, glistening proud, the silver dollar. He returned the coins to the purse. Lifting her hair, he looped the slender rope around her neck, and tucked the pouch beneath her shift. 'Hide it. There are those who would snatch it without a second thought.'

'I don't know your name,' she said.

'Antonio.' His throat closed over the last syllable, and he coughed. 'It'll get better. Take one day at a time.'

She met his gaze. Grey eyes. Clear with certainty. He should have understood what they were telling him.

He watched her as Enzo steered the cart away. He watched her grow smaller. Then he watched the space into which she vanished, obscured by the dust thrown up by the wheels.

A Letter to Luisa

El Mesón del Sol, Valencia
Valencia, 24 mayo del año 1756

Mi vida, Luisa,
It seems that the war in Europe could not be prevented, and even as a soldier – perhaps especially as a soldier – I know that war is never a good thing. Heads of nations argue over land that belongs to others and it will not be they who pay the heaviest price.
I remember we talked about it that evening on the terrace of your hotel. I cannot recall if I said so then, but Señor Martinez was wrong to opine on what is 'a fitting subject for a woman.' In a world full of hot air, your voice means everything. You matter. Now my mind is full of that evening, and a most welcome memory it is too. Your maid, Marta, showed me where you were. A good woman. I knew her little but recognised her as kind and wise. I hope she is well. I owe her my thanks for leading me to a memory that stays with me yet. You and I sharing a glass of brandy, watching the stars, over the Port of Barcelona.
As for the thing I mentioned previously, I have done what I can, though I fear it is not enough. The actions I took compromised me, and I suppose I shall have to come to terms with that, because I cannot regret them. No harm has been done and

maybe, God willing, some good. I have added another name to my daily prayers.

I know I must shed this cloak of melancholy, for I do not believe it suits me. I have air in my lungs, clothes on my back and fine friends.

Misery only generates more sadness. When I think of you, I see you laughing under the same sun as me. Perhaps wearing that hat with the blue ribbon that you wore to escort me around town.

Be happy, amore mio. My heart would break once more if it were otherwise.

Suyo en cuerpo y alma

Antonio

Postscript: Another thing I was right about that evening. Blue is your colour, like the sky above our heads, as infinite as my love for you.

A Society Courtship

May deepened into June, bringing longer afternoons, and Rafael became a regular visitor. Their time together, always easy and filled with laughter, became a welcome counterpoint to the responsibilities that kept Luisa tethered to El Marqués.

On one such long afternoon, Luisa sat at her desk, tallying the endless columns of her accounts, the scratching of her quill, and the shifting of invoices the only sounds breaking the stillness. The air smelled of lemon wood-polish, and sun filtered through lace curtains, patterning the floor. She rubbed the bridge of her nose, and let her gaze drift to the courtyard outside where the gardener was tending to weeds in the borders.

Footsteps tapped in the corridor outside, then Rafael spilled into the office like a sunbeam through a break in the clouds. Only he did this – demanded her attention without so much as a moment's notice. And got it. She sprang to her feet, circling the desk to greet him.

'A gift, mi querida,' he said, spinning her before drawing her into his arms from behind. He smelled of outdoors. Resting his chin on her shoulder, he handed her a small rectangular package.

'What, are we dispensing with *buenas tardes,* now?'

He kissed her ear. 'Open it.'

Luisa turned it over in her hands. 'This is too beautiful to disturb. Your work?'

'Of course.' He'd wrapped it in blue silk with a matching ribbon. 'The closest match I could find to the dress you were wearing when I first saw you. You were a celestial vision.'

She wriggled out of his arms and turned to face him. 'I'm caught by surprise; I should have prepared a gift for you.'

'*Open* it.' Rafael nodded at the package.

Beneath his humour, she could tell he was in earnest. When she untied the ribbon, the silk wrapping slid away, pooling in her hand to reveal a polished wooden box with a golden clasp. She ran a thumb over the grain and unlatched it.

Inside lay a gem on a white velvet cushion. She turned it against the light. Its colours shifted through a spectrum – chocolate, gold, green, maroon, and even black – as light and shadow caught different planes.

'Only a base stone, but precious because it exactly matches your eyes.'

'I don't know what to say.'

'So you don't think me miserly, I shall have it set in diamonds.'

'No! I love it exactly as it is, because you chose it.'

His expression melted. 'May I?'

She gave him her back, and felt his fingertips, ghostly, against her nape. With the necklace fixed, he ran his hand down her arm, planted a kiss on the inside of her wrist and twirled her around.

'Beautiful.' He nodded at the stone nestling in the hollow at the base of her neck. Hands on her waist, he pulled her in. She tucked her chin so his kiss missed her mouth and caught the tip of her nose. She pretended not to notice.

They sprang apart when her mother swept in – a tempest in lilac silk.

'Don Rafael! This is unexpected! What brings you here unannounced, scandalising my daughter? Oh, don't look so apologetic, I jest.' She brandished a cheek, receiving his kiss without breaking flow. 'I hope our guests don't learn of it; we shall be the gossip of La Ribera. And I hope you haven't compromised her. Well perhaps just a little.' Did she just wink at him?

'Mama!'

A change of subject was called for. Luisa lifted her chin to show off the stone. 'Rafael brought me a beautiful gift, see?'

Inspecting with both eyes and fingertips, her mother sniffed. '*Cuarzo.* Is that the value you place on my daughter?'

If only the ground would swallow her.

'If I believed her to be for sale, Doña María, I would arrive with a coachload of diamonds and still know it to be inadequate.'

They discussed her virtue and her price the same way her father discussed trade: coffee beans, bolts of silk, a daughter's virginity.

Luisa *tsched.* Rafael squeezed her fingers.

It doesn't matter; she told herself. What is virtue anyway? Perception. Performance. Reputation. A mistake buried.

Calification

His skin tightened, shrinking from doubt. He might have misread. Hope does that – shows you what you want to see. He turned it over, checked the broken seal. No, even his dreams would not conjure this miracle; they were never so specific; they circled but never took shape. The Lord's doing then. At last, and praise be. And about time too. Fausto devoured the words once again, hardly daring to blink, in case they vanished.

Royal Palace of the Inquisition of Valencia
18 mayo del año 1756

> *BY THE AUTHORITY VESTED IN US BY THE HOLY OFFICE OF THE INQUISITION.*
> *In connection with a current case being examined by this Tribunal of Valencia, we require knowledge of any prior proceedings, accusations, confessions, verdicts, sentences, or other records pertaining to the accused individual:*
> *Don Antonio Albrono,*
> *or his lineage, within the jurisdiction of your Most Reverend Tribunal. We request that you conduct a thorough search of your records and archives and communicate any findings to us at your earliest convenience, that we may proceed with the case in accordance with the sacred duty entrusted to us.*
> *Your response will be received with the gratitude befitting your devotion to the Holy Office.*
> *In Nomine Patris, et Filii, et Spiritus Sancti.*
> *Don Ignacio Ortes de la Peña.*
> *Primer Inquisidor Licenciate, Tribunal of Valencia*

'Su Excelencia?' Señor Alcacid crumpled his brow. 'Are you quite right? Shall I fetch the physician?'

Fausto waved his hand. 'Sometimes I grow so weary. Yet another heretic.'

'I can only imagine the strain.'

'It is my calling,' Fausto said. 'I fight for every soul, no matter how lowly or how heinous their crime.'

He put aside the letter and leafed through the accompanying papers. Four witness depositions, all consistent, no irregularities. And here was the Calification – the theological review of evidence to determine the charges. Fausto pored over them, pressing his lips together lest he give voice to the joy bubbling in his chest:

> *… the heretical practice of necromancy, insult to the sacred ceremonies of the Catholic faith and Holy Mother Church.*

Of course, he had known Albrono harboured an unclean soul from the moment he laid eyes upon him. By his untroubled posture, his lustful gaze, his unseemly ambition. If ever a soul needed saving…

To think he had rescued Luisa from the clutches of a heretic. She would need him now. He would break the news himself, comfort her, educate her on the folly of a woman's heart and the need to strengthen her relationship with God. He reached the final line:

> *… declared unanimously that the person under qualification be pronounced under suspicion de levi.*
> *Signed: Fr. Francisco Sileta, Fr. Augustin de Vinaros, Fr. Juan Ba. Lopes, Padre. Juan-Antonio, Doctor Pedro Montez, Secretary.*

De levi. Valencia must be rotting from the inside with cowardice. He lifted the document to his nose, as though he might catch the stench past the tang of ink.

Outrage is more satisfying for being shared, but the secretary was nowhere to be seen. Fausto must have been more absorbed than he realised, because light had given way to long shadows, restless against flickering candlelight. The letter. A formality demanding a simple reply. He folded it and tucked it under his arm.

Lineage. That word nagged as he left the grand hall.

Crossing the shadowed courtyard, a breeze tugged at the folds of his robe. Seville would have received the same request, and they'd reply in the negative. Not a problem. Except the prisoner, too, would be asked – it was a standard question.

He climbed the stairs, passed along the mezzanine, ascended another level, to his chamber and more pacing, slippers on stone. The thought swelled with every step until doubt became certainty and inconvenience a disaster.

No. He exhaled. He'd yet to meet a crisis that prayer and planning couldn't avert – which meant, of course, that he'd yet to meet a crisis. He stood before his tall crucifix and clasped his hands.

A coarse laugh broke the stillness, and he glared at the interruption – the open window – then stepped across to look. Just guards. The cathedral bell tolled midnight. He searched the sky for inspiration, because it was what men did. The tall silhouette of Santa Agata's church opposite broke his view; a single light flickered in one of its windows. A verger preparing for service?

No use. His mind was too full.

'Juan!' he called. The novice had a knack for soothing him.

Sure enough, his breathing steadied as Juan trembled before him. And answers came with penance. Eight this time.

It was obvious, really. In view of his concerns at the *de levi* assessment, duty required that he deliver his reply to the Valencia Tribunal in person. And in view of his prior knowledge of the defendant, duty also required that he grasp the case with both hands.

Fausto slept with righteous contentment, and woke before the cathedral clock struck four. He pushed Juan from his bed, and by the time the sun rose, he'd passed the walls southwest of the city, his friar trailing on a mule.

A Society Betrothal

The proposal came in June. In a quiet moment, as natural as any of their conversations. Shall we dine in town tonight? Do you think it will rain? Shall we marry? No grand gestures, no poetic speeches, just two people deciding to join their lives.

Her mother had, of course, hoisted the news like a banner, casting Luisa as triumphant heroine in a play she hadn't staged. Soon Luisa couldn't leave home for being congratulated by people she hardly knew. Indoors was no better. All morning it had been one well-wisher after another; for everyone that made an appointment, another dropped in unexpectedly. She should be happy, but the more she talked, the more the words lost their shine – like an heirloom passed between too many hands.

In the end, she hid in Marta's room. Not to be ungrateful, just for the peace – a couple of hours without having to answer the same questions a dozen different ways.

She perched on Marta's window seat, twisting the betrothal ring – not nervous, she told herself, but to enjoy the sparks it threw over the walls.

'Nice,' said Marta, peering at the ring. 'Are your parents happy?' She returned to her darning.

'Oh, thrilled, what it won't do for their status.'

'He's your choice, though.' Marta sucked the end of her thread and poked it into her needle, squinting.

'He is. I care for him.' She knotted the other end for Marta.

'You make a fine couple, the most handsome in Barcelona.'

'He's a good man. And muy, *muy* inteligente.'

'You don't need to tell me that. I'm lost when you witter on about his books.' Marta clipped the torn part of the stocking into the sewing hoop and passed the needle through for the first stitch. 'Are you happy?'

She opened her mouth to speak, but couldn't think what to say. Marta sewed – loop and pull, loop and pull – Luisa watched. After a while, Marta dropped her work to her lap and looked up.

'Señorita?'

'Can I help?'

Marta looked down. 'Ffff. Your help means more work for me. Last time you sewed stockings you stitched the leg closed, remember?'

Luisa stifled a laugh. 'I learned from it. Let me try.'

'Your talents lie in managing the hotel, mine in managing you. Let's keep to what we know.'

Luisa scrunched her face and stuck her tongue out at the top of her maid's bent head.

'And you can put your tongue away.' Marta looked up, and set aside her sewing. 'You didn't answer my question. Are you *happy*?'

Luisa turned toward the window. A grocer walked towards the trade entrance below, a crate of vegetables on his hip, curving his body to balance its weight.

'Is it the Genoan?'

Luisa couldn't reply. Why did her throat feel so tight?

'If he ever came back here, I'd… I'd have things to say to him.'

'I loved him.'

'He didn't deserve it, muchacha.'

'I thought I *knew* him.'

'Apparently not.'

Luisa turned the ring again. 'The truth is –' Luisa hesitated, embarrassed. '– I'm afraid I'll never have with Rafael what I had with Antonio.'

'What you *thought* you had. It didn't take him long to move on; three months after he left you, was it not? His last letter?'

'I know. I *know*. So why do I think of him every day? Even –' Luisa stopped herself before she admitted her deepest shame, that she compared Rafael's touch to that of Antonio.

'Listen.' Marta grasped her hands, her own dry and warm. 'Rafael is good for you, kind; he'll never hurt you; you enjoy each other. People marry for less. Look at your parents.'

She did. Often. Her mother had been practically a child when her father had set his sights on her. At sixteen, she'd had no choice. He'd been her guardian. Luisa *did* have a choice. She could carry on pining for a ghost, or marry a good man, a man who respected her.

But should she?

'Marta,' Luisa swallowed. How to say this? 'Do you think Rafael would marry me if –'

'Don't say it.' Marta squeezed so hard her thumbnail dug into Luisa's palm.'

'Ouch.' Luisa tugged her hands away; her gaze was another matter – Marta had it trapped, her own unrelenting.

After a moment or two her maid nodded, as if to herself. 'You're entitled to your secrets.' She said *secrets* as if they were laundry that could be folded and put away. 'Yes. And to happiness.'

Luisa sat with that. Absently rubbing her palm where Marta had pressed. And thinking.

'Rafael does make me happy. If I think about losing him, my heart hurts. That must count for something.'

'It counts for a great deal.'

She studied the ring again. She meant every word; happiness was hers to take. Antonio, no doubt, was with another woman this very moment, telling her he loved her, asking her to say his name, so he could leave her with a shattered heart.

She'd paid enough for believing the wrong man. What purpose would be served in raking it over with Rafael? When ink's been spilled, it's best to turn the page.

The Lord's Work

They rode well, covering almost twelve leagues every day and resting each night in monasteries. From his final rest stop, outside the city walls – the Monasterio de Santa María – Fausto sent word of his arrival. Two days later he received an invitation for a meeting with the Tribunal – in three days' time. He screwed the missive into a wad and threw it into a rosebush. He had paced every step of the cloister, attended mass, held audiences, admired the gardens, heard confessions. Enough was enough. Three days? No. Today.

He arrived at the Monasterio San Francisco, close to the end of his patience, and almost reached it when the Tribunal's secretary, a Doctor Montez, explained the misunderstanding. Apparently, Montez had *assumed* that Fausto would appreciate a longer rest after his journey. Well, Fausto put him straight in that regard, and Montez proposed a slot directly after the weekly meeting, later that very afternoon. In essence, the secretary removed any room for grievance, and Fausto entered the meeting smouldering, like embers denied air.

Fausto took his seat at the centre of the table facing two Inquisidors: Don Ignacio Ortes de la Peña, and Don Antonio Inviola. Juan took a chair against the wall, where the shadows swallowed him alongside the other assistants. A rather arch man in secular dress took the seat on Fausto's left: Doctor Lorenzo Balleza. With small eyes and hair brushed forward to cover a high forehead. The most disturbing aspect of his face was that it bore no lines –

unsettling for Fausto, because it made him unreadable, apart from the moment Montez introduced him by his dual role as both Physician and Confessor. Then he lifted his chin, a small but noticeable tell. Pride. As if nobody else ever held two positions.

'Su Excelencia, it is a pleasure to see you here. We are humbled.' This young Doctor Balleza certainly didn't lack confidence. 'How fares the Inquisition in Barcelona? I imagine we share the same challenges?'

'And what *challenges* would they be?' Fausto asked.

'Oh, well, finance, efficiency…'

'Those are not our biggest challenges, Lorenzo.' Ortes interrupted. At least Fausto thought it was Ortes; the two Inquisidors looked so similar. 'Freemasonry, intellectualism, new ideas coming from Europe. Being a seaport has its challenges, a landing point for the undesirable and corrupt. I am sure you see the same in Barcelona, Su Excelencia. Perhaps worse.'

'Indeed, you are exactly right…' Fausto coughed to conceal his confusion about the Inquisidor's name. 'These are testing times.'

'And we regularly uncover secret meetings, men sharing impure ideas that would undermine the very fabric of our Holy Faith,' said Probably-Ortes.

'Voltaire!' shouted the other Inquisidor, Probably-Inviola.

The grey-whiskered secretary at the end of the table jerked upright at the exclamation. Fausto brushed his mouth to conceal his amusement.

'We uncovered a copy of his latest manuscript,' Probably-Inviola went on. 'A heinous tract. He compares humans to insects, suggests our world is one of many, our faith something to be mocked.'

'Most of these *progressives* are intellectuals,' Fausto told them. 'They fill the institutions in Europe. They would indoctrinate our children and expect us to rewrite doctrines that have served us well for centuries. I wonder why we do not close our borders.'

'I fear our country is already polluted. Good Spanish people are not safe anymore.' Probably-Ortes shook his head.

'You are right, Ortes,' said the other, settling their names. 'What these progressives forget,' Inviola continued, 'is that we tried integration. What did that achieve? Conversos and Moriscos practising in secret, leading people astray, stealing from us, eating our pets, a terror to anyone with children.'

They all shook their heads, unified in dismay.

'Is there something we can help you with? Su Excelencia?' the physician-confessor asked.

And so, to business. Good, he was ready. 'I read with interest your case against Antonio Albrono. I came to confirm that Barcelona has had no prior case against him or his ancestors.'

The two Inquisidors raised their eyebrows. Fausto had expected them to be perplexed that he journeyed here on such a routine account; he'd rehearsed for it. 'I've encountered him; he is one of those progressives.'

'Really? Interesting,' Ortes said.

'He attempted to seduce a noblewoman of the city; to run away with her.'

'Abducted her?' Inviola said.

'Kidnapping a noblewoman…' Ortes said.

Fausto left the misunderstanding to fester, and flapped his right hand, shifting the subject on. 'I read the Calification. Such serious charges. And so, to my point in coming here, I wonder why your office considers them *de levi* offences.'

Ortes swung his head towards the secretary. 'Montez, can you shed any light on the *de levi* judgement?'

The secretary twitched and blinked.

Ortes sharpened his question. 'Was Friar Francisco being sentimental again?'

'The friar did influence the decision,' said Montez, 'but the panel followed due process; shall I fetch the record?'

'Will this Friar Francisco be involved in the trial?' asked Fausto.

'Su Excelencia, I hope you trust we will conduct this case appropriately,' Ortes said.

'With respect, My Lord Inquisidor, I detect a tendency towards leniency that does your Tribunal no credit.' Fausto gave him the benefit of his stare and watched the colour rise in the other man's cheeks.

'Perhaps you would prefer to take the case yourself,' Inviola interjected. 'I can assure you there will be no value in the defendant's confiscated goods. If he ever had wealth, he lost it. He's been living on a soldier's wage this past year.'

'Are you suggesting my interest is financial?'

'Of course not. Trials are expensive though, are they not?' Inviola smiled at his own recovery, pitiful though it was.

'Su Excelencia,' said Ortes, 'I wonder if you would excuse us, so we may confer.'

Fausto dipped his chin. 'Of course.'

They waited. The Valencians clearly expected him to leave, which he took as an insult. The impasse stretched until it had to break, and they both made a grudging exit.

Secretary Montez shuffled his papers, but Doctor Balleza matched Fausto in silence: still, relaxed, unreadable.

Ten or so minutes later, the two Inquisidors re-took their seats. It was Ortes who spoke.

'We are awaiting approval from Madrid; we still require the necessary confirmations from eleven Tribunals; we only have yours and that of Granada. So, we do not expect to arrest him until the end of June, which introduces a complication.'

'The regiment of the accused – the Asturia – is shortly to be demobilised from Valencia and moved to Barcelona,' Inviola said. 'By the time we issue the arrest warrant, they will probably have completed half the journey.'

Fausto had to study the insignia on his ring to hide his glee. This really must be the Lord's work. They were delivering Albrono into his hands, and he had not even had to argue for it.

'Given your existing intelligence, and that the accused will be in your jurisdiction by the time of his arrest,' said Ortes, 'there is an argument for handing the case over to the Tribunal of Barcelona, if you agree of course.'

Fausto stroked his chin. 'Will you provide me with the services of your confessor? So that my officials fully understand the evidence?'

'Of course.' Ortes looked across the table at Lorenzo as he spoke. 'And should Article Fifteen be necessary, he can also act as Physician.'

Fausto eyed Doctor Balleza, who sat impassive. 'A case as straightforward as this, we will not detain him for long.'

'Very good,' said Ortes. 'We have other denunciations to pursue. Perhaps one day we will be able to return the favour.'

'Doctor Montez will see to it the documentation is forwarded to your office,' said Inviola.

'If there is anything I can take with me now, I would be happy to carry it myself.'

'I hope you plan to stay a few days,' said Ortes. 'We will show you our fine city. Perhaps you would bless the docks project and say mass at some of our monasteries and convents.'

'Nothing would please me more.' A lie. It would be odd, though, to travel such a distance only to turn around again.

'That settles it,' Ortes said. 'Doctor Montez will put together an itinerary, and Friar Josef here will find you a room. Your friar can share with him.'

'Gracias, but our needs are modest. Juan shares with me.'

Doctor Montez closed the meeting. It had been a triumph.

So Let It Be Done

'Bread, cheese, march. Bread, cheese, march.' Gianni grumbled to the rhythm of his footsteps. 'We were to have reached Reus in eight days, and this is the ninth.'

'Strange. The march didn't trouble me until yesterday. At around the time your complaining began.' Antonio frowned at his left boot, wondering if the sole would last all the way to Barcelona or if he should seek a repair. He could ask the division's cobbler to fix it; perhaps ride with Enzo in the meantime. His friend had secured a place among the camp followers, driving one of the supply wagons.

'Why are you so eager to be in Reus, Gianni?' asked Luca. 'We shall be there but a few days, and after that, upon the march once more.'

'A few days is all I ask to break the routine.' Gianni sighed. 'Is this not interminable?'

'I hope someone has warned the chicas of your arrival.' Felipe glanced at his camaradas, pleased with his joke, but his grin dropped when he saw it had fallen flat.

The group marched in silence for a while, each man inside his own thoughts. They'd been walking for four hours, and the July sun pulsed high in the sky as if invested in their discomfort. They were due to take a break in another two hours; it would be a lunch of more bread and cheese, and if they were lucky, some cured ham.

Miguel broke the peace. 'Don't you have someone in Barcelona, Antonio?'

Antonio blinked, then he remembered he had once walked with Miguel to post a letter. 'Once.'

'But you still write to her.'

'A habit. Or perhaps dumb optimism.'

Luca swung his head around. 'You're an enigma, Antonio. You never speak of this woman. Why so secretive?' Then he stumbled on a protruding rock and returned his attention to the path ahead.

'Nothing to tell.'

'Ha! Is that not what people say when there's *something* to tell?' said Felipe.

Antonio pressed his lips together. His camaradas all appeared to be following the conversation; he should never have let Miguel see him with the letter.

'What's her name?'

'Is she beautiful?'

'Is she from a good family?'

'She is tu novia?'

'Will you meet in Barcelona?'

The questions came, and Antonio studied the back of the head of the man in front, the grime that had deposited from his neck and hair to the collar of his shirt, and the white flecks of dandruff on his back.

'Enough! The man's silence is all the answer we need.' Gianni cut the questions dead.

Antonio looked at the face of the big Milanese and nodded his thanks.

'Di niente, amico.' Gianni spoke Italian, his voice low. 'I think this woman is important to you.'

An understatement. Damn it. Now she filled his mind. The small scar parallel with her jaw, the crinkle at the top of her nose when she laughed, her thick hair separating between his fingers, the dent between her collarbones that tasted of vanilla and honey… He breathed in hard. A warm hand landed on his shoulder, Gianni's, a gentle smile lighting his features; a side of him Antonio had never seen before. And then he tripped and had to grab Gianni's arm to stop himself falling.

'*Maledizione*!' The sole flapped like a laughing mouth under his left boot. His walk became comical – he had to lift his left knee high to avoid tripping, and with each step his sole slapped the ground, mocking him further. This wouldn't do. He swerved out of the group and found a large flat rock. And there he sat, waiting for the wagons.

The soldiers of his company marched past, striking the dirt in unison. In the distance to the rear, the canvas covers of the wagon train glinted in the sun. The line of infantry snaked as far as his eye could see, both ahead and behind. Incredible that human endeavour transformed the meaningless travails of individual souls into a single, proud, man-made unit, capable of changing the future of entire nations.

A shout cut through his philosophising.

'Antonio!' Matheo wove towards him, against the direction of the soldiers, frowning so hard his eyes were reduced to glints under his dark eyebrows.

At first, Antonio expected Matheo to reprimand him for falling back, and he raised his foot to show his difficulty. But his sargento ignored it and sat on the rock with him. He looked into Antonio's eyes, and opened his mouth, then took off his hat and stared into it as if searching for something. His grip flexed, knuckles whitening, then he exhaled sharply and ran a hand through his hair.

Antonio's skin prickled at the performance. What distressed Matheo so? He placed a comforting hand on his shoulder, and it must have worked, in its way, because the moment his touch landed, Matheo straightened his back and pulled his hat onto his head. His jaw bunched, and he took Antonio's hand from his shoulder, slowly, deliberately, his grip firm. 'There is a matter. I'm to take you into custody.'

Antonio stared at Matheo's lips, replaying how they'd moved, so he might disprove the words that had fallen from them. He forced a laugh, making a jest of it. Then he noticed Matheo's eyes, and the sound died in his throat. This was no joke.

A thousand questions formed and, by way of reply, Barbieri appeared in his line of vision. The two men locked eyes. It seemed to Antonio that Barbieri smirked, twisting in his direction as he marched past with his new sección. Then Barbieri's features blurred, shrinking into a small circle, before fading to a speck.

Matheo still held his forearm; the weight of his grip a puzzle… '*A matter,*' he'd said. That sole was a mess. He placed his foot on his knee and poked at it. It might be beyond repair, detached all the way past the instep. He pulled at it, watching the leather bend. Matheo stopped his hand.

'Antonio.'

'My boot…'

He slid it off. The stitching had disintegrated, what with all that marching. He tore the sole, and it came away with a satisfying rip. The rough stones under his stockinged foot felt pleasantly uncomfortable. He wiggled his freed toes.

'Antonio.'

'Sargento?'

Matheo stood, pulling Antonio up by his right arm in the same movement. 'I won't humiliate you with shackles. I trust it won't be necessary.'

Shackles? He allowed Matheo to lead him, walking by his side in the reverse direction to the soldiers. A few looked their way; one gave him a tight smile, wry sympathy for a fellow soldier holding a broken shoe. Antonio looked towards his shoe, then to Matheo's face, and it struck him his problems went beyond footwear. The knowledge began as abstract, but with each step it settled further into his chest and abdomen like molten ore, heating and squeezing his internal organs, pushing his breath into his throat. He clung to the periphery of his growing awareness, to details and practicalities, choosing to watch the unfolding scene from outside himself, because it was the only way to not be crushed by it. 'Let it be Enzo's wagon,' he said.

Matheo eyed him. 'If you seek to escape, do so without implicating your friends.'

'I don't look to escape.'

Matheo nodded, and Antonio knew he believed him. He also somehow knew that if he did abscond, Matheo would do little to stop him, or to seek him afterwards. But what would that achieve except to add desertion to the weight of whatever charges already existed?

Matheo's state concerned him; his face had turned grey, and sadness had carved lines Antonio had never noticed before. He patted his shoulder to comfort him, and his sargento's expression shifted to one of surprise.

Enzo's vehicle bore no distinguishing features, so they would have missed it had not his friend seen them. Antonio watched him steer out of the train and, with a tug on the reins, pull up at the side of the track, commanding the horses as he did so. '*¡Izquierda! ¡So!*'

The four creatures obeyed in perfect unison; a testament to their driver, Enzo. He had hidden talents. The version of him observing from outside realised he would normally ignore such details, but now the horses fascinated him more than the conversation between Matheo and his friend.

Hands took each of his arms and steered him to the back of the wagon, and without thinking he climbed in, taking a seat on a low box inside. He tugged at a piece of loose skin on the side of his thumb, fascinated by the bead of blood that swelled there. Then two brown hands took both of his, and he looked up.

Enzo squatted on his haunches in front of him, his face a hand's breadth away. His forehead glistened, his skin had a yellow tinge, and his eyes peered into his. How had he not noticed their striking green before?

'Amico mio,' said Enzo, 'what can I do for you?'

His sargento perched to his left. A wonder three full-sized men could find such space in here.

'Don Antonio,' said Matheo. 'You do understand what's happening?'

'Sí, entiendo.' Then he looked at Enzo. 'Capisco.'

'I'm to deliver you to the Inquisition. The charge –'

'I know the charge,' Antonio cut him off.

And he did. It had to be either helping Catalina or the other thing, and he'd gotten Catalina away; nobody had been any the wiser. But the other thing… Barbieri, in the cellar, jabbing his finger, all glassy eyes and wine-slurred sibilance. More fool Antonio. Had he not been living under its shadow since Bellvís two years ago? It had been biding its time, waiting, this particular sin.

'Heresy.'

The word, a serpent's hiss, lingered, then shifted into the high scrape of chains – a memory. *Catalina.* Her face sharpened by pain. Her eyes glistened. Tears. Not for herself. No. She wept for him. For Antonio.

The sound came from deep inside, a groan, building and fading even as it reached his own ears. He jerked to his feet, and leapt for the exit, too fast for the men to stop him. But they need not have worried; he didn't seek escape; he leaned out and splashed the ground below with vomit. He didn't stop retching until every last scrap of half-digested bread and Manchego cheese decorated the dust behind the wagon, glistening in a pool of green bile. Somehow the sour smell satisfied him. More fitting than the clean scents of earth and sun-baked brush that had marked the place where his future ended.

Enzo climbed down. Antonio knew him by the buckles on his shoes; felt him waiting while he caught his breath, bent double, hands on his knees. Waiting for gasps to become shuddering sighs. Waiting for Antonio to compose himself.

Antonio took the water pouch Enzo offered and tipped it, swirling the liquid around his mouth, spitting it onto the ground.

Another deep draught and this time he swallowed, feeling the cool liquid trickle past his abused pharynx, cleansing the bile at least from his mouth, if not his soul. Antonio looked into Enzo's eyes and saw his plight written there, and when his friend reached out his hand, he took it.

The three men sat in the wagon and talked in low, sober tones.

'Every man in the sección will speak for you, Antonio,' said Matheo.

'I'm not afraid.' Antonio didn't believe his own assertion, and the frown on Matheo's face told him neither did his sargento.

'The Inquisition will look to take everything you own,' Matheo said. 'Even if – when – you are found innocent, they will claim it for their costs.'

Enzo's eyes widened. '*Figli di puttana*!'

'Sí,' said Matheo, his mouth a grim line. 'It's fitting they wear the black of vultures.'

The men's sentiments did little to lift Antonio's spirits.

'You'll leave everything here,' said Matheo. 'We'll keep it for you. I will see to it myself.'

'It's no good to me.' Antonio's voice cracked. 'Take my purse. And everything I have.' He handed his knapsack to his friend, then stood and twisted open the first button on his jacket, then a second, working down the line.

'What in God's name are you doing?' said Matheo.

'Returning my uniform, Sargento, they shall not profit from a single thread of it.'

Matheo exhaled hard through his nose, shaking his head. 'You're a stubborn bastard, Antonio.'

A minute later, Antonio stood in shirtsleeves and breeches.

'Keep your papers, my lord.' Enzo removed everything but Antonio's proof of identity, which he returned to the knapsack and passed back to him. 'It will surely help if they are aware of your nobility.'

Antonio doubted it, but slung the strap of the bag over his head and across his chest.

'I will fight your case, Antonio,' Enzo said, 'This shall not stand.'

Antonio knew Enzo's confidence was an act, but then, so was his. 'What now?'

'Reus,' said Matheo, 'where I have been instructed to transfer you to the care of the military prison. From there one of the familiars of the Inquisition will collect you and escort you to the prison of the Tribunal in Barcelona.'

'Very well.' Antonio took a breath. 'So let it be done.'

How We Deal with Informers

Someone watched from the side of the track. The stare drew him, intense, the kind you feel first, the kind that takes you by the chin and turns your head. Two men side by side on a rock, shoulders slumped. One had a hand on the other's arm. It had taken a few moments for their features to fall into place. Why did Albrono – he'd be damned if he called him *Don* – sit with his sargento, on a rock, letting the Asturia pass them by? Then again, who cared. Let him sit there like a dog with its master. The past was the past.

He turned from the men who'd judged him, planting one foot, then another, listening to his sección bounce from subject to subject without structure or reason, too fast to follow. Even when he thought of a retort, by the time he'd prepared it on his tongue the moment had slipped. One step, then the next. And after a thousand or a million, or a thousand million of those, dwellings began to appear – slumped, hollow-flanked things, their roofs curved down like the spines of underfed oxen. They rose in ones, then twos, and then in whole clusters, crouching as if in prayer around a spire.

A thousand or a million steps more and lanes became streets, packed earth walls became stone, and Barbieri, along with his sección, entered Reus. After nine days marching, finally they were permitted to break ranks. They didn't need telling twice.

Hours later, emerging from a tavern, he knew he'd drunk too much because his knees no longer spoke to each other. Good thing he had a rest day ahead. His stomach turned, and he tasted an acid version of his supper at the back of his mouth. He let go a long belch, and his guts settled, probably only temporarily. A quarter-hour, if that, the journey from his lodgings to the tavern had taken, so the return didn't daunt him. Pointing himself in roughly the right direction – so he hoped – he set off.

The ground was lost to shadows so he bounced off the walls, letting them guide him with the optimism of the drunk. As luck would have it, he travelled in the right direction, away from the tavern, but deeper into darkness.

He couldn't pinpoint when it began, the prickling on his skin. A bark startled him – a dog, distant at that. A rustling above – just the wind threading between branches. Something creaked to his left – only the flapping door of an empty dwelling. He laughed then stopped, caught by that noise. His heels against the stone echoed impossibly loud. A creature darted across his path, a cat. *For the love of God, just a cat.* His heart pounded fast inside his ribcage.

Did someone call to him, or was it the breeze again? He froze, ears straining. There it was.

'*Barbieri.*'

No. Remarkable how far a murmured conversation would carry in the still of night, twisting sound, feeding fear. He resumed walking.

'*Informer.*'

Loud this time, and close, from a side street, barely wide enough for two men abreast. He peered in. Derelict buildings rose black and jagged each side. He strained his eyes against the shadows cloaking the path. There it was again. Air moving in the shape of his name. Stepping into the alley, he felt his way, fingertips against the wall until his eyes adjusted to the dark and discerned shapes ahead. The shapes of men.

He registered the whites of eyes at the same moment as the blow to his guts. Winded, he staggered back against the wall, retching and wheezing. A second blow to his stomach creased his waist, then an upward strike to his jaw jerked him straight. Searing, ripping pain in his cheek and even as he registered the warm wetness on his neck, his back met the ground in a hard flat landing that emptied his lungs. His bladder gave way. As if pain needed its friend shame just to round out the party. A thudding boot to his chest, and he would have shouted for help had there been air in his lungs. More blows threw his body this way and that, like rags shaken by a puppy. They each took their turn, leaving no time for one agony to fade before the next arrived. He howled as a rib gave way under a stamping sole. Then his thighbone. His hand flew up to shield his face, and time slowed as his hand – the one that wrote his name, saluted, cleaned his weapon – folded like paper, knuckles kissing his forearm. A final kick to his chin snapped his head backward, cracking it against the stone cobbles. White-hot pain radiated from the back of his skull to his eye sockets. He couldn't move, only stare, bewildered, at the shadows standing over him. He recognised the voice addressing him, but not the contempt within it.

'Informer.'

He wanted to protest. *Not this, no. The rest, fine, flog me for it. Hang me if you must. But not for this.* His lips moved, but no sound came.

As his vision dimmed and his life slipped away, pain was replaced by unfathomable sadness. He had achieved so little, done so much that shamed him. But for all his sins, Jorge Barbieri was not, and had never been, an informer.

As Crimson as Christ's Wounds

A hole in the wall, high up. Meant for a window, more a taunt. Light seeped from it, reluctant, like it had been sent. Enough though to light the stone where it sweated.

A cot, also stone – a ledge really – with straw that hissed if he shifted his weight and sent up dust and fumes that burned his nose and throat and the spaces behind his eyes. The sting was settling now. A kind of mercy.

Outside: steps, scraping, rattling – a place of errands, keys, and places to be. A loud clatter, followed by hoarse curses. A wet splattering – a bucket or bowl, its contents thrown. A child laughed.

Antonio looked up, as though that laugh was for him. He raised a hand to the light and turned it over. *Here*, he thought. *I'm really here, in this place.* He ought to be afraid. If not, he was lost. He snatched his hand back, a guilty thing.

Beneath him, the ledge ached up through his bones. The floor stank of piss and rot. He drew his feet back, heels tucked in, draped his arms over his knees and lowered his head to think in the dark.

Everything he'd done, he could explain – demonstrate even. They'd see reason.

He straightened his shoulders. His legs ached, and he longed to use them. *Ignore the filth*, he told himself. *It's either that or stay crouched on the ledge until your legs forget what they're for.* He stepped into the thin light, lifting his face to the window, eyes closed; warmth would mean God hadn't forgotten him.

Steps outside the door, drawing closer. He wouldn't turn yet. Let them see composure, not fear – the calm of the innocent. A key scraped. Let it mean deliverance. Perhaps Matheo had explained. He might return to his sección, maybe even today.

The door creaked open, then clicked closed. Someone entered – a large person, by the way the air compressed. He opened his eyes, took a breath and turned. Faced his visitor.

He saw the crucifix first: a massive cross, a masterpiece in gold and silver filigree, studded with rubies as crimson as Christ's wounds.

He raised his eyes to meet those of the man before him. A man he'd last seen two years ago, and who now towered over him, with a smile too gleeful to be holy.

And as Don Antonio Albrono looked into the face of Don Fausto de Alenya, he knew he was doomed.

Part Two - Incarceratio

Imprisonment

Articles of Faith for Conduct of Activities of the Inquisition of Spain. Issued by Tomás Torquemada to the General Assembly of Inquisidors, Seville, 1474.

Article X
Persons guilty of heresy and apostasy incur the loss of all their property and the administration of it, counting from the day when they first offended, and their said property is confiscate to their Highnesses' treasury.

Article XVI
The accused shall not be supplied with a copy of the depositions against him, but he shall be informed of what is declared in them, whilst such circumstances as might lead to the identification of the deponents shall be withheld.

If the accused should demand an advocate, he shall be supplied. The advocate must faithfully assist the accused, but if he shall realise that justice is not on his side, he shall at once cease to assist and inform the Inquisidors.

Article XX
If any writings or trials should bring to light the heresy of a person deceased, let proceeding be taken against him.

Arriving in Barcelona

23 July 1756

I have been in Barcelona ten days. I know the number because every time a new day's sun shines through the window of my cell, I scratch another mark on the stone next to my cot. Or rather, I scrape over a mark already there. I'm one in a long line of prisoners who have occupied this living tomb.

They give me coarse bread and vinegar-water that makes my stomach cramp. It seems my body is under siege both from what I put in it and what it lacks. Running my hand across my abdomen, I trace valleys between my ribs, and when I touch my face, it feels hard and tight under my new beard. The skin on the back of my hands fascinates me; it has become crepe, and when I pinch it, there remains a raised tent, thin enough for light to pass through when I hold it up to the window.

I have company. Yesterday, I awoke to a searing pain in my ankle and found a rat gnawing as if I were a roasted guinea fowl. I cleaned the wound – vinegar-water has its uses after all – but it shouldn't still be so tender. Now I'm afraid to sleep. When I do, I pull a wool blanket around for protection, knowing its stifling heat will force me awake before I'm ready. The rat returns in the daytime and watches from the corner of my cell, and I think my mind must be slipping because in the last few days I've begun to greet it.

The mosquitoes are worse. They leave raised welts on my skin where they have feasted. The itching is madness.

How I complain. It's only been ten days. What of men and women who are sentenced to exist this way for years? And what of me if I become one of them? But more likely, I'm a dead man. Fausto would have it so.

I live from one moment to the next. My empty gut makes the next piece of bread a banquet. I crave human company, so a glance from my jailer thrills me. Perhaps I can exist this way until the moment the noose is around my neck or faggots at my feet. It would be better than entertaining hope – therein lies torment.

Routine keeps my mind whole. Rise with the sun. Walk a thousand steps. Then, I perform the bodyweight exercises I learned as a cadet in Vienna; they are harder with each day that passes, but the rat counts with me.

My jailer arriving each day is an event; I talk to him whilst he performs his duties, bringing food and changing my soil bucket. This morning, for the first time, I caught his eye. A small triumph. One day, God willing, he'll return my greeting.

For a while each day a beam of sunlight shines into my cell, marking prayer time. Positioning myself in its warmth, I close my eyes and repeat the Pater Noster, Ave María, and Credo, first in Italian, then German, then Spanish. Then, I practice a form of meditation I believe I've invented; I recall a scene from the Bible and position myself within it as a bystander. Sometimes I'm bold enough to speak a word or two to Our Lord, or one of the disciples. They always reply kindly. This morning, I talked with Judas, suggesting ways he might put his silver to use. He looked like Barbieri.

I complete my prayers and meditation by saying Grace. Then it's time to eat, which I do slowly: half the bread, twenty mouthfuls. After my first meal of the day, I snatch a short sleep, if I can. Then more steps. Then Grace again. Then my second meal. Then school, which means closing my eyes and recalling a lesson from my old professor in Vienna, or perhaps one of our many conversations on the new philosophers: does anything exist beyond immediate perception? To that great question, I would add my own: Does it matter?

School is over when my cell grows dark and I pull my blanket around myself, and say my final prayers.

That's how I keep my reason during the day.

I've resolved to impose a similar discipline on my nights, by reliving my time with Luisa in every detail. It will make each return to reality an agony, but I see no other way to preserve myself against blackness greedy for my sanity.

April 1754

I arrived in Barcelona a little over two years ago, aboard a three-masted brigantine named *La Fortuna* – some luck she brought me. I'd travelled with Signor Enzo Gallo, the Albrono family lawyer. Though he'd spent most of the journey sick in his bed, on the day of our arrival he emerged immaculate, from the shiny buckles on his shoes to his powdered wig.

We watched from the deck as marinaio threw ropes to the dockhands waiting on the jetty. The water churned; shirtless workers shifted cargo while merchants in waistcoats and hats marked ledgers and shouted. It reminded me of Genoa – my port of departure – though more sunburnt, more chaotic; not so much built as thrown together. A trade hub with warehouses lining the wharf, all bearing names of the merchant families whose wealth built the city.

I saw Luisa for the first time as we descended the gangplank, before I'd even set foot on Spanish soil. I didn't merely see her; I *recognised* her. An impossible thing, for I'd never laid eyes on her before. Standing beside the loading bay of the '*Navas*' warehouse, she did nothing remarkable, nothing to draw attention to herself; she merely talked with a man who marked a paper resting upon a barrel. So why couldn't I tear my eyes away? To me, her simple grey dress and plain white fichu outshone the finest Parisien gown. She glowed. Perhaps I stared too long, because she lifted her eyes towards mine, all the while still talking with the man beside her. When I nodded, she may have dipped her chin; I couldn't be sure.

I'd almost reached the quayside when an almighty yelling began from the ship next to ours. A scuffle, a chase, and a man in torn breeches and shirtsleeves leapt from its gangplank, barely clearing the water. He sprang to his feet and took flight, with three others in pursuit, shouting. Some onlookers gave chase. Some watched. As for me, I'd spotted the stack of crates in his path. It all happened fast: I ran, he collided with the boxes, the uppermost ones teetered, and I lunged forward in time to shove her out of harm's way. The woman I had been admiring not a minute earlier, landed against the warehouse wall like a sack of vegetables, while I hit the ground on my stomach, the falling load crashing onto my lower legs.

Two men dragged me to my feet, berating me in Spanish. '*¡Bestia! ¡Bellaco*!' No use expecting Enzo to help. He rolled his eyes and took a seat on a nearby sack, legs crossed, arranging his features like a cleric dealing with an errant parishioner.

She must have been a woman of note, because a throng gathered, clamouring and bustling: '*¡Llama a un medico! ¡She is hurt!*' That puzzled me. I'd just seen her scramble to her feet and straighten her hat. '*¡Retrocedan!*' '*¡Denle espacio!*' Ironic, the crowd calling for space at the very same time as pressing her. The fuss worked in my favour, for in the competition to display the most concern for '*La Señorita*,' the men forgot me in favour of joining the crowd bearing her away. Glad of the reprieve, I sank onto a crate to examine my injury.

'You made quite an entrance, Antonio.' Enzo peered at my foot, bottom lip protruding in a frown. 'Is it bad?'

'Non è niente.'

Not exactly nothing. I had to force the boot back over the swelling, and when I stood and attempted a step, pain shot along my leg. I made some progress leaning on Enzo, and resolved to limp along in that manner until we found a place – any place – to stay.

I'd not taken many steps before another woman approached. Older than me, around Enzo's age, neatly dressed, eyes like polished walnut. She introduced herself as Marta. Her mistress desired me to be brought to her hotel.

So, I came to stay at *La Posada del Marqués,* one of the most prestigious hotels in Barcelona, a guest of its manager, the woman I'd come to love. Luisa Navas.

Shoes on My Head

23 July 1756

I jerk upright, woken by bright sunlight. Too bright. 'What time is it?'

Marta pours water into the lavabo. 'It is late.' Her mouth is a tight line.

'My head hurts.' I massage my temples and lower myself tentatively against the pillow, wincing at the fresh pain set off by even that soft contact.

'From the brandy.'

'You disapprove, but I was cultivating my intellect. Rafael has been teaching me about modern thinking.'

'Modern thinking, is it?' Marta unfolds a towel.

'Yes… reason, not traditions. People choosing their own leaders rather than having to follow someone who inherited a title. And… and… all people are equal…' Is that right? My head really is a torment.

Marta chuckles drily. 'In that case, Señorita, perhaps you will wash *my* hair for me. And arrange *my* petticoats. And follow me around for hours while *I* go courting.'

I have no answer, and not because of my headache.

'Pffft, do close your mouth; you are not a cod. Now come here and allow me to get you bathed and dressed. I declare, if you had to do it yourself, you would leave the house with your shoes on your head!'

Two hours later, still thinking about Marta's remarks, I'm in Rafael's library, tracing the spines of his books with my fingers. I'm not as interested in this bookcase as in the secret shelves that appeared last night when he performed that strange rotating trick. It would be presumptuous, though, to try the feat without him.

Given his height, how is it that the first I know of his presence is when he places his hands upon my waist? I jump, then catch myself and laugh.

'Good morning, mi dulce prometida.'

Prometida. Clunky. Too many syllables bumping together. The wedding comes fast, too fast.

'Are you looking for a particular book?'

'Browsing. I enjoyed our conversation about *Inequality Among Men.* I thought I understood, and then Marta challenged me this morning, and now I'm right back at the beginning.'

Rafael laughs, hard. 'Did she say it's hypocritical for people such as you and I to preach on the matter?'

'Well, yes. She quite halted me in my tracks.'

'Be careful, mi querida.' His smile remains, but it's doing less work now. 'These books are prohibited.'

For some reason, I think of Don Fausto.

'Why don't we save our minds for when the sun isn't shining, and ride out?' he says.

A wonderful idea. I love Rafael's country home; with its books and curiosities, its bright rooms and corridors, and its exquisite formal gardens, but most of all I love the undeveloped land up in La Collserola. 'Give me time to change. I'll call Marta – no. I'll manage.'

I stretch onto my toes to kiss his mouth, change my mind and aim for his cheek, then pull away, embarrassed, and dash out.

I *will* dress myself; how difficult can it be? Shoes on my head indeed. Upstairs, I scramble into my riding breeches. I check myself in the mirror, decide, and pull on my boots.

Marta enters.

'My lord told me you were changing. I see you started without me.' She shakes her head. 'You have put your boots on before your skirt. Let's put this right.'

'No need. Have the afternoon to yourself. I'm ready.'

Marta gapes.

'Pffft, do close your mouth, Marta, you are not a cod.'

I only took a few minutes, but I cannot find Rafael. I learn from María, his housekeeper – my future housekeeper, I have to remind myself, when she frowns in disapproval at my attire – that he already left. Unlike him to be so rude. Now what? Should I cancel? No, I'm dressed for a ride, looking forward to it, and I'd like to know why my future husband rode out without me.

I expect to find him at our favourite spot, the highest point on the estate. And, sure enough, when I arrive, there is his stallion, Sol, secured to the hitching post. But there is a second alongside, a chestnut thoroughbred. Rafael sits on a rock – our rock – talking with another man, his arm outstretched, gesturing over the city below. They both turn as I approach, and Rafael jumps to his feet, followed by his companion.

'Luisa! What are you wearing? You look remarkable.' He takes my shoulders and spins me. 'All the ladies of Barcelona would dress this way if they saw how well it looks.' He drapes his arm around my shoulder – a comradely gesture. 'This is a very good friend, Jean-Pierre Vauvignarde, from Marseille. Jean-Pierre, this is mi prometida Luisa Navas, the most intelligent and beautiful woman in the whole of Spain.'

I elbow him in the ribs and hold my hand out to greet his friend.

He lifts it to his lips. 'Enchantée, Mademoiselle.'

He's striking. Around the same age as Rafael, with blonde curls escaping their ribbon. I can only imagine the line of sherbet women he must have vying for his attention.

I turn to Rafael, half a dozen questions ready, which he shouldn't need me to ask out loud. *Who's this? Why is he here unannounced?* And most of all, *why did he forget his manners and ride off with him?*

He says nothing. *Nothing*! The Frenchman offers something, though it's hardly adequate.

'Pardonnez-moi, Discúlpeme, Señorita Navas, I made an impetuous decision. I should have written, but I wanted to surprise my friend.' His French accent is heavy, but his Spanish is clear enough.

'And you did!' Rafael is grinning like a boy who just dreamed up a prank. 'I thought I'd faint, Luisa. It's been almost a year. Jean-Pierre is my closest friend. I can't wait for you to get to know each other, the two people dearest to me in the world.'

Touching. So dear he's never mentioned him before.

'Sit with us,' Rafael says.

Now I'm second guest.

'I've been telling Jean-Pierre about our plans for an observatory.'

'Ours? The imagination is all yours,' I say. And it is. I hadn't known the heavens offered so much, until Rafael explained his ideas to me. Constellation Hill, he calls this spot.

We settle on the rock, me in the middle. I ought to be less sour, I know, so I paint on a smile. 'Rafael is the cleverest man. Isn't this the perfect viewpoint?'

'En effet, il l'est, et c'est parfait. For where else can one see the city, sea and sky laid out before one's eyes all at once? A divine triptych. Ce sera magnifique.'

His enthusiasm spills out, like that of a child, but his seamless switches between French and Spanish sound sophisticated. At least to my ears. Despite myself, I'm drawn. 'Monsieur, are you familiar with Barcelona?'

'Jean-Pierre, please.' His smile could melt ice. 'Non, I have never had the privilege of visiting your city. The architecture is something I have always wanted to see for myself.'

The rock feels too small; there is more contact between us than Marta would approve of.

'Then we shall show you the sights!' says Rafael. 'We three will light up the city. Luisa, where shall we take him first?'

'How is Barcelona by night?' asks Jean-Pierre.

'Dreary.' Rafael laughs. 'Not what you're used to. But by day it's beautiful, both within the city and from the water.'

'How long will you stay?' I ask.

He shrugs. With only breeches between us, his thigh presses heat through mine. How awkward. Do I shift my leg, or will that draw attention to our contact? Worse, when I look to see if he notices, he's watching me. He holds my gaze, unblinking, while my face floods with heat.

'Let's go to town!' Rafael's exclamation is sudden, and so that we know he's serious, he leaps to his feet. 'Luisa, perhaps you should change first. I'm not sure Barcelona is ready for a woman in breeches.'

They stand together, and each extends a hand to help me up.

'That is Barcelona's loss then.' The Frenchman looks me up and down. 'Women in pantalons would soon be la mode if you were to hold your nerve.'

'Ha!' My laugh sounds loud to my own ears. 'How much there is for you to learn of Barcelona, Jean-Pierre.'

'And how much there is for you to learn of Europe, Luisa,' he replies.

'Come, mi amor,' Rafael places his arm around my waist. 'Let's return to the house and change for our trip to town.'

I sense him watching as Rafael leads me back to our horses, and sure enough when I look back, he is. That gaze could set fire to dry grass.

First Interrogation

28 July 1756

Uncle Luigi invites me to sit, but I might sully the damask. Stone walls have been replaced by ivory silk wallpaper, straw flooring by marble. My mind is performing sensory tricks, I know, but still, my neck aches from staring at the stuccoed ceiling with its paintings of cherubs. I must pay attention; he's speaking, and something tells me his words are important. Heat coats my skin like warm pitch, and the air is so thick I could chew it.

'The Spinelli accomplishments were funded with Albrono money.' His moustache moves with his lips as he speaks. It looks like a dancing slug. Do slugs dance? 'The debt has been passed through four generations.'

'Why was the debt never collected?' I have him there; I'm sure of it. Have I not asked this before?

'Genoa has long been at the centre of one power struggle or another. France or Spain. The Bourbons or the Habsburgs.' His lower lip is pink under his moustache, wet like that of a small child. 'The families that survived were those who found safe positions. For a long time, it was safest to disavow connections with Spain.'

'So why me? Why now?'

'You are anonymous. No political ramifications.'

'Anónimo Albrono?'

He laughed. 'That's it. Anónimo Albrono. If you're successful, then consider my obligations to your father discharged.'

'And if I'm not successful?'

'Then still, consider them discharged.' His laugh is loud now. 'Antonio, I'm saying with respect, *vafanculo*. Fuck off. This is all I'm giving you, and only because I like you. Your father was a disgrace. Quite frankly, he's lucky to have died at Velletri, because I'd have had him killed if he'd shown his face here.'

I should decline the debt; it must be a fool's errand. But I'm intrigued. Uncle Luigi is still laughing. I wish he would stop. The sound beats a harsh rhythm inside my skull, and I fear it will crack from within. '*Anónimo* Albrono. Ha!'

I'm a furnace, yet my teeth chatter. The room shrinks. Silk and damask recede. My stomach lurches. Stone rises. A tomb. A woman is screaming. Catalina. Here? I pull the blanket up. Blanket? The dream splinters. I draw my knees in. Anónimo Albrono. Nobody Albrono.

The screaming isn't Catalina. It's here, and it's now. It must be another prisoner, in a different cell. To treat a woman thus. *Another* woman. I press my face to the stone, so it draws heat from my skin.

The night fades; a ribbon of amber lines the stone edge of the window. The screams have dwindled to whimpers, and I pull my arms over my head to block them out, listening to my own rasping breath instead.

An immeasurable eternity that might also be minutes. A ray of sunlight spills into my cell, marking the start of another day, illuminating the rotten straw I pushed into one corner. I drag myself up on my cot, and the cell pitches and rolls. Something is wrong. Not just that I'm underfed, that I lack water; something more. Heat seeps into my skin, into my bones. Trembling, I grip the sides of my face to still my knocking teeth, but my hands feel distant, unwilling. And those dreams?

Routine. Breathe. I use my spoon to once again scratch faint freshness into a mark on the wall. Rat watches from the corner of the room, and I nod, announcing the day. 'Fifteen.' Rat lowers his head and sets to work pushing straw around his corner of our dwelling.

I'm at prayer at the top of my cot, knees drawn up, forearms draped over them. I don't move when I hear the key clicking in my cell door. Nor when I hear the door swing open. It's only when I hear a voice addressing me – the first since they brought me here – that I lift my head and drag open eyelids coated on the inside with sand.

'Don Antonio, of the Genoa Albrono family.'

My mind must have slipped once more. The man watching me is too neat to belong here. Too sanitary. His stock and shirt are too white, his frock coat too black, his buttons too shiny. He peers at me over a long nose, through beady eyes, with an expression devoid of humanity, and I realise he's waiting for a reply, but he has not asked a question. I can only watch as he steps into my cell, careful where he places his shoes. He brings a wooden chair, sets it against the wall at the foot of my cot, next to the door, and takes a seat. One of his buckles catches the light as he swings a knee over the other. There is a smear on it; he must have polished it in a hurry this morning.

'I am Doctor Lorenzo Balleza. Confessor of the secret prison of the Holy Office.'

I wait. He does not need me to introduce myself.

He allows silence to build, and something tells me he practiced that inscrutable facial expression before a looking-glass. The thought amuses the far-away version of myself that still recognises humour.

'I have come to hear your confession.'

'Are you a priest?'

'I am your confessor.'

'*My* confessor?'

I drop my head back against my wall, relieving my aching neck. We both allow the silence to stretch. Eventually he breaks it.

'A deposition has been made against you, substantiated by several witnesses and documented. You are charged with several counts related to heresy: necromancy, abuse of the sacred scripture and insult to the holy sacrament of mass.'

'Substantiated? By whom?'

'Article Sixteen protects them from being named.'

'My camaradas would never speak against me. You deceive me.'

He drops his foot to the floor. 'You accuse *me*?'

So, he's capable of emotion. I can see I need to retract the insult; he may be a self-important official, but he's my only bridge with the world.

'Forgive me,' I say.

A beat, while he examines me along the length of his nose.

I comb my fingers through my beard. I've caught myself doing that more and more of late – I've never grown one beyond my chin before. 'May I see the charges?'

'In due course. Procedures dictate it is for the Inquisidor to decide.'

'When did I allegedly commit these offences?'

'That is for you to confess.'

'How shall I confess that which I don't remember?'

'Your heresy is all the graver if you forgot.' He sits back and crosses a leg once more, the other one this time.

I always thought I could read people, but when I study his face, I find nothing to interpret, no means of closing the space between us. He's young. Unlined. Clever, no doubt – to be in the position he is in – but his face shows no emotion, no scars, within or without.

He lifts his chin. 'In accordance with Article Eleven, if you confess your faults, and the faults of others, entirely and without reservations, your penitence will allow the Holy Church to offer you clemency.'

And the faults of others. My skin prickles.

Doctor Balleza goes on: 'However, in accordance with Article Fourteen, if heresy is proved and a defendant persists in denial, he shall be declared an impenitent heretic and sentenced accordingly.'

'What does "*sentenced accordingly*" mean?' I think I already know, but there is a clawing creature inside the cavity of my chest demanding an answer.

'Once a crime is juridically proved, by refusing to confess his error the convict does not permit the Church to use him mercifully.'

Jesu. Is euphemism the language of the Inquisition? 'Spell it out for me,' I snap.

My temple throbs. I rub at it, and my fingers come away wet. I tug at my collar, peeling fabric from hot, damp skin.

His gaze flicks to my hand before he answers. 'An impenitent heretic would be abandoned to the secular arm.'

Apparently so. Though I glare at him, he will say no more. I shift direction.

'Am I entitled to a lawyer?'

'In accordance with Article Sixteen. You may be represented by an advocate. At your own expense.'

He knows his Articles, for that I have to credit him. 'And if I don't have the means?'

'Come now, you are an Albrono.'

'I'm an Albrono without means, *and* accused of heresy. How much further can I damage the family name? Though I'm not the first of my family to be pronounced a heretic in Spain.'

His expression slips: a frown, a small but real shift. 'What do you mean, "*not the first*"?'

'You don't know?'

He pulls on the blank confessor's mask once more.

'There is a man who has nominated himself as your advocate. Señor Gallo.'

Enzo. 'Why have I not been told this before?'

'This is the first time I've spoken with you.'

'I have been here for –' I look at the scratches on the wall. '– over two weeks.'

He too looks at the markings. 'I do not dictate the timetable here. There are procedures to follow, particularly in transferring a case between Tribunals.'

He fades and re-emerges, as if fog swirls between us. I can hold him still if I squint, but then my head pounds. I cannot do this alone.

'I wish to speak to my advocate.'

'That can be arranged. First, I must advise you. Choose a lawyer schooled in the faith. One who will advise on your sins. Because a lawyer defending a guilty man is in breach of Article sixteen – and as such will have to answer for his own sin against the faith.'

I'm starving. I'm feverish. And now it seems my hearing is failing.

'So, if I plead innocent, and am found guilty,' I say, 'so is my lawyer?'

There's nothing wrong with my hearing. He nods, once, slow, eyes fixed on mine. I thought myself doomed; now I know it.

'Shall I arrange for Señor Gallo to visit you?' he says.

'No. That won't be necessary.'

'Have you given thought to how you will plead?'

'I *am* innocent.'

'That is for the Holy Office of the Inquisition to determine.'

'Then why did you ask?'

'To understand your version of the truth.'

'Isn't truth absolute? Surely the issue at hand is whether the Inquisition has the capacity to learn it.'

'You doubt the Inquisition?'

'Here I am.' I lift my hands.

'Here you are.'

The confessor's face is blank. I maintain his gaze despite the hammering in my temples. Eventually, he breaks the silence.

'Suppose you tell me why you believe you are here.' Very good. Throw a net and you never know what fish you might catch.

'Your Inquisition brought me here,' I say. 'Suppose you tell me why, so I might examine my conscience?'

He shifts his weight. 'Have you claimed to have the power to divine a thief?'

'Yes. Have you claimed to have the power to divine a heretic?' Perhaps it's unwise to toy with the man, but anger energises, despair emboldens.

His eyes glint. 'Have you invoked our Lord in exercising your *powers*?'

'Have you?'

'Are you comparing yourself to the Blessed Mission of the Holy Office?' His voice swells.

'No. That I would not do.'

I set my voice quiet against his outburst, and it rattles him, his eyes swivel from left to right. He licks his lips, then draws a huge breath and sighs.

Now I take the initiative. 'Isn't *Thou shalt not steal* a Commandment? Is it a sin to unmask a thief?'

'It is a sin to practice magic. And it is blasphemy to claim to invoke the gospel in doing so.'

'No magic,' I say. 'I tricked a gullible man into revealing himself.'

'A trick? Explain it to me,' he says.

I describe how I trapped Barbieri with a child's ploy. To his credit, he listens.

'How did you add the ink to the water unnoticed?'

'In a darkened room, everyone watches the last candle.' I'm sure there is a metaphor there. 'I added the ink when all eyes were on the act of extinguishing it.'

'And then your thief withheld his finger for fear of being marked, only to realise too late that his unmarked hand spoke of his guilt.'

'Exactly,' I say. 'It was hard not to laugh when he proudly brandished his finger as proof of his innocence.'

He actually smiles. Then he catches himself and becomes the pompous confessor once again.

'You would not be imprisoned without compelling evidence of sin. In the name of our Lord and his blessed Mother, bethink yourself and confess the whole truth so you may be afforded mercy.'

'To say any more, I'd have to invent it.'

'Is that your confession?' he asks.

'I suppose it is,' I reply.

'Article Eleven requires that you confess the faults of others. Who indulged with you?'

I recoil. It's a physical thing, as if hands press me back against my wall. 'Nobody "*indulged with me*". The ruse was of my own invention.'

'Who did it benefit? Who encouraged? Who believed?' Shots fired before I even finish my denial.

Holy Mother of God, now I see how the gluttonous Inquisition grows corpulent: names begetting names. 'Go feed elsewhere, Doctor Balleza. My actions were on my account, in benefit of my own vanity.'

He gives me a long, hard stare.

I return it.

'I shall leave you to reflect, Don Albrono. I exhort you to use the time well.'

As he turns to leave, I roll a die – though it might be only a pebble. 'Tell me, Doctor Balleza, does it strike you that Don Fausto has an unseemly enthusiasm to see me damaged?'

He stops mid-turn and regards me, eyes narrowed. His lips part. Perhaps he thinks better of whatever words he's shaped, because he walks out. A clang of iron, a key grinding – the sounds that come with the labour of burying a man alive.

The session has taken more of my strength than it should. My mind is restless, but my body lethargic. Pacing is impossible; my legs are too soft; even small movements on the cot rob me of breath. The sun spilling through the window is intolerable. I've sweated through my shirt, and my ankle is aflame where the rat took its meal. Though I dread to look, I must. The skin around is too pink, too sponge-like, and it smells like yeast. The bite itself is tiny but moist where it should be scabbed. I rip a strip off my shirt and soak it in my water bowl, wrapping the wound, wincing at the bite of vinegar against open flesh.

The confessor did a fine job. I exhaust myself guessing what he knows, building defences against every possible scenario. Hope is folly, so why do I indulge it? My fate is decided not by what I've done, but by what Fausto believes I deserve.

Another matter nibbles at the edge of my mind.

The confessor knew nothing of the previous heresy charge. Surely such a detail would have surfaced in light of my current accusation.

Unfinished business.

No, Enzo. I have more pressing concerns than a fifty-year-old case against my grandfather. At least *his* was posthumous. Mine, it seems, will prove fatal.

Light Through a Canopy of Leaves

28 July 1756

Jean-Pierre lies on his side, propped on one elbow, a blade of grass between his teeth. 'You must be the most uninterested bride in all of Spain, Luisa, leaving it all to your mother.' Though he addresses me, he gazes down at the view from Constellation Hill.

'Not true. She was interested in its location,' says Rafael.

I shrug. 'I only said, "*Not the cathedral.*" I cannot bear pomp.'

'To her madre's disappointment,' adds Marta.

'Mama isn't getting married.' I regret the edge in my voice and soften it. 'At least she gets a new wig, and it will make the society pages. That will make her happy.'

'And what about you, Luisa? Will you wear a grand wig and be parcelled in silk and ribbons? Delivered to your husband as a gift?'

Is that sarcasm? Rafael hears it too. He glares, but Jean-Pierre just chews his grass, unbothered.

'Are you cynical about marriage, Jean-Pierre?' I ask.

His mouth smiles, but his eyes don't join in. 'Ignore me, ma chère. It is not my business.'

Rafael frowns, but Jean-Pierre doesn't notice – or chooses not to. It makes an odd kind of sense that he mocks marriage. After all, what would a free spirit gain from it? Whereas women… we live by permission – that of a father or a husband – the best we can hope is one of those will set us free. Father wouldn't know how. Rafael wouldn't know otherwise.

As for the past… I could pine for *the great love*, or I could accept I've been deserted and make an adult choice. Who knows? If I lay the hearth and stack the wood, perhaps the flame will follow.

I follow Jean-Pierre's gaze down into the basin of the city and the sea beyond. It's hazy and distant, but I know exactly where I first saw Antonio. For that matter, I could point at the spot where I met Rafael. The first time I saw Rafael, I found him pleasing. By contrast, the first time I saw Antonio – disembarking from *La Fortuna* – I was drawn. And he kept pulling.

May 1754

We didn't actually meet until the following day, when I pulled up a chair as he sketched in his notebook. Inexplicably, his hands fascinated me: laying down confident lines, now and again stopping to smudge charcoal with his stained thumb. He wore a ring on his smallest finger – brass and milky quartz, plain and grounded.

I saw the pencil stop before I realised, I'd been staring. When I snapped my eyes up, he was watching me with that curious expression I'd come to know: eyes crinkling for a smile, mouth still deciding. How strange, it only then occurred to me to introduce myself.

'Luisa Navas.'

'Antonio Albrono.'

Perhaps I imagined his thumb tracing a soft line over my fingers. When he bent his head, I suppose I might have imagined he took a moment longer than the act required. But I didn't imagine the way my skin tightened in anticipation.

It didn't come, of course. To kiss a woman's hand on first meeting would be scandalous, and when he raised his gaze to mine once more, I released my breath slowly so he wouldn't see I'd been holding it.

'Antonio,' I repeated.

And he smiled as if I'd told him a delicious secret.

I grasped for a way to distract myself, if only to cool the heat rising from my décolletage to my neck, so I made work of collecting a footstool for his injured leg while he veered between protest and amusement.

'Is it just Señor Martinez that you find interesting enough to sketch?' I asked.

'No, I drew Gabriel too, but it's not a good likeness.'

Antonio knew our mayordomo's name.

'Do you draw?' he asked.

'No. Sí. A little. Badly.'

I should have answered otherwise, because he passed his book and pencil to me. And I could have sketched anything, but I chose the most difficult subject: him. I'd like to say I did marvellous work, but it was dreadful: flat discs for eyes, a jaw too sharp, ears like tankard handles… as for his mouth – if he couldn't decide between smiling and thinking, what chance did I stand? I dropped the pencil.

'Are you ready to reveal?'

When he tried to look, I flattened my hands over the page.

'No. Truly it's bad.'

He stretched out his hand. '*Dámelo.*'

I snatched the book to my chest. 'Let me tear out the page.'

He grinned, devilish. 'Show me the picture.'

I peered down. Worse than bad. 'Oh. I cannot.'

'I don't believe anything you do can be so poor.'

I resigned myself to ridicule and handed it over. He watched me as he took it, then dropped his gaze to the drawing. His eyebrows shot up. A few seconds passed in which my cheeks burned.

'You're so wrong. This isn't bad. It isn't bad at all.' He lifted his eyes to mine. 'It's truly terrible. Horrible.' His chuckle rippled outwards, tilting me. 'Really. It's an uncommon talent you have, to create a drawing so… *monstruoso*.'

'Perhaps that's how you appear to me.' I feigned pride and stuck out my chin.

He turned the page upside down. '*Buon Dio.* Then it's more than my foot that needs help.'

That did it, my laugh bubbled up and burst out, and just like that any space left between us vanished.

Teasing turned to quiet talk, the kind that meanders like a stream, and I forgot he was a stranger. And time. I forgot that too until Mama burst in, fussing and fanning, putting an end to our encounter.

Antonio intrigued me. He *reached* me. Like sunlight through a canopy of leaves.

To Withhold the Truth

31 July 1756

A false kindness I know, but today they've brought meat. Boiled. Goat, I think, floating in watery stock. Perhaps it signifies my trial will be soon – I suppose appearances wouldn't be served by a skin and bone defendant. Or perhaps my trial is delayed and they need to keep me alive longer than they'd planned. I cannot second-guess the Inquisition.

I grasp a sinewy scrap between shaking fingers and swallow. My stomach clenches, but I breathe hard, and somehow, I keep it down. When the ceiling stops swaying, I sip the broth.

From his corner, Rat watches. Funny, while the room fades and tilts, he's still. I greet him with a nod. He's silent, enigmatic, and it strikes me he bears an uncanny resemblance to yesterday's visitor. I snort, spraying broth from my nose. It *is* him. Those beady eyes glinting over the long snout, analysing, concentrating. The hair brushed forward over the sloping forehead, ears pricked, listening.

'Doctor Balleza, it's good to see you again so soon.'

He tilts his head to his left.

'I apologise for the state of my chamber.'

He twitches his nose, and two incisors appear over his lower lip.

'What did you say? Cleanse my soul?' I nod and arrange my face into a frown. 'You first.'

The teeth disappear; his lips are sealed.

'Tell me about this heresy charge against my grandfather.'

His eyes drop to my plate. I have him.

'Aha! Come now, Balleza, Article *Eleventeen* requires you to bear witness against sinners.'

He lifts his eyes to mine once again. We watch. Seconds pass; neither of us prepared to blink first.

'Very well, a trade. I will confess, then you.'

He drops his eyelids. The bargain is struck, and now I realise it's a heavy one. So my strength does not fail me, I breathe in hard, then exhale through my nose. The back of my head finds the wall, and my eyes close. My sins are many; where shall I start?

'I confess to enjoying the amazement of my camaradas. I confess to pride…' I open an eye and squint at Balleza. Is this what he wants to hear?

He watches.

'I confess to vanity. Boastfulness.' My own words shame me, and I drop my head, examining the bowl in my lap. It's incredible, but despite hunger and thirst, I lack the strength or will to eat. I place my food aside.

Balleza Rat waits. He's good at this.

'I confess to obtaining money by deception.' Joaquim's face appears behind my eyelids. Yet, no matter how hard I try, I don't feel the regret I should. I open my eyes again and look to my implacable confessor for understanding. 'But he was greedy, Balleza Rat, is that not a sin of equal gravity?'

There's a dent on my finger where I wore the ring; the skin is paler there – white, almost. I touch it with my thumb.

Balleza follows the movement, then looks at my face.

'He believed in magic; does that not make *him* the heretic?'

It's written all over Balleza's face, his judgement, as clear as the spoken word. '*His sins do not lessen yours.*'

He has a point.

How did my hands get so filthy? My skin is grey, black underneath the fingernails. My whole body is corrupted with dirt. I touch my hair; it's grown out and matted. And my face… good thing

I don't see my reflection, I'm not sure I'd recognise the owner of these sharp edges, this ragged beard.

My confessor waits; he has the patience of a saint.

'Since I'm cleansing my soul –' I take a shuddering breath. 'I should have told her the truth. The moment I discovered who she was.'

May 1754

It was the day we met. By that I don't mean the day I first saw her – I didn't see her again after the drama on the wharf – it was the next day. She introduced herself, then repeated my name.

'Antonio.'

Each syllable a separate breath. I never stood a chance. If my name on Luisa's lips is the last thing I hear before I die, I shall die content.

Once again, I had that sense I already knew her. It struck me I'd like to have Luisa's handiwork in my notebook, so I persuaded her to draw, and for a few precious minutes I had nothing to do but study her. I could have stayed there all day, watching light catch the twist of dark hair pinned behind her ear, the dent at the centre of her upper lip. And her eyes. Polished onyx, flecked with gold.

But what a poor attempt at drawing she made. I was sure to tease her, and the space between us shrank further. We talked the way old friends do, about many things and nothing: the running of the hotel, eccentric and interesting guests, and those infuriating types who are never satisfied. I'd have talked to Luisa all morning, but for the force of nature that was her mother.

The door to the salon flew open and a striking woman spilled in. An older version of Luisa, but more styled, more coiffured, and wearing the widest day-dress I'd ever seen, talking before she had even completed her entrance.

'Luisa! What is this? You cannot be in the salon with a gentleman unaccompanied. What of your reputation? Where is Marta?' She turned to me. '¡Señor! You should know better.' She fixed me with an expression so haughty I didn't know whether to shrink or laugh.

'The last thing I'd do is compromise your daughter. As you see –' I shifted my foot. 'I'm incapacitated.'

She narrowed her eyes. 'Are you the man who attacked her yesterday? I heard you jumped upon her.'

'Mama!' Luisa exclaimed. 'But for Don Antonio, I'd have been badly hurt. He saved me from Father's coffee crates.'

The woman looked from Luisa to me, and back to her daughter. Then slumped into a chair in such an abrupt manner I had to admire her skill in folding her skirts down with her.

'Ffffffhh. If you say so, Luisa.' She looked at me. 'Forgive the misunderstanding, Don Antonio. There has been quite some gossip about yesterday's little incident.' She straightened. 'And it *is* most improper for Luisa to keep company with a man, alone.'

I liked her.

'Daughter, are you going to introduce us?'

'Sí. Mama, this is Don Antonio Albrono from Genoa. Antonio, this is mi madre, Doña María Spinelli, from Bellvís.'

I must have gaped, then I forced a neutral expression. Fate is a strange thing. While Enzo searched Barcelona for a clue as to the location of Alejo Spinelli, I'd been sitting in the hotel belonging to his family.

Now what? Was Luisa to believe I'd arrived in her hotel by coincidence? I hardly credited it myself.

The Sea Beyond the Port of Barcelona

31 July 1756

How enchanting. Golden rocks rise above water blue as a deep-set gem. The sky is scraped clean; the air sharp with salt. We're in a faluca, a six-berth wooden sailboat that Rafael somehow secured this morning, along with its single crewman. The two men insisted they could sail, and that may well be, but Marta refused to climb aboard without a professional. Me neither; I'd have said it if she hadn't.

Although the shadows are long on the deck, it's still warm; the men are in shirtsleeves, Marta and I bare-shouldered.

'¡Señorita! Look!' Marta points out to sea, one hand holding her sunhat.

'A dolphin,' says Rafael over Marta's shoulder. He points. 'There's another.'

'*Hermoso,*' I say, and they are indeed beautiful.

'Tursiops truncatus,' says Jean-Pierre, 'Bottlenose dolphin. Intelligent creatures.'

'Is there any subject upon which you are not an expert?' Marta asks.

Such impertinence, but Jean-Pierre chuckles. 'Name a subject I have not mastered, Rafael.'

'I cannot.' Rafael looks for the wine jug, finds it and takes a swig. 'No wait. Women. You're hopeless when it comes to women.'

'All that charm, and nothing to show for it,' I say, taking my turn at the wine.

'Thank you, Luisa,' Jean-Pierre nods at Rafael, as if to say: *See?*

I hadn't meant it as a compliment.

The Frenchman catches Marta's left hand. 'Dance with me. Let's prove Rafael wrong.'

Marta snatches her hand back and I fear she's offended, but Jean-Pierre persists and now she mirrors him in the starting pose for a minuet. *Marta.*

He takes a step, but she falters; she's laughing too hard.

'Finish the dance or my heart will break,' he says. He does look crestfallen. 'I mean it, I shall throw myself into the sea.'

'What, and frighten away the bottlenose dolphins?' says Marta.

He peers over the side. 'Gone. My dance, Mademoiselle.' He holds out his hand.

Marta sweeps past him; I pass her the wine, but she won't drink from the jug, and begins hunting for a mug. She collects one from under the bench, and now she can't decide between the jug or a dirty mug.

'You don't believe me?' The Frenchman climbs onto the first rail of the bulwark and leans over the edge.

I doubt he'll jump, but if he doesn't fall it will be a miracle. 'Come down!' I don't like this one bit, and Rafael is no help, standing around smirking.

A splash; the boat lurches; I stumble; Marta's drink sloshes onto her chemise; fat droplets of water land on the deck, spattering my skirt. He's vanished. Swallowed by the sea. Gone beneath a widening circle of ripples and foam.

Marta squeaks; it would have been a scream, but she clapped her hand over her mouth.

How will we report the drowning of a Frenchman? What of his family? Does he even *have* family? Wine surges up my throat, along with ham, herring, egg, and those sugared fancies I've been snacking all afternoon. 'Rafael?'

But my betrothed merely rolls his eyes. *What's wrong with him?*

Jean-Pierre surfaces, spouting water in an arc.

Better if he'd drowned because I could murder him myself. '*¡Bellaco!*' If only I had a stronger word. 'To frighten us so!' He's too ridiculous.

Rafael shakes his head. 'You're a child. Now we'll have to travel through the city with you drenched.'

While Jean-Pierre struggles to heave himself from the water, Rafael watches, arms folded. But it's clear the Frenchman cannot climb out unaided.

'If you don't help him, I will,' I say.

'You've no idea what you're asking.' He shakes his head.

'I know we cannot leave him there.'

He gives me a long look I don't understand, then sighs and reaches for his friend.

Jean-Pierre has braced a foot against the side of the vessel and pulls hard, yanking Rafael headfirst into the water. Now I understand. With his hair plastered to his face, Rafael breaks the surface, spluttering. He finds Jean-Pierre's head and pushes him under. The battle begins.

'Oh, you are boys! Come out at once!' Marta scolds.

'We cannot! You will have to help us!' Jean-Pierre holds out a hand.

'You think us fools?' I say. 'We cannot swim.'

We have no intention of leaving them in the water. Marta has already fetched the crewman who shakes his head, and drops a short ladder. The two juveniles are soon back on the deck, dripping and shoving, wrestling and only half-chuckling. What is it with men and contests? They'd fight over air given half an excuse. Marta stalks off, but I'm oddly fascinated – though a touch vexed. Jean-Pierre wraps an arm around Rafael's neck; Rafael somehow flips him around; they both lose balance but Jean-Pierre is first to steady himself and barges into Rafael while he has the advantage. Rafael stumbles into me. I totter, and he yanks me into his arms – he has to, its either that or I pitch onto the deck.

A shock of cold and I shove him away. 'Oh, you are the devil!'

At first, he laughs, then his mouth falls open. I'm shivering too much to wonder why, until I see Jean-Pierre, his own laugh frozen, his eyes wide, and I follow his gaze downwards. My wet dress. My shift. Every intimate detail. Breasts, skin raised in bumps, the outline of nipples, the shape of me rendered in wet gauze. I throw my arms across my chest. I'm not cold now; I'm burning. Where is Marta? My mantilla, where did I leave it?

'Tiens.' Jean-Pierre offers my folded shawl. He nods, not averting his eyes – which would make it worse – but fixing his gaze on my face. Then Rafael steps in, draping the fabric around my shoulders, restoring my dignity. I nod a thank you to Jean-Pierre, but he doesn't see. He's suddenly fascinated by the shoreline.

By the time we turn for home, the sun is low. I sit alone with my back against the transom, watching the wake frothing behind us. Rafael and Jean-Pierre are on the main deck. Their voices drift over the wind and churn, too fragmented to reassemble into words. Marta is somewhere back there too, asleep, I think.

In the distance, a ship carves the water – *La Fortuna* – no doubt laden with its usual cargo from Genoa. An elegant sight lifting and dropping against the horizon, sails aflame with evening sun. Hypnotic. My eyelids grow heavy and behind them, unwanted memories surface of the man who stepped from that ship and left my heart scattered like flotsam behind.

May 1754

Wednesday and Friday evenings, I – and my parents if they were available – would dine with the guests. That particular Wednesday, two days after Antonio arrived, I dithered over what to wear. First the blue silk, then not, as though I'd become a fluttering ingénue.

'Madam, I have nothing else prepared!' Marta stood before my armoire, eyeing the folded silks and brocades, all in need of hanging.

'Then I shall go as I am.'

'In a day-dress? Unthinkable!' She folded her frustration into her fists and planted them on her hips.

'The green then. I wore it yesterday, so you won't need to prepare it.'

'The same dress for two days? This is a fashionable hotel, Señorita! Why not the blue?' She stepped to where she'd hung it – over the folding screen – and brushed at the skirt, loosening a speck of dust only she could see.

'It's too nice. I shall look as though I'm trying.'

Marta fixed me with one of her stares, the kind she had used to get me to confess when I stole candied fruit as a child. 'This isn't about the dress, is it?'

I tugged at my stays.

'Is it the Don from Genoa?'

My face warmed. 'Perhaps. A little.'

Her smile widened. 'I have never seen you this way about a man. And why not? A noble name. And handsome, no?'

'It's not that. I mean, sí, he's handsome, and has a good name, but there are plenty such men in the city.'

'So…?'

'So. I feel… He *sees* me.'

'Oh, he "*sees*" you, Señorita.' She chuckled. 'He does not take his eyes from you.'

'I don't mean that. Although –' I touched my collarbone, remembering the way his eyes lingered there. '– I mean, he's curious; he seeks to *understand.* Don't you find that many men only talk about themselves? Especially when they seek to impress.'

'I do. They talk of wealth, or business conquests, or some sporting feat. And our role is to listen endlessly, to gasp and be amazed.'

'Exactly! I can read about accomplishments in the society pages. Perhaps the true measure of a man's worth is how well he listens.'

'And the Genoan listens well?'

I recalled our conversation in the salon, the way he leaned in, furrowed his brow at a tale of a rude patron, his intelligent questions, and the spaces he left for me to finish my thoughts. 'Yes, he listens well.'

Marta nodded. 'Very well. The blue dress but with a plain scarf. Simple jewels, but flattering.'

When Mama and I entered the dining room, the guests had already taken their seats: Señora and Señorita Cadiz, Señores García and Martinez, Monsieur Dupont, Signor Gallo, and Antonio. As usual, Mama soaked up all the attention in a brocade dress depicting parrots and exotic flowers. All attention but Antonio's. He watched me, and I watched him.

As hostess, Mama took her position at the head of the table. She'd placed Antonio on her right, and Señorita Cadiz on her left. I was seated a full table-length away, so I had to spend the evening watching the hopeful woman peer at him from under her lashes. She was flawless, the epitome of demure femininity. The way Mama looked between us, I expect she found me wanting in that regard.

At my end of the table, Señor García prated on about the price of coffee, then diverted to the tensions between Britain and France in the New World – something interesting at last. But Señor Martinez interrupted him.

'This is perhaps not an appropriate subject for the dinner table.'

A deep pink glow rose from the neck above Señor García's scarf, all the way to the edge of his wig. 'Ah. I –'

'Or indeed for conversation with women.' Señor Martinez looked at me. 'I am sure Señorita Navas does not want to hear about fighting in the Ohio River Valley.'

'Quite,' said Señora Cadiz. 'Luisa, you must let me speak to your cocinero, I am dying of curiosity about the herbs you have used for this capón, such a delicate flavour.'

I'd rather have talked about the Ohio River Valley – wherever that might be – but all now ahhhed and cooed over the delicious capón, and a hostess must let the conversation take its course.

Several times I caught Antonio watching me, eyes crinkling as if he was about to smile – an expression I'd begun to recognise.

He left the table early – his lawyer eager to discuss some pressing matter. After that the meal became a chore. Señor García offered me a marzipan with a flourish so gallant one might think it had come from his kitchen, not mine. I nibbled politely, smiled in all the right moments, and made my excuses as soon as I could.

I have a private space, off limits to guests – a favourite wicker chair on one of the terraces. A place for myself at the end of each day, watching the ships in the harbour, enjoying the salt-laden breeze and listening to the late-night bustle of a port that never sleeps. That night, as usual, I sipped a brandy, and closed my eyes.

Something shifted, no, stilled. A warmth. A presence. The body is attuned to such things. My eyes flew open.

Antonio stood at the balustrade, looking out over the ships below. I glimpsed Marta behind him – her small smile, for my benefit – before she vanished inside.

He turned and rested his hands on the wrought iron rail, watching me with that frank, open expression of his. 'Forgive me, I hoped to discuss a matter, but not if it meant waking you.'

Light from the terrace lanterns danced over his face, revealing him a line or shadow at a time. Marta was right; he was handsome, not because his features were well-proportioned and arranged – they were – but because he carried himself like a man who knew his own mind. And because of that quiet curiosity, the kind that made me feel I was the only other person in the world. A dangerous talent. I should have been more careful.

'So where is this Ohio River Valley, and why are the British and French so vexed about it?' I asked.

His eyes widened, and he gave me a small laugh. 'As I understand, it lies in New France, near the British border. A transport route both sides wish to claim for their empires. It will come to war soon.'

A depressing thought. 'I suppose that means Spain will support France.'

'Do you think Spain will be inclined towards conflict?' he asked.

A good question. I shook my head. 'I think no, not under King Ferdinand.'

He nodded. 'I suppose it would be an awkward reversal, since he's made peace his slogan.' Before I could answer, he tilted his head to one side and narrowed his eyes. 'That dress – it's your colour, I think.'

I don't know why I looked down, as if I'd forgotten what I was wearing. I said the first thing that came into my head. 'I suppose dress design is a more appropriate conversation for a woman.'

His laugh tumbled from him, rich and full, set in velvet like a gift. He pulled up a chair beside mine and sank into it, so close I could smell him. Linen and a trace of cologne: citrus and herb. His fingers rested on the arm of his chair, a whisper away from mine. I folded my hands together to stop myself touching them.

'*Appropriate conversation for a woman*,' he repeated. 'I'd like to see them try to run a place like this.'

Now I really did feel seen.

He dipped his gaze. 'And blue *is* your colour.'

I waited for my skin to heat, to feel the flush of embarrassment, but it didn't come. I felt a different kind of warmth, a glow that began in my stomach and unfurled like silk through every part of me.

'War could break out right now, in the port there.' He gestured with his chin. 'I'd still be more interested in that blue… against your skin.' His eyes met mine. 'I know I'm not supposed to say that.'

My senses lit up like fireflies. But was he mocking me?

I offered him my brandy glass. He took a sip, then handed it back, his fingers brushing mine – warm skin, cool glass. I drank, my lips where his had been, and caught him watching my mouth. Then he smiled, shaking his head slightly as if something perplexed him, dragging his eyes away to peer out at the sea once more.

A distant ship's bell clanged. Lanterns flickered below, catching the silhouettes of workers heaving crates and sacks. Brandy, wood smoke, and beside me, the solid presence of a man who – inexplicably – offered both the magic of an undiscovered place and the familiarity of a favourite pair of gloves.

But the moment tensed. Something shifted. His fingers curled and he coughed quietly.

'Luisa, there's a matter I need to discuss with you.'

I wasn't prepared for '*a matter*', and in no mood to break the peace, so I cut him off. 'It can wait, Antonio. Surely?'

He opened his mouth, then snapped it shut.

We both rested our heads against the back of our seats and sat in silence, sharing a brandy, watching the stars reflected in the sea beyond the Port of Barcelona.

The Buzzard Circles

1 August 1756

I barely manage to scratch the nineteenth mark on the wall, blinking away memories, or were they dreams? The terrace. The words I meant to say. *'It can wait, Antonio… surely?'*

Doors clang. Feet stomp outside the window above my head. Soldiers are changing shifts. One of them is called Benet. He's had the night patrol for the last two weeks and must soon be due to change his pattern. At least there were no screams last night; what happened to her? Instead, a man wept. It was me.

I dreamed of food too. If I close my eyes, I can still smell, still taste. I remember mopping up the deep red-gold oil of pan-fried chorizo with a hunk of bread, feel my teeth tearing through the flesh of succulent mutton, taste the caramelised edges of roasted beef melting against my tongue… I'm driving myself mad.

My limbs shriek as I unfold myself from the bed and do my best to stretch my aching body so I may breathe in the fresher air closer to the window. My vision blurs as though I'm watching my surroundings from under the surface of the sea. Images bend and fracture. The bars of my window twist into wrought iron, and I smell the musk and leather of a horse. Now I'm beside Luisa as she steers our carriage along the Carrer Ample.

With her hat shading her face, Luisa gestures toward the intricate twisting metal of the balcony of Señor Xifre's house. 'One could almost pick one of those grapes,' she says. Her voice is light, but my heart is heavy. Here she is, giving me a personal tour of the city, and I still cannot tell her what she needs to know.

I taste sour air and am back in my cell. My legs crumple, and I slide down the wall to meet the floor, and wait for the dizziness to pass. It worsens. I fall sideways; the stone floor lands cool against my cheek. Strange, I no longer mind its stench: mildew and rot, and something like rusted metal. A large bug scuttles before me, its hard carapace iridescent, antennae quivering – a scarafaggio. Raising one leg, it begins cleaning itself. The creature has no fear of me, and it can only be because I'm dying. I may as well close my eyes and enjoy it.

'La Plaça del Rei,' Luisa announces. She tugs the reins; steers the calesa around the square, the Palace of the Inquisition. *Oh, I know Luisa; I know it better than you can imagine.* A laugh surges up my throat, and I clamp it behind my teeth because I fear where it will lead.

Blending past with present is a construct of my mind. I'm not so far gone that I don't know it, just as I know that if I concentrate hard, I can still separate the two. It's not now; it was then. The day I saw him for the first time. Fausto. In El Plaça del Rei. His black robes billowed as he strode through the square, crucifix swinging, eyes fixed on Luisa.

Years ago, in the forests of the Wienerwald, my friend Sebastian and I found a bird's nest. Just children playing. We meant no harm, but try telling that to the buzzard that swooped upon us, rending the air with its shrieks, talons outstretched. What paralysed me as it reared into my face, were its eyes. Polished black marble. Cold as the grave.

As Don Fausto stood before Luisa, I saw that buzzard again: though his lips smiled, his eyes were as dead as the bird's. And when Luisa introduced me, the air between us shifted. Though I knew not why, I became his prey that day. I still am.

My jailer arrives and leaves; I barely notice. He brought bread and vinegar-water, but I cannot hope to reach them, and what does it matter anyway? Hunger and thirst are abstract things. Twin beasts standing over me, conferring over which will have the pleasure of taking me, while I lie on my side in the dirty straw, arms protecting my abdomen lest they decide to kick.

Luisa. I close my eyes to summon her again.

We're in the casa de café, I study the dark liquid coating the inside of my cup. 'I'm sorry, Luisa. It became harder with each passing hour to tell you.'

'*How* hard?' Her eyes are shards, I flinch. 'How *difícil* was it to say, "*I am seeking a debt between your family and mine*"?'

Now she thinks I have been seducing her to further my cause. She's hurt, because I hurt her.

'Forgive me, Luisa.' I squeeze my eyes to hold her here, so she might hear my apology. But she fades.

'Don Albrono.'

Here is my confessor. Not Rat Balleza: Doctor Balleza. I know because shoes appear. Two identical men watch me from the polished silver of their buckles. I pity them, with their sunken faces and cracked lips. They'll die soon, surely. I try to raise my hand to touch them, to comfort them, but cannot summon the strength.

Shouts. Hands under my armpits, my shirt is displaced and cold stone scrapes my back. Grey. Light. Faces. Jailer. Balleza. My head falls to the side. Rat Balleza is here, watching, incisors exposed, nose twitching. I look from Rat to Doctor and back to the rat again. Brothers surely. I laugh. I cannot stop. Pain rips through my guts. I want to stop. I need to stop. The laugh is monstrous; it has me in its claws and will surely rip me in two: 'Confess,' says Balleza. 'Heretic,' says Barbieri. 'Liar,' says Luisa.

The buzzard circles, claws outstretched, ready to seize its prey.

Truth

1 August 1756

Somehow the barest touch, his fingers on mine, reaches every part of my skin. I turn the glass a little, sipping the brandy from the same spot his mouth touched. I know he sees because his eyes linger there.

I wake mid-breath, heart thumping, sweat trickling across my collarbone and between my breasts. Why does Antonio invade my dreams? He doesn't deserve it. I will be married in days.

Rafael. My best friend, not yet my lover. On the faluca, soaked through, his wet shirt and breeches left nothing to guess. Water slid down his face and neck, into the dark curls on his chest. If there exists an angel called *Temptation*, he looks like that. So why wasn't I tempted?

Does he sleep, or does he think of me? How disloyal, to lie here contemplating another man. I cover my face with my hands. If only I could as easily block out the last traces of my dream.

I must put this right. Commit to Rafael. End the torment for good.

I'm decided. Before thought stops me, I fold back the bedcovers and swing my feet to the floor. This is me, no affectations, no excuses, barefoot. Just me in my skin – unless one counts my muslin nightgown, just enough for modesty on the journey I am about to take.

I've never been to his room, but I know where it is – along the corridor, down the west staircase, up the east staircase. *Dios mío*, this house is big! I pray my resolve doesn't crumble before I reach him.

I'm outside his door. He must be awake because a faint orange light flickers beneath the heavy oak, painting my toes amber. I shake my hair out and pinch my cheeks. When I turn the handle, it's with the most tentative of touches so I don't make a noise. I know that doesn't make sense, but in truth I don't know what I'm doing. I'm forcing my instincts into a direction they resist. My heart thumps so hard I'm sure to him it will be as loud as a knock. I hold my breath and push the door.

My eyes won't accept the vision, so I hear first. Voices whispering, familiar: Rafael and Jean-Pierre.

And now I understand. I know what I'm looking at. The two of them entwined. Naked. They move together, sighing, touching, kissing. And this is impossible.

They freeze. A tableau. It crosses my detached mind that their bodies are beautiful in the candlelight – an Italian sculptor would be proud. A laugh escapes; it's like breaking glass. I don't know where it came from, for none of this is funny. I must have broken a spell because they scramble apart.

Though the two naked men snatch up sheets, cover themselves, they cannot undo what I've seen. And I laugh once again. I've lost my mind.

'Luisa –' Rafael steps towards me, one arm outstretched, and trips over his own sheet, falling to the floor. The worst moment of my life made comedy. What an affront. I turn away.

I pace my room. I don't remember getting here.

Lovers.

How is it possible? It's unnatural. A sin. I lean back against my wall, hitting my head backwards against the plaster as if I might knock the images from my head, or knock myself unconscious – I care not which. Sliding to the ground, I pull my knees up so I may rest my head against them. And there I crouch until morning.

Marta finds me. I don't know if I have been asleep or in a trance. Her hands fly to her face. She rushes to my side. 'Luisa. ¿Qué pasó? Oh. Luisa.'

She helps me stand. Her arms are tight, but I still tremble.

'Shall I fetch Rafael?'

I shake my head so hard my neck clicks. Her eyes are one big question, but I cannot answer. Not today; perhaps not ever. She cajoles me into bed, but I won't lie down; I sit with my knees hunched under my chin, and she pulls the covers around me just as I am. Shaking.

'I'll call a doctor. You have had a shock.'

Ha! A shock!

What would I say to a doctor?

Marta is at a loss. I put my hand on her arm to reassure her, and because it's my only hope of being left in peace, I find words. 'Let me rest. I had a bad dream. Just a dream.'

'I cannot leave you like this.'

'Por favor.' My voice is little more than a whisper, a prayer – that she will leave me be.

She does, for now. I know she won't leave me for long.

Unburden Your Conscience

2 August 1756

Luisa

The fresco is quite ridiculous. A grown man – naked but for a wreath perched on his head and a pale blue cloth draped to protect his modesty – lifts his gaze and arms heavenward, offering a golden chalice to the skies. I suppose he's magnificent, with a rippling muscular torso and impossibly large thighs. His body is arranged in a pose the artist perhaps considered angelic: broad chest thrust out, waist and hips narrowing beneath him. His legs are bent; toes pointed like a leaping dancer. The perspective is all wrong: his feet are huge; his big toe is longer than his entire hand. I wonder why he grimaces so. Perhaps he knows he's ludicrous. Or he regrets the crime that earned him the sentence of being frozen in time above the bed in the guest bedroom of a noble family until the ceiling plaster crumbles or paint fades.

I have been staring for hours, watching him emerge from the fading night. Although I have been in my bed for a day and a night, I'm exhausted. And numb. But that's my choice, because if I allow myself to feel, I'll cry, and I don't think I'll ever stop.

The heavenly man has no more to offer, so finally I lower my gaze. And jolt. Rafael watches from the chair by the door. How long has he been there? When our eyes meet, an unspeakable sadness passes between us, and I turn away. I cannot stand to look at him.

I only pretend to sleep, so I hear him leave: the creak of the chair, the door clicking shut. And now I do cry. Tears soak my pillow, wrung from my twisting insides.

Rest is a reward for the honest. I once named Antonio liar. Rafael could teach him a thing or two about lying. Now I think about it, so could I.

Antonio

A cloth is pressed against my head, wiped across my face, then my lips, and a drop of liquid enters my mouth. I hope for more, and by some miracle it comes. There is a monk. He tends to me, his unlined face impassive, eyes almost black, expressionless. I allow my head to sink back onto the pillow and close my eyes.

I wake again. It's dark, and the window, normally behind, is at the end of my bed. How did it move? The moon watches, serene.

Liquid drips into my mouth, and I flinch from the cold shock. But when it reaches my tongue – sweet, soothing, I crave more. The monk is feeding me through a cloth. I grab it and suck until all I taste is stale linen. He takes it back and dips it. Now I see the source, I snatch the mug and gulp. Although hunger still chews my insides, my head is clear – the monk has done a decent job of sustaining me, and I'm grateful, until I remember he's part of this machine: the Unholy Office of the Inquisition. This is all for its benefit, not mine. I lie back and fade once more.

This time when I wake, the sky is muted, and the long shadows of the window bars stretch across the end of my cot. Now I understand; I'm in a new cell, no larger than my last, but less corrupted with filth.

A shift in the air to my right tells me I'm not alone. Pain skewers the back of my skull as I turn my head. It's not the monk. It's Balleza. He peers at me over his long nose, and oh, how I envy the ease with which he has slung one leg over a knee. I doubt I can lift mine. He affects the relaxed patience of a man who's been waiting a while, yet has nowhere else to be. How long has he been here? Perhaps always. Perhaps there's nothing beyond him. My whole life. Balleza and me.

'Don Albrono, it is good to see your health improving. Juan has looked after you well.' He leaves no space for a reply. 'We must continue your confession. Time is running short before your trial, and it will go better for you if you have unburdened your conscience beforehand.'

Luisa

'Tell me the truth, Rafael.'

It had been my idea to come to Constellation Hill. I crave fresh air. Though did I ever enjoy lavender? It clings inside my nostrils like cheap lye soap.

'Why haven't you run from me, Luisa?'

The truth is, I don't know, and I may yet. This morning, I sought him out in the library to tell him I was leaving. For a while I watched him opening and closing books, brushing their spines. *That's nice. A peaceful morning, reading.* But then he rested his forehead against the edge of a shelf and his shoulders slumped. And when I approached and saw his bloodshot eyes, and lines where his skin had been smooth not three days ago… I couldn't simply leave.

So here we are, in our *magical* place. Ours until that other man came like a tempest, leaving chaos.

'Help me to understand you.'

He shrugs. 'I'm unnatural.' His jaw is set, bitterness sits behind his eyes.

'Is this why you never told me about Jean-Pierre? Has your relationship always been thus?'

He nods and pinches the bridge of his nose. 'He's gone now. He feels terrible for hurting you.'

I blow out a breath. 'Does he.' It isn't a question.

Rafael turns to face me. 'He –'

'This isn't about *him*.'

'You said you wanted to understand. That's not possible with only half the truth.' His voice is steady, his eyes intense.

Give me strength. 'Rafael, I don't know why I'm still here. You're incompatible with God.'

His face tightens. 'So they say.'

'But I *know* you. I don't understand…' I lose my train of thought; probably didn't have one, just swirling notions and principles, bumping and tumbling.

'Luisa, I hurt you, and for that I'll never forgive myself. But God help me, I cannot help the way I am. I've tried. We both have – more separations that I can count.'

He speaks the truth; he always does.

Apart from the small matter of his cheating with another. My chest burns as though I ate something too hot, too fast, and I can no longer sit beside him. I step forward to where the ground begins to curve downwards, looking out over the city beneath – my city – the place where I thought I knew right from wrong, up from down, natural from unnatural.

When I face him again, he's slumped forward with his elbows on his knees and his fingers laced in his hair.

Whether or not he's at fault, I didn't come here to destroy him. Besides, didn't I ask for the truth? I should at least hear it, however difficult. If Rafael has taught me anything, it's that to judge without facts is to set sail in a grand ship without a navigator – no matter how strong the vessel, it will most likely end up broken on rocks. He's also taught me to think in similes.

I drop before him so our faces are level, and take his hands. 'Tell me then.'

The things I learn, there, on that rock. And I have a sense that it's only the outside of the matter. He starts slowly, but then it's as if he's been waiting to tell someone all his life. He and Jean-Pierre have been lovers for fifteen years; they live for each other and apart. They didn't choose; they found. They're two people in love who pretend otherwise – sometimes even to each other – because the world says they cannot be.

'Can you imagine having to deny who you are, every day of your life?'

I cannot.

Yet he cheated. I've every right to be angry. 'What of me, Rafael? Why all this?'

He shrugged. *Shrugged.*

'No.' I leap to my feet; take a step back. 'You turned my life upside down. Don't feign as though… as though you brought me the wrong colour ribbon!'

'I thought, hoped, that if I acted the part, it would become who I am.'

As if that could ever make sense.

Something shifts, and when he speaks his words are measured, gentle, but nonetheless a challenge. 'Can you tell me, Luisa, that you haven't been doing the same?'

I look up at the sky – because the ground isn't helping. It returns my gaze, impervious. He's right. Damn him.

'I always knew there was someone else,' he says. 'You shrink from my touch, you can be distant, we've never even kissed…'

'That doesn't mean…' *It does though.* I won't deceive him.

'This is us,' he gestures, palms up. 'Both wanting one person, but needing another.'

He's unrelenting, and my face burns. When I press my palms to my cheeks, the heat only spreads, dampening my neck and brow. Of course he knows. He's always known. I manage a nod.

'We've been playing the same game,' I say.

'Almost fooled ourselves,' he replied.

Two *idiotas.* We sit together, each inside our own head. He's warm – strange, that his nearness calms me. The minutes stretch, and my thoughts unscramble.

'I love you,' he says. 'You know that.'

'But not in *that* way, Rafael. Just as I love you – not in *that* way.'

'I don't disgust you.' He says it flat, his tone dead.

He should, if everything I've been taught is true. But it's Rafael sitting beside me. Not some corrupt, corrupting… *other*. I take his hand. It's the same as it was a week ago.

We sit until the air cools, then he swings an arm around me and chafes warmth into my shoulder. Its unromantic, very him, and it's right.

'I'm glad we understand each other,' he says. 'I'll never forgive myself for hurting you.'

'And me, you.'

'My betrayal was the worse.'

'Is it a contest now?'

His smile is the best thing that's happened for days, a cool cloth on fevered skin. I kiss his lips, and for the first time it feels right.

'What next?' he asks.

'I'll go home; I need to think.'

He nods.

'Will you go to Jean-Pierre?'

He scrubs his mouth. 'He's gone. I'll go back to Carrer Ample. I've been neglecting business.'

I peel away, so we may ride down together.

'Luisa. This isn't goodbye. Is it?'

I choose my words: 'I don't know what the future holds, but I want you in it. Can we manage that?'

'Always. You have my word.'

Riding back side by side, I keep stealing glances at him. He stares ahead, focused on something beyond the track. Is he thinking about his lover? About the future they might have? I'm not so good a person that I can wish them happiness. Life has schooled me once more: never believe in promises. What a dreadful student I've been, to need the same lesson twice.

Lulled by the rhythmic clip of hooves, my mind drifts to another ride, another companion, another betrayal – all the promises Antonio made on the road to Bellvís.

Antonio

'Time is running short before your trial; it will go better if you have unburdened your conscience.'

'*It will go better.*' I doubt that very much. In any case, what more might I confess? My mind may be failing, but I could swear I already gave a full account.

The stone is rough against my shoulder blades. This position – perched on my cot in the corner, leaning against the wall with my forearms draped over my knees – has become mine by habit. There's comfort in it.

'When is my trial?'

'Soon, days.'

Though I search for an emotion – turning the news over in my mind – my heart cannot summon the interest. It will come soon enough: apprehension, anxiety, terror even. I might as well appreciate this exhausted numbness while it lasts. I watch my visitor from beneath half-closed eyelids.

'¿Cómo está usted, Doctor Balleza?' I've spent so long alone in my own thoughts, Spanish feels forced.

He flinches at my question. He does look like the rat, but it's not funny anymore.

'Your friend, Señor Gallo, has repeated his offer of representation. I know you said –'

'No.'

'Is that your final answer?' By Christ, he's persistent.

'The matter is closed.' I shut my eyes and rest my head back against the wall.

'Will you give me your confession, so your case may be looked upon kindly?'

Now that *is* funny.

'Why do you smile, Don Albrono?'

'I don't expect kindness.'

'Why do you insist on making this difficult for yourself?'

I raise my head and examine my visitor. Today he wears a different waistcoat; this one has brown embroidery, the colour of dried blood. 'You and I must be of similar age. How did you reach such a grand position so early in your career?'

He narrows his eyes. 'We are not here to talk about me, Don Albrono.'

'Are you a doctor of law or theology?'

'I am a physician.'

I didn't expect that. Both physician and confessor. A more ironic combination I cannot imagine.

'Did you study here in Barcelona?'

I can tell he's uncomfortable by the way he shifts in his seat, but I cannot help myself; he's a far more interesting specimen than I.

'I studied in Valencia, where I live. I am here assisting with your case.'

'Why would a man of healing choose to work for the Inquisition?'

I don't mean to irritate him, but see I have. He uncrosses his legs and folds his arms.

'Why don't you tell me about yourself, Don Albrono? What brought you to Spain? How did you, a nobleman, come to be a foot soldier? And what were the circumstances that led to this charge?'

'A lot of questions.'

'I have time.'

'Don Fausto will be able to tell you what brought me to Spain. I joined the Asturia Regiment in Seville, because soldiering is my profession. This charge came about because I tricked a thief into revealing himself. There's nothing more to tell.'

'Nothing more? We have the sworn testimony of witnesses; enough to consider the case more than semi-proven.'

My camaradas wouldn't testify against me. Is he lying? He may be a cold bureaucrat, but I think he would find dishonesty beneath him. My temples throb, I rub them. 'How many times? I have nothing else to say. There *is* nothing else to say.'

'Who indulged your trickery? Who did it serve?'

'Myself.' The word falls from my mouth, as truth will.

'Bethink yourself. Witnesses denounced you. Why do you protect them?'

'To each their own conscience.'

I have no other words to offer, though I know the danger. I have a sense of floating, here on this cot, unmoored, unanchored, and like to be dashed against rocks.

He presses his lips together, exhales through his nose – I'm an errant child who won't be told. 'In that case, I am compelled to advise you, Don Albrono, that Article Fifteen allows for the Inquisition to use stern measures to assist you in your confession.'

Article Fifteen, is that what they call it?

I knew this would come, but for all my self-talk, all my resignation, the thought of torture pierces my bravado. The cell tilts and sways like a vessel in a gale, so I drop my head between my knees to both contain nausea and hide my face. I understand this terror is a torture in its own right, designed by the *Inquisition* to crush one's will. Yet I never anticipated the physical nature of fear, the way it hammers inside your chest, bruising your heart and lungs, and the cold… *Dio mio*. The cold. I pull my forearms around my shins, folding in, to contain the shivering that threatens to overwhelm me.

Then his '*Valencia*' falls into place and with it a new realisation. Icy fear melts into hot anger, and I raise my head once more to look into the eyes of the bureaucrat who recites *Articles* to fool himself he's better than a butcher.

'Did you give the same advice to Catalina Margueles?'

His eyes widen; a child emerges. 'How do you know –' He jumps to his feet so fast the floor shrieks at his scraping chair. 'I remind you, Don Albrono –' He has added a lofty tenor to his tone, an affectation wasted on me. '– it is not *I* who broke God's laws.'

He can peer down his nose all he likes; I know what he is.

'Did you interrogate her? Were you there? Did you oversee it?'

He turns, giving me his back, but not before I see the truth in his eyes. I grip the edge of my cot because, God forgive me, I want to rip his heart out.

'You destroyed a defenceless woman.'

He thumps the door. 'Guard!'

'And yet you put *me* on trial.'

Footsteps. The jangle of keys.

He looks back over his shoulder. '*I* did not destroy her. She took her own life. Her final insult to God.'

His words punch a hole in my guts.

Catalina is dead?

The world cracks.

Though I open my mouth, any words crumble.

Catalina is dead.

By now the cell door is open, and a guard stands alongside Balleza watching me. '¿Has terminado aquí, Doctor?'

'You did not know?' Balleza whispers.

Somehow, I spring up and lunge for him. And yes, my intention is murderous. But the guard clips me about the head with probably no more than his own heavy fist. In my state, I collapse, head bouncing against the side of the cot. I sit on the floor, wiping blood from my mouth, looking up at a man who has replaced his bureaucratic mask and examines me as one would an artefact.

'How?' My own voice floats, as though it comes from outside.

'She threw herself from the Puente de Serranos onto the rocks below.'

I suffocate. I drown. Whatever substance it is I'm drawing into my lungs scorches me from inside.

The door clangs shut, and the lock scrapes back into position.

Catalina's face swims before me, eyes filled with trust; I let her go into the world alone; she stood no chance. And here I am, as Catalina was. Perhaps it's justice.

The shadows of the bars lengthen until they cross my body, imprisoning me anew until darkness comes to erase them. I don't seek to escape into my memories; I'd prefer oblivion. But they arrive anyway. I started something and can't stop it. I dream of the road to Bellvís, and what happened there.

What Happened on the Road to Bellvís

May 1754

Luisa

Discovering Antonio sought payment of a century-old debt swiped the ground beneath me. Not for the money. But for the humiliation. His meetings with Enzo, the whispering in corners, the shared looks… how well they'd planned. How they must have laughed. Reeling me in like a fish on a hook, all the while scheming after my family's wealth. Surely, I knew better than to allow myself to be seduced by a beautiful face and a lingering smile. I'd got one thing right. He *saw* me. Didn't he just? He saw me coming from a hundred leagues away.

That evening, with Papa still away, and Mama sleeping off one of her headaches, it fell to me to host dinner. It would take all the resilience I possessed to see to my guests' needs while *not* tipping the tureen of broth into Antonio's lap. I seated him next to Señorita Cadiz at the far end of the table. Of course, her face lit up when she spied the place settings. With luck, she'd monopolise him all evening.

Yet if I cared nothing for Antonio, why did I strain to hear their conversation? Difficult, given that she whispered, and he contributed only an occasional nod and smile.

'Oh, what a shame! Leaving tomorrow?'

I heard *that.* Not that I cared.

But when I studied the plate before me, the food had turned into pebbles.

'Señorita Navas, are you quite well?' Señor García peered into my face. 'You haven't touched a morsel.'

Though he had not been particularly loud, every diner stopped talking, and seven pairs of eyes swung towards me.

'Mademoiselle, you are pale.'

'¡Un poco de agua para la Señorita!'

Señora Cadiz fanned me with her abanico. Monsieur Dupont scraped his chair back to give me space. As for Antonio, was that a smirk? Curse him. And curse me for noticing.

'What is this? Is my daughter indisposed?'

As one, the guests rose in recognition of the head of the household. Before the chairs had finished dragging, the staff had moved my place setting and built a new one for him.

'Are you well, Luisa?' he whispered.

'Sí, Papa,' I muttered back. 'Just not hungry. May I retire?'

'Very well. I'll host. See me later.'

Then we faced the guests, and I spoke up. 'What a pleasure! Mi padre is a day early. Papa, allow me to introduce our guests.' Each man bowed, and each woman dipped as I recited their particulars. '… and this is Don Antonio Albrono. He travelled from Genoa with Signor Enzo.'

Whereas Papa had simply nodded at each guest, now I could have sworn I saw a flicker of something. Did his eyes narrow? His breath catch? I dismissed it. Perhaps I was over-sensitive where Antonio was concerned.

Though he had been gone only a week, Papa and I had business to discuss, so later that night, I went to find him in his study. As I approached the closed door, the low hum of voices drifted through the wood, one of them familiar.

Nothing short of necessity could induce me to spend time with Don Fausto, so I turned away. Then, a name floated above the conversation, rooting me to the floor.

'He's an Albrono,' said Don Fausto. 'He's not here for the climate.'

My father said something too muffled to discern, I leaned in.

'That is as may be,' Don Fausto said, 'but this needs to end. For good this time.'

'By what means?'

'Whatever it takes. Gonzalo. Or we might be undone.'

Eavesdropping becomes nobody. But should I steal away or announce myself? I had no choice really; besides, curiosity threatened to swallow me whole. Gathering my skirts, I pushed the door and breezed in.

'Papa! I'm so pleased you're back!' I turned to Don Fausto. 'Uncle, to see you twice in one day is a blessing.' I was referring to our earlier meeting in the Plaça del Rei, when I introduced Antonio. 'Have you eaten? Shall we prepare a plate for you?'

'Luisa, how wonderful to see you.' Fausto's eyes crawled upon my skin like wall lizards. 'Your father said you were out of sorts. I hope it is fleeting.'

I stepped into Don Fausto's hug; a duty I preferred to get done than dread.

Papa spoke as I disentangled myself. 'Thank you for bringing this matter to my attention. We'll talk again.'

Don Fausto took the hint and swept out in a cloud of incense. I patted my hair where it had caught in his crucifix. They were an odd pair, Father and Don Fausto. Inseparable since boyhood, yet I never sensed any real affection between them. From what Father had told me, they'd grown up in neighbouring streets, matriculated together, and been drawn into my family's orbit as young men. Father became the Spinelli family secretary, and Don Fausto followed his vocation, mentored by my Uncle Luca. With all that history, one would think they might like each other, but I never saw them engage in any tone other than tetchy.

Their meeting today had left Father in another one of his sullen moods, and he leaned backwards against his desk, drumming his fingers against the wood behind.

'Papa, how was your trip?'

'I understand you've been spending time with that man from Genoa.' Straight to the point, as always.

'He hurt his foot saving me from some falling crates. It was the least I could do.' I concentrated on the space between his eyes at the top of his nose, a trick I'd learned as a child.

'Is that all?'

'We got along well. He's leaving tomorrow.' I considered telling him about the Spinelli debt, but my father isn't one for inviting my confidence.

'You are not to see him again.'

I didn't expect that, nor did I like it. 'Papa. I'm not a child.'

'On this matter, you'll do as I say.'

'What will you do? Lock me in my room?'

'If I have to, yes.' He held me in his stare, then collapsed into a chair. 'I've had a trying week. Trust me on this matter.'

I picked up a discarded abanico from the mantelpiece and fanned my burning face. I've never been good at hiding my feelings.

'I insist you obey. It's for the best. A father's judgement.'

'Why should I, when you cannot trust mine?'

His eyes hardened. 'Because I am your father.'

End of conversation, as far as he was concerned.

That night, sleep eluded me. Too many questions: Why had Father reacted to Antonio? What had prompted Don Fausto to visit? What '*needs to end*'? Why had Father been so fierce? By morning one question had risen above all the others: *What was Papa afraid of?*

Antonio

It suited me, Enzo's silence. No doubt he was preoccupied with thoughts of the long ride ahead. Four days if we made good time.

The courtyard bore that crisp stillness peculiar to the moments between night and dawn, silent but for the snort of our horses and the creak of leather. I ran my hands along my gelding's flank, feeling his warmth, and the ripple of firm muscle. *Castagno*, I'd call him, in honour of his chestnut coat. Enzo had opted for a white mare, small and strong. He had done a good job in hiring our mounts; by the look of their gleaming coats, they were fit and well-fed. Both now stood quietly, flicking their ears at the sounds of our preparation: the jangle of bridles, the clinking of buckles. Every now and again, one of them shifted or scraped a hoof on the paving slabs, as if to say, '*We're ready, what's taking so long?*'

I tightened the girths, tugging the leather to test its strength, while Enzo secured the packs. I was ready. I looped the reins over the saddle horn. Enzo cinched his last strap.

'What will you call yours, Blanco?' I asked.

Enzo considered his little mare, from head to tail. 'Gigante,' he said with not a hint of a smile.

He always could raise a chuckle in me.

'¡Señor, espera!' The hotel's mayordomo flew into the courtyard as if running from a fire.

'Gabriel?'

'Señor Navas sent me to fetch you.'

Curious.

'Come, Enzo,' I said. 'Let's see what this is about.'

Luisa's father sat at his desk; round glasses perched on the end of his nose. Although he pretended to study a paper, his eyes didn't move. 'Forgive me for delaying your departure. There's something I would discuss with you, and who knows –' He smiled. '– perhaps I might save you the journey.'

'Journey?'

'Bellvís, no?'

Luisa must have told him of the debt. 'Sí.'

'Well then, I would speak with you –' His eyes flicked to Enzo. '– de hombre a hombre.'

It almost warranted an eyeroll.

'I'll check the tack,' Enzo said. 'Again.'

Señor Navas waited until the door clicked shut. 'A lawyer who knows when to leave, I hope you pay him well.'

He no doubt thought himself clever. Not at all like a man who rehearsed *gravitas* before a looking-glass.

'Enzo is also a friend.'

'Travelling together makes amigos of men.'

'Forgive my impatience; we've a long journey. What do you wish to discuss?'

'I understand you seek payment of a debt from the Spinelli family.' His eyes darted over my face.

I waited, knowing he would go on. After all, he'd requested the meeting.

'The debt is over a century old,' he said. 'Why do you think you will succeed where others have failed?'

'Others?'

He blinked twice, fast. 'You surely cannot be first in all this time. The debt must either be settled, or have been declared invalid.'

'Yes, more than likely,' I said, 'I have been tasked with discovery. If the debt is cleared then so be it.'

A long silence. He worked his mouth. Then: 'I am prepared to make you an offer.'

'Why? It's between Alejo Spinelli and my family.'

'I'm his guardian.'

'I'm told he's nearly fifty.'

'I've never stopped looking out for him.'

Horseshit. 'Admirable. I'm sure you understand, my uncle, Luigi, will have questions if I return without resolving the matter.' I lied. Luigi couldn't care less.

'Your uncle will have questions if you return empty-handed – as you will – when you had a chance to make a settlement. At least hear my offer.'

I'd no intention of *not* hearing his offer, but I'd make a poor negotiator if I snatched at it.

'Five thousand reales.'

I concentrated on not blinking, but I must surely have given something away. Five thousand reales. More than six hundred silver dollars. I had to accept.

But why would a successful businessman like Señor Navas make such an offer? Unless the true prize was bigger.

Did I need a bigger prize? I'd not come to Spain to ruin a family, or create rifts.

'Take it, Antonio, with my goodwill and that of the Spinelli family.'

I could. Walking away had its attractions.

I would.

'I'll need Enzo to review the terms,' I said.

'And that brings me to a matter, as far as *terms* are concerned.'

Here it came.

'I'll require you to sign that the debt is settled, and to undertake never to see my daughter again.'

Now the man before me shrank; his beady eyes – already magnified behind his glasses – grew. Gonzalo Navas became a weasel peering over its snout.

'Does Luisa know you are doing this?'

Of course she didn't. I let his silence make my point, then shook my head and turned to leave.

'I care about my daughter, Antonio,' he called after me.

Something about his tone… Faster than thought, I strode back to his desk.

'I defer to your knowledge as a merchant,' I said. 'You plainly know more than I about the price of a daughter.'

The weasel returned, this time with his head retreating into his neck.

I braced my hands on the desk. 'A poor businessman, I. Yesterday she told me she never wishes to see me again. Yet I'd pass up your *five thousand reales* for the smallest chance she might change her mind.'

I let my words hang there. It struck me if I said 'boo!' he would topple right off his seat. As fast as my anger had risen, it vanished.

I turned on my heel and left him there. Gonzalo Navas and his reales.

Luisa

He would not! I tried the door again. It rattled but stood resolute. Unbelievable! Father locked me in. Yes, Father. Who else?

What of Marta? Had he sent her off on an errand? Locked her in too? I rooted through the wardrobe and found my front-lacing stays – old-fashioned, but all I could manage on my own. The wool of my plain grey skirt snagged in its waistband. In my hurry and rage, I misbuttoned the chaqueta and had to start over. Last of all, I pinned my hair into a loose knot, and jammed a mobcap on top. Now what?

I hardly knew what I threw into my portmanteau – anything, useful or not: hairbrush, a spare shift, scarves, maybe even a candlestick. I'd show my parents I'd not be imprisoned like a… a *felon*. Now, to get out.

Through the keyhole, the tip of the key blinked. How hard could it be to turn it? A hairpin might do it. But my poking only served to nudge the key backwards. If it fell, I *would* be trapped. Squinting into the hole, I took a breath and inserted the pin alongside the metal, pushing sideways and down. My fingertips whitened; the pin bit skin. 'Heavenly Father. Forgive my anger, and for disobeying my parents. Please. Give me this one thing and

I will say an extra mass on Sunday.' The pin began to bend; surely it would break. 'Every Sunday for a month.' The key began to move. I pressed – a slow firm motion. 'Two months!'

The key clunked and shifted. I could have cried. Free.

I greeted Barnabas, the stableman, with a breezy '*¡Qué hermosa mañana*!' as though it were the most natural thing in the world for the hotel manageress to appear in the courtyard, carrying her own luggage. Other than to take the first vehicle available, I'd no plan. A horse would do if need be. I was in luck. He'd prepared the calesa for my mother. Ignoring his protests, I leapt into the driver's seat, and with a clatter of hooves, I sped out of the courtyard and onto the street beyond.

I'd no plan until suddenly I did. Papa had been unnerved by Antonio, and since he wouldn't explain why, I'd find the men who might. They couldn't have gone far, and I knew which way. The road to Bellvís, to my uncle, Alejo Spinelli.

Antonio

A couple of hours into our journey, Enzo got around to the obvious question. 'Are you going to tell me what he wanted?'

Castagno's ears flicked at his sudden voice.

'He offered me money to abandon the claim,' I said.

'How much?'

'Five thousand reales.'

He pulled up, so I had no choice but to do likewise.

He dropped his hands to his pommel. 'You should have accepted. We agreed a deal was your best chance. That was a good offer.'

'I didn't like the terms,' I said.

'What terms?'

I squeezed my calves against Castagno's flanks. 'He's not a man I wish to do business with.' Why did my horse not move?

'We're not here to make friends. What offended you so?'

'It matters not; it's done now. Let's go; we've already lost an hour.'

'Reconsider. Turn back.'

'I shall not.' But though I nudged Castagno with my heels, he merely snorted and shook his mane. 'He wanted me to leave his daughter alone.' I pressed again, harder. '¡*Arre*!' Now, my gelding jolted forward, almost unseating me. He was going to take some getting used to. I pulled the reins to slow him back into his easy trot.

'For the love of God.' Enzo broke into a trot beside me. 'You told me she'll have no more of you. What am I missing? Where is the loss?'

'Agreeing a price on his daughter? I'll have no part of it.' I patted the side of Castagno's neck, finding heat and wiry hair.

He muttered something that sounded like, 'Heaven protect me from men of principle.'

'I'd rather be a man of principle than a weasel like Señor Navas,' I retorted.

He looked at me sideways. '*I* would rather you had done a deal with a weasel. Then we could have been on the next ship home, instead of facing four days on horseback on this godforsaken road.'

'Look at all this.' I waved my arm at the golden-red landscape, spread like an artfully draped quilt. 'What awaits us in Genoa, anyway?'

'My bed! I haven't slept well for weeks now.'

'We will get you home to your bed. Tell me what you know of the Spinelli family.'

That worked. The only thing Enzo loved more than his research was reciting its findings.

'Did you know the Spinelli line originated in Genoa?' he said.

'I didn't, but now that you mention it, it's not a very Spanish sounding name.'

Uncle Luigi must have forgotten that part, or deemed it irrelevant. He'd told me all about the Albrono loans. To Alessio

Spinelli so he might raise an army on behalf of King Phillip the Fourth.

'The position of Marqués de Bellvís was created as a reward. Four generations of Spinellis, not one of them inclined to settle the debt.'

Nothing stopped Enzo once he got going. His cadence rose and fell with the up and down of Gigante's gait.' An excellent rider, he occupied his saddle with light grace, sending his cues with a knee-shift here and a tilt there – maybe even by thought. I rarely saw him tug the reins; they hung slack against his fingers. As though for decoration, not utility.

'Here's an interesting thing,' he said. 'Carlos Spinelli – Luisa's grandfather – had a brother, Luca, Archbishop of Tarragona. He met a violent death, murdered by robbers on this very road.'

'Ouch. I didn't know that. When?'

'Thirty-four years ago. Same year Carlos died. Same year Alejo inherited.'

'Luisa's father told me he was Alejo's guardian back then,' I said. 'The boy was only sixteen at the time.'

'He was Carlos Spinelli's secretary,' Enzo said. 'I wonder how it came about that he became guardian, and indeed married so high – his wife, Maria, is Alejo's twin sister.'

'He must have been an excellent secretary,' I laughed.

'It's akin to my marrying your aunt,' said Enzo. 'Not something I'd entertain.'

'I don't know. *Uncle Enzo* sounds well.' I shot him a sideways look, pleased to see him smile, finally. 'Wait, did you say Luisa's mother is Alejo's twin?'

'That's right.'

'So, Gonzalo Navas was also *her* guardian, and he married her.'

'Many a gentleman has secured a pretty young wife through guardianship.'

I pictured María Navas y Spinelli and wondered how much of her marriage had been her choice. A distasteful line of thought, and one I pushed aside. 'He mentioned previous claims to the debt. Did you discover anything about that?'

'There is no recorded legal case in Barcelona, but that doesn't mean it didn't happen. Your uncle, Girolamo, spent some time here, but if it was to pursue the debt, it was under his own initiative. It would be hard to discover his movements – business transactions, perhaps.'

I let his voice blend with the echo of the horse's hooves while my mind drifted to the landscape. Spain is a truly beautiful country with its rolling hills and unbroken blue skies. In the distance, I wondered if I saw the glimmer of rooftops, or it might have simply been the heat bouncing from the track.

'… records can be problematic outside of large cities… Antonio, are you listening to anything I'm saying?'

'Sorry, amico, I have to be honest, you lost me when you started talking about business transactions.'

'I suppose you were thinking about Señorita Navas.'

'On this occasion, no. She has occupied far too much of my mind this past week.'

'She's an impressive woman. I would think every eligible man in Barcelona is taken with her. Though she did seem to make a place in her heart for you. God knows why.'

'You jest, but you're right. God knows why. It would take an admirable man to deserve her.'

'A woman could do worse than you, my lord. A man of uncommon integrity.'

'Enzo, did you just compliment me?'

'A slip, it won't happen again.'

I tried to shake Luisa from my mind and concentrate on the landscape, the steady rhythm of the horse. The peace didn't last.

At first, we ignored the rumble in the distance – the Camino Real is a well-travelled track. But it grew louder.

'Someone's in a hurry,' Enzo said.

Three clouds of dust. Three horsemen. We shifted aside to give way. But, as it turned out, they were coming for us.

The riders wore dusty, mismatched clothing, once fine, now grimy and weather-beaten: low-brimmed hats, scarves pulled over their faces. Too late, I realised. Briganti. Bandoleros.

Enzo drove his heels into his mare's sides, urging her into a gallop. But I knew by the time we roused our horses the men would be upon us, so I held my ground and braced myself.

The first gave chase to Enzo. The other two converged upon me. Both held knives. One was huge – a mountain of a man. Good. Size is rarely an advantage for a rider. I tightened my grip on my reins. 'Easy, Castagno… steady… espera.'

I hoped the big fellow would attack first, and my prayers were answered. He lunged. A blade flashed. I veered my horse away, and with the same motion, swung my booted foot hard against his shoulder in the direction he leaned. Thrown off balance by his own momentum, he tumbled from his horse, landing with a crunch.

The second assailant had been charging, and his horse only avoided the falling hulk by rearing onto its hind legs. He balanced precariously as he struggled to steady his mount, so for a second, the initiative was mine. I steered alongside and lunged, grabbing his mask, trying to yank him down.

He was too strong. I didn't topple him, but I saw his face. A few days of black beard growth, and a vertical scar running from the tip of his nose into his upper lip, giving it a strange puckered appearance. This was not his first fight. *Va bene*, nor was it mine.

He gripped his reins in one hand and slashed at my face with the other. I knew little of it – a streak of metal, a hiss. My forearm shot up, meeting his in a bone-jarring clash that numbed my arm and sent shockwaves through my bones. Sunlight flared as the blade hissed past my eye, close enough I felt the air whisper over my lashes. Then fire tore across my forehead, spilling coppery warmth down my face.

I had no time to catch my breath. No time to steady the hammering in my chest, or nurse the throb in my arm. No time to consider how close I'd come to losing more than blood. For he was lining up his second blow, across his body and downwards.

I saw it coming, and every sense sharpened – the world narrowed to the path of his arm. I ducked under it, forward, leaving him slicing space, tilting sideways in his saddle. I surged back up, thrusting my shoulder into him, in the direction he was already swaying. His flailing arm reached for my horse – *my* horse – to steady himself. But Castagno, unnerved by the chaos, was already shifting. I barely had to press my heels before he lurched forward, leaving nothing for my attacker to grasp. I looked back once. The fellow lay on the ground, a red circle spreading beneath him. He'd fallen on his own knife. I hoped it wasn't fatal. Violent death, even of a bandit, requires explaining.

Enzo was in trouble. When I reached them, both he and his assailant were on their feet. One of Enzo's arms hung useless by his side, and he circled his mare, using her as a shield while the other prowled the opposite side, wielding his knife. I couldn't imagine the strategy working for long and didn't wait to find out.

I ran my horse at the thug, using my thighs for balance, swinging my right arm behind, gripping the reins. As I rode alongside, I cracked the leather across his face, slicing air with sound, splitting the bridge of his nose, and sending his knife flying.

When I brought Castagno about, the thug was still staggering backwards, still holding his face. But his howls had shifted from raw shrieks to coherent curses, and I knew he wasn't done.

Sadly, Castagno was. Neither pressure nor pleading would induce him to run at the assailant again. I didn't blame him. I leapt down, ignoring protests from my ankle, and closed the distance. My mind emptied. No thought, no feeling. Perhaps true anger isn't fire – it's ice. A cold, stilling clarity.

I acted fast, before he could compose himself, driving my fist into his ribs, feeling their hard ridges against my knuckles even through flesh and clothing. With the crunch of impact, his body buckled. I couldn't afford to let up – couldn't risk it. While he still gasped and choked, my knuckles found his jaw, the force snapping his head to one side with mechanical efficiency. The shock rippled through my arm, clean, my wrist aligned to absorb it. I seized his collar, using my weight to pull him off balance, and drove my knee into his stomach. He crumpled to the ground with a strangled groan, clutching his abdomen.

The danger hadn't passed. He was already clawing the ground, trying to get up. And back along the track, I wasn't sure I'd taken the big guy out of the fight. As for Enzo, he lay vulnerable and half-conscious. I yanked him to his feet and pushed him towards his horse.

'Enzo, get out of here.'

He placed a foot in Gigante's stirrup, but his injured arm only flailed at his mount. I heaved. Astride the horse, he collapsed forward. Jesu. If he couldn't sit upright, how could he ride? He would have to. I thrust the reins into his good hand and slapped the horse hard. *'Corre!'* The animal reared slightly, then cantered off, carrying him away.

I didn't make it to my own horse. By the time I'd dragged Enzo away, his attacker had scrambled to his feet, eyes locked onto mine, amber, bloodshot, furious. He edged towards his knife lying in the dirt. I let him think I hadn't noticed. Waited for him to lunge. Then, drove my boot into his back, sending him sprawling. He reached for the knife. I was faster. My heel came down hard. Something snapped.

He screamed, shattering the air like glass, cradling his hand to his chest, his fingers so mangled I had to look away. When he lurched to his feet and ran for his horse, I let him go, folding his knife – a *navaja* – and slipping it into my pocket.

But there was no reprieve. The big guy appeared, feet pounding down the track, barrelling toward me like an enraged bull – if bulls waved knives. Out of ideas, I slapped Castagno's flank with all my strength. The gelding reared, hooves climbing the air. In the chaos, the big guy hesitated just long enough. I planted one foot and drove the other into his knee. My weak ankle protested, but held. I can only imagine the pain he endured, for his leg buckled backwards, grotesque, unnatural, and he fell. He clutched, he rolled, his mouth opened and closed, but shock took his scream.

I'd been driven by fury and fear, and now I had nothing left. And my horse had bolted. When I slapped its flank, it must have decided enough was enough, and disappeared up the track, in a blur of pounding hooves and clay dust. So much for our emerging bond.

I squatted and studied the thug on the ground; his mask had long ago dropped. I saw a battle-hardened man, perhaps fifteen years older than me, hair cropped to his scalp, and a large face beginning to sag around the jawline. 'What am I supposed to do with you?' I asked.

He spat blood-streaked mucus onto the ground in reply. His two front teeth were missing; those that remained were brown.

'I should turn you in, but as you can see, I'm without transport.' I gestured at the empty road. 'And it appears, so are you.'

He was pale and trembling, his hands pressed against the remnants of his knee. I knelt, pulling them aside, examining the damage. Broken, but he'd live.

'I'm sure someone will find you,' I said.

I set off along the track, back towards the city, every muscle in my body screaming for rest, my ankle weak and loose. A breeze awoke the stinging on my forehead, and I wiped at the blood trickling from the cut. I passed the spot where I'd knocked the two briganti from their horses, marked by stained earth – as though someone had spilled a flask of Bobal. Of their horses, or the third brigand, there was no sign.

Enzo was somewhere ahead, but how far? With no better plan, I walked, hoping I'd find him around the next bend.

Luisa

Two hours on the Camino Real and no sign of them. But what had I expected? They were on horseback; I was in a calesa built for city errands. Had I taken leave of my senses? I might lose a wheel, or worse.

I brought my horse to a halt and considered my surroundings: rolling red terrain, vineyards rising to the north, olive groves stretching to the south. The sun thrummed relentlessly above. I had water pouches; between me and the horse, they would last a day. This must be the most bizarre flight of reason I'd ever succumbed to. Why? My father's proprietorial behaviour. Even thinking upon it had me grinding my teeth. To lock me in my room… but then, what judgement had I shown, taking flight this way?

I would return, but not home. No. I had to show my father he couldn't simply lock me away. How long since I last visited Marguerite? Too long. I turned the horse and set off at a comfortable trot toward the city.

I hadn't travelled a hundred yards before the thunder of hooves rose behind me. Bandoleros. My stomach lurched. 'Arre… Sombre… ¡ARRE!' My mother would be beside herself if she knew. After all, her uncle had been killed in an ambush on this very road. Poor judgement indeed.

Sombre had no stamina for the open road. He gave a token jolt, then slowed to a lethargic trot as though we were parading down the Carrer Ample. In any case, no horse hooked to a calesa can outrun a galloping rider. I'd have to face my assailant. I'd hand over everything, and pray it would be enough. Dust filled my nostrils. My eyes stung. He was almost upon me. I should be trembling; instead, I felt numb. For sure, my heart hammered, but it was somewhere outside my skin, barely within earshot.

It was Enzo. Even slumped forward, his face pasted in blood, I recognized him.

He drew up beside me, one arm swinging limp at his side. He clutched his ribs with the other.

'Enzo. ¿Qué pasó? Here, sit. What happened? You were attacked?'

'Briganti.'

'Bandoleros?'

'Yes'

'Antonio?'

'Half a legua.' He waved back the way he'd come with his good arm.

Barely a ten-minute ride away. 'Is he hurt?'

'Not when I left him, but there were three.'

I moved quickly, helping Enzo into the carriage and tying his horse to the back. The saddlebags would have to stay on the mare – no room. He grabbed his satchel and cradled it to his chest. Some bandoleros – leaving their target with his possessions.

'Señorita. It's not safe.'

I set off. Yes, I knew I might be leading us into danger, and yes, I was afraid. But I couldn't shake the image of a man lying injured, perhaps close to death, in the road. Even if he deserved it. No. Nobody deserved that, and in any case, Antonio owed me answers.

No matter how I urged Sombre onwards, the track unravelled with mocking nonchalance. My heart jolted at every shrub or rock, each masquerading as a broken human form until I drew close enough to see the grotesque mimicry.

In the distance, a dot blinked in the shimmering heat, growing bigger, taking on human form. A tall man limping; slow at that – no hat, hair loose, untucked shirt billowing over his breeches.

I pulled up and met him on foot.

'Now I know they ended me,' he said. 'Here comes an angel.'

Oh please. Now I knew he was fine. Still trying to charm me.

But for all his bravado, he was a grisly sight. A cut ran from his eyebrow to his hairline – crusted, its edges jagged and raised; it seemed he'd used the hem of his shirt to mop blood. More had gathered at his collar. As for his face – half of it was smeared red, putting me in mind of a grotesque devil's mask I'd once seen in a religious play, one eye blinking clear through the paint.

'What happened?'

But he spotted the little white mare. 'Enzo!' He hobbled to the calesa. 'Stai bene?' The carriage tilted and settled as he clambered up.

Enzo's head lolled, and even as Antonio reached for him, he slumped into a heap on the floor.

I checked his breathing while Antonio felt for his pulse. Both strong.

'Dislocated,' he said, cupping his shoulder. 'That's got to hurt.'

'There's a monastery near here,' I said, 'Sant Cugat. They'll know what to do.'

Antonio crouched, frowning. 'Now is the time, while he's out.' He lifted Enzo's arm.

'What? Wait…' I'd an idea what Antonio might be about to attempt, and didn't like it one bit. 'Do you know what you're doing?'

'Been shown. Never done it.'

'And now is when you decide to try?'

He chewed his lip, thoughtful. 'A rope would bite. Fabric. Linen.' For a second he seemed about to sacrifice his shirt, and there was no need for that.

'Momentito.' I circled behind to my portmanteau on the back; pulled out my spare shift. 'Here.' The day became ever stranger.

He glanced at it. 'Twist it into a line.'

'A *por favor* would be good,' I muttered, but did as he instructed.

'When I lift him, loop it under and across his chest.'

He'd already begun; no time to ask what he meant. It didn't matter. I soon worked it out.

'Here, take the ends.'

'Are you sure this will work?'

'Absolutely not. Pull.'

It took a few minutes, manoeuvring and sweating, but it happened: *crack*.

I thought we'd broken something. Enzo shrieked. Then inhaled a loud, rasping breath, followed by a stream of curses. '*Cazzo! Figlio di Puttana!*'

'Such language in front of La Señorita,' Antonio said.

Enzo jerked away. '*Sei il diavolo!*'

With his face like that, Antonio might indeed have been the devil.

'Better?' he asked.

The lawyer poked tentatively at his shoulder, then harder, and his expression softened. 'What did you do?'

'A trick I learned in the army,' he said. 'Luisa did all the work.'

'Not that you deserve it,' I said. 'Enzo rest. I know a place. Antonio, for the love of Our Lady, will you clean your face up? I cannot travel with you looking like that.'

Antonio offered to take the reins, but I wasn't about to cast him as gallant rescuer, so he perched beside me, hands loose on his thighs, watching the horizon – perhaps for more bandoleros, maybe the same ones.

I found the turnoff for Sant Cugat and drove Sombre slow and steady, every now and again checking on Enzo. He lay pale, eyes closed. Not asleep though; he winced every time I hit a bump.

The loud rattle of the wheels only served to amplify our silence. To break it meant broaching the subject sitting like a third person between us. And though I'd come for answers, I didn't know where to begin. A dust devil whirred in the distance; I watched it spin and settle. A pair of vultures flapped up, leaving behind a strewn carcass that might have started the day as a cat. I steered around it, holding my breath against the rotten funk.

'What were you doing on the road alone, Luisa?'

'It's just as well I was!'

'I cannot deny that. But why?'

'I don't know what possessed me.'

'Imagine if they found you first?'

'Are you reprimanding me?'

'That I wouldn't do.'

A hawk circled overhead, low enough for its shadow to flicker across the plain. We both watched it wheel once, then twice, then disappear.

'But Christ! What were you thinking?' He glared at me.

Sounded like a reprimand to me. Even Sombre's ears flicked up. I ignored him.

I ached. Top to toe: neck, arms, back… even the soles of my feet. Bundles of nerves telling me they'd had enough, shrieking protest at every new movement. I rolled my shoulders.

'Here.' He handed me the water pouch, unstopped, and took the reins. 'Shall I drive now?' His voice was gentle.

Thirst dealt with, I took the straps out of his hands.

The water served me well at first. Too soon though, the protests began again, starting in my neck – which I tried to stretch without him noticing – then spreading once more into my shoulders.

'You're struggling.' He touched my forearm.

'I'm fine,' I replied.

A beat. He watched my face, then, bafflingly, nodded to himself. 'Were you following me?' he asked.

'Sí.'

I kept my eyes on the road, but felt his stare hot on my skin.

'Don't be flattered,' I said. 'It concerns a disagreement I had with my father. I think there are things you haven't told me, and I don't like being taken for simple.'

'That I *certainly* wouldn't do.'

'Why does my father dislike you?'

'There's a question. I never met your father before yesterday.'

'The *truth*, Antonio.'

I looked then had to look away. Those eyes – all mahogany and innocence – had clouded my judgement too many times already.

'I wouldn't lie to you, Luisa.'

Could he hear himself?

I turned to check on Enzo, apparently sleeping now – face slack, lips parted. 'To withhold the truth is to lie,' I said.

To his credit, he didn't speak, just resumed watching the track unfold.

We had time; I might as well learn what I could. 'The day you arrived, you knew I was a Spinelli, didn't you?'

'No,' he said.

'Then why did you watch me?'

He laughed under his breath.

'You find me funny?'

'*No*, Luisa,' he huffed. 'God's *teeth*. Must you be so…?' He bit his own sentence off.

'Must I be what? Angry… cynical… guarded. All the things I should have been when you were drenching me in charm and worming your way into my affection so I'd help you with your money-making scheme.'

He turned away, jaw tight, staring at only he knew what: red plains trimmed with grey scrub – brittle as bone. Here and there an awkward patch of green, like a visitor at the wrong address.

He could sulk all he liked. I'd have my answers. 'Why did you watch me if you weren't looking for Luisa Navas y Spinelli?'

'I might as well admit defeat. Because you'll find my answer hard to credit.'

'Let me judge that.'

The wheels shook, the track curved uphill, and I felt his eyes upon me once more.

'I couldn't *not* watch you. I've been unable to stop.'

Damn him, my chaqueta tightened against my ribs.

He toyed with the fabric of his breeches. His knuckles, I noticed, had been scraped raw. 'I learned you were a Spinelli when you introduced your mother. At that exact time, Enzo was at the municipal offices enquiring after a family of that name. We were both astounded at the coincidence.'

'Yet didn't tell me.'

'For four more days. Because I knew how it looked. And the longer I left it, the harder it became. I'm not proud of myself.'

I let that settle. My head told me not to believe him. My heart, my belly, even my spine – they had other ideas. But whoever prospered taking advice from vertebrae?

'What are you thinking, Luisa?'

'That I don't know what to believe.'

'There we are then.'

His eyes grew distant once again.

The skin around the cut on his forehead looked horrible – purple, swollen – the wound itself angry. Three bandoleros. They could have killed him. I rubbed my arms, cold suddenly in spite of the sun.

'Your head,' I said. 'We should ask the monks to examine you too.'

As though he'd forgotten, he blinked, and raised his fingers to the cut.

'Does it hurt?'

He turned to me then, fixing his eyes on mine. 'I should have told you the moment I knew. I'm sorry.'

In spite of myself, my chest loosened. I steered us to the side of the track and brought us to a stop. Dust gave way to musk and leather, clattering wheels to the chirrup of insects. I rubbed the frayed edge of the reins with my thumb, collecting thoughts, shaping questions.

'How does my father know you?'

He thought for a moment. 'He cannot. But he knows of the debt. Do you remember when you introduced us? He didn't react to my face, only my name.'

He'd seen it too, that reaction.

A lizard darted past, flicking dust in its wake; we both watched.

'What about Don Fausto?' I asked.

'Don Fausto?' His eyebrows shot up – and I'd have sworn *that* was genuine. 'The cleric we met in the square?'

'Last night he and my father were talking about you in his study.'

Antonio straightened. 'What were they saying?'

'I don't listen through doors.' *Except I had.* 'After, my father was angry; he forbade me to see you, and…' I tailed off, embarrassed.

'And what?'

'He locked me in my room.' I forced a small laugh.

'That's not funny.'

'He's a protective father.'

'Who is he protecting?'

I pressed my lips together. This conversation made me a disloyal daughter, and Antonio must have understood, because he relented. He exhaled slowly and fell silent. I was close to interrupting his thoughts when he finally spoke.

'I won't pursue this debt if it causes trouble for you.'

That I didn't expect. 'You'd give it up?'

'I would.' He looked behind. The lawyer had shifted position – shoved his precious satchel under his head as a makeshift pillow – but apparently slept on. Antonio grinned as though we were talking about a prank. 'Enzo will kill me.'

Tempting, but how could it be right? Besides, this might be another of his tricks. 'I'd sooner let the law deal with the debt,' I said.

He looked at me for a long moment. 'Then how can I win back your trust?'

I tugged the reins and gave him a hard look. 'You'll just have to try.'

Sombre stepped on a rock, stumbled and corrected – I lurched with the calesa and Antonio caught my arm.

This time he didn't ask; he took the reins. 'You're exhausted.'

Because he was right, I didn't argue.

The wheels picked up the horse's pace; the way they juddered I doubted they had an hour left in them. Enzo shifted and moaned. The white mare panted behind. Thankfully, the spire of Sant Cugat appeared over the next rise. My eyes grew heavy, my limbs soft, but I held myself stiff, so that I didn't fall against him. That effort became a whole new torment.

'So… affection, is it?' Antonio said.

A smile played about his mouth.

'What?'

'I wormed my way into your affection. That's what you said.'

I looked away. 'Presume nothing. Antonio.' I lingered on his name, separating each syllable.

He blew out a long breath.

'You're merciless,' he said.

Shadows were long on the ground by the time we reached Sant Cugat. We passed vineyards tended by monks in long black tunics, sleeves tucked up with string. The weathered walls of the monastery grew larger, folded square around a spire. Finally, we rattled to a halt in front of a door cracked with age and banded with iron, its studs rusted red. The friars swept Enzo to the infirmary and attended to Antonio. For now, their journey would have to wait.

I hadn't got my answers, only more questions. I would stay with Marguerite for a while, until I understood better the forces disrupting my life.

A Glimpse of Compassion?

3rd August 1756

I wake to the sound of her name, and I realise it fell from my mouth. I was there on the road to Bellvís. I close my eyes and wish with all my heart sleep would take me back there, for I remember well what came next. There can be no torment worse than waking in a stinking cell, starving and filthy, with thoughts of the purest, most perfect moments, lost forever.

No, there is worse. I had a few moments of forgetting. Precious seconds. But now reality crashes upon me anew. Catalina is dead. Murdered by a machine, and my ineptitude.

When I turn my head, pain crashes through my skull. I have been told to wish for death is a sin. Well, so be it. What will God do? Punish me?

Something moves in the corner. No, someone. I'm not alone. A young monk sits watching. How long has he been there?

'That's some talent, to sit as still as the grave,' I try to say, but what escapes is a croak. My tongue is swollen, my throat raw. I change my approach. 'Water.' That I can manage. I laugh. Where is my mind?

He brings me a mug. I struggle upright to drink, and the room tilts. The water tastes clean – of pewter, herbs, and something else. Orange peel. Oranges. Luisa. Is this mockery?

He tips the mug to my mouth but I snatch it and gulp. Half of the contents run onto my shirt and I suck the fabric dry. After all, waste would be another sin. Another chuckle bubbles up; I bite it back. The monk watches with sad eyes. I decide to gather my senses – apparently, I'm still able to make that decision.

'Ancora acqua, per favore.' I seem to have forgotten my Spanish.

No matter, he understands; he pours from a clay jug. This time I sip, controlled. Then I close my eyes, enjoying the coolness unravelling in my body. 'Mas. Por favor.'

He shakes his head. 'You mustn't drink too fast.'

'So, you *do* speak!'

He smiles. At least his mouth does; his eyes are more wary.

'What do you think of all this?'

The silence stretches so long I assume he won't answer, so when he finally speaks, it startles me.

'I think it is sad to see a man suffer so.'

I cannot believe the *Inquisition* allows such an indiscreet answer. I make a performance of raising my eyebrows. He looks away, embarrassed, hesitates, then returns to his seat by the wall.

'There will be food soon. You need to build your strength.'

I open my mouth for a sarcastic reply, but change my mind. He's only a boy; none of this is his doing. 'What is your name?'

His eyes dart to the door then back. 'Juan.'

'Juan,' I repeat, appreciating this new human connection. 'I'm Antonio.'

'Sí, I know.'

'Of course you do.' I smile to take the bitterness out of the comment. 'Gracias Juan. It cannot be easy for you to watch over me.'

He shifts in his seat. I think he prefers me raving.

'I'm told my trial will be soon. This will be over then, for both of us.'

His nervous expression drops. 'I hope it ends well for you, Antonio.'

His reply catches me – surely not permitted. 'You do?'

His nod is firm.

'Why?'

His lips tighten. I pressed him too hard. Perhaps I've been imagining his sympathy. Perhaps he's being polite after all. Our silence is interrupted by the rattle-click of a key.

'Your food is here,' says Juan, rising to his feet.

At least that's improving. I think I spy three specks of grey meat floating in the liquid and, praise be, is that a fragment of carrot?

A watery repast will only relieve hunger for a little while. I close my eyes, seeking memories to transport me, before the beast returns.

What Might Be Between Us

June 1754

Antonio

There was no satisfying the boy. 'Again, Señor!'

'Again? There'll be no oranges left. Then what will your mother say?' I'd finished my supper of rice and vegetables and was entertaining the son of the proprietor at my table outside. He was a boy of perhaps six or seven, with a freckled face and black hair stuck up at the front, as though a cow had licked his forehead.

'Why do you have grapes growing from your ears?'

He felt them. 'I do NOT!'

'Then what's this?' I plucked a grape from behind his ear.'

'¡Señor!' His laugh exploded from him. His new front teeth hadn't finished descending – the left had progressed further than the right and crowded its space.

I leaned in, as if we were two men sharing a secret. 'Do you think if I throw this grape into the air, we could make it come down an orange?'

'No. Es imposible,' he whispered back.

'I think it can be done.'

I sensed her before she spoke, even before the boy's gaze shifted behind me. I didn't look up when she rested her hand on my shoulder; I didn't need to.

'Watch.'

A small tureen, left behind from supper. I removed its lid; at the same time, I showed him the grape. 'I'll throw it, and catch it in this pot, then we shall see.'

I pretended to launch the grape. The boy tracked its imaginary flight, and I flicked at the pot to create the sound of an orange landing. When I showed him the pot, of course it contained an orange – I'd placed it there earlier.

He clapped his hand over his mouth, eyes dancing above his fingers.

Luisa took a seat beside me, warming the space between us through the layers of her clothes.

'Juan-Luis, bed now. It's late,' called a voice from beyond a doorway.

'Mama! I am entertaining your guests!'

His mother emerged, strands of hair escaping from her mobcap, hands red from her work in the kitchen. 'I hope he hasn't inconvenienced you. Oh.' Her gaze flicked to Luisa. 'Can I get you anything?' She looked exhausted at the prospect of another guest.

'Thank you, no. I came to discuss some family business with my brother here.'

I never imagined she could lie so easily.

'Antonio, will you escort me to my driver?'

We stepped from the warmth of the courtyard into the hush of an orange grove, far enough for privacy, but not so far we'd lose our footing in the dark. And not quite hush. When one cares to hear it, night in the country is as loud as any tavern – what with chirping crickets, toads calling, and creatures rustling through brush and branches. To all that noise we added our own: gravel crunching, twigs snapping, the swish of Luisa's skirts, our conversation rising and falling.

'What are you doing here?' I said. 'Will your friend not miss you?'

She pulled her shawl around her shoulders and crossed her hands at her waist. 'I retired early, then slipped out through the back of the house.'

'You're serious?'

'I know. A second escape. It seems I've a talent for creeping about.'

'Will you be trading hotel management for burglary?'

'I'm not a clever enough burglar,' she said, stooping to pick up a fallen orange – ripe, recently fallen by the look of it. 'There'd be little profit in an orange heist.'

We walked on, our path emerging from darkness one step at a time. The matter walked with us. The one we hadn't resolved yesterday and that now we skirted around with small talk. To which I added.

'Was your friend surprised to see you yesterday?'

'Very.' She dug her thumb into the skin of the orange. It dented but didn't break. 'Pleased though. It's been too long.'

'Shall I try?' I held out my hand.

She looked at my hand, then back down at her efforts. 'No. I'll manage.' Then she jabbed hard, splitting the peel, her thumb vanishing up to the first knuckle.

'Won't your parents want you home?'

'Pfft. They can want.' She sucked her thumb and set to work peeling, then looked around for somewhere to place the rind – as though we were in a parlour.

I held out my hand again. 'Here.'

She dropped a curl of the skin onto my palm.

'What did you do today, apart from shopping?'

She made a point of looking me up and down – I'd found a farmer willing to sell me a second hand camisa and waistcoat for only twice the price of new. Blood-stained travellers, it seems, are a profitable market.

'I visited our patient.'

'How is Enzo?'

'Sore and grumpy. They've got him flat out on a cot and told him not to move. He hates that.'

'Is there anything I can do?' She piled peel upon peel – a small pyramid now.

'You've done enough. We're both indebted to you.' I wanted to touch her face, so I focused on the orange. 'Show it some mercy, Luisa. It's starting to look like those two vultures have had a go at it.'

The last section of peel landed on my hand. I threw the lot onto the ground.

She traced its arc – pale fragments swallowed by shadows. 'Why did you offer to –?'

'So you'd get on with peeling your orange.'

She laughed, then separated a segment. Handed it to me. The best thing I ever ate. She took a segment for herself, then threw the rest after the peel and looked at her hands.

When she blew out a long breath, I assumed she was wondering how she'd clean them, so I patted my pockets for a handkerchief.

'Antonio.'

The way she said my name…

'I've been thinking about our conversation on the road yesterday. I was angry.'

'Yes.' As if I needed reminding. I handed her the square of linen.

'You said you would win my trust. But it's impossible. There's no way for you to do it.' Left then right, she rubbed at her hands.

My chest tightened.

'I mean, what could you do?' She laughed gently and folded the cloth; sharp citrus caught the air. 'Not fail me? How does one find evidence of not being failed?'

A good point. 'We could always ask Enzo.'

She punched my arm. 'Don't tease. Besides, he's not impartial.'

'Now who's teasing?'

'Is this how it's to be between us?' she said. 'Never serious?'

Between us. I was sunk. I wondered if she knew it.

'Anyway. What I was thinking… about trust, and the nature of it, and what's real and what isn't and whether trust is given or received… I'm waffling.' She laughed, but it was joyless. 'I need to come to the point.'

No. The last place I wanted her to come to was *the point.* Because from what she'd said so far – notwithstanding the waffling – it didn't sound like a destination I'd be sharing. 'Luisa –'

'Here's the thing,' she said, and took a deep breath.

'Luisa –' *Don't say it.*

She tucked the handkerchief back into my waistcoat pocket, and gave the pocket a pat. 'I think I have to decide to trust you.'

I'd braced for a blow that hadn't come. But still, I had no idea what she meant. 'Luisa –'

'No, let me finish before I lose my nerve.' She tugged the edges of her shawl together. 'You said I wouldn't credit your reason for watching me, that first day. But I watched you too. And I criticised you for not telling me, but I knew you'd something to say when we were on the terrace, and I stopped you.'

'Luisa –'

'Let me *finish.*' Her eyes flashed in the darkness. 'I will trust you because it's too difficult not to. But don't give me reason to regret it. Promise me honesty. And that means telling me *now* if I'm wrong. If what might be between us is false, then find the honour to walk away. Otherwise, you'll hurt me, and I don't believe you'd do that. You're not a cruel man.' She spoke the words faster and faster, one on top of another. Then stopped. And waited.

Now she finally gave me space to speak, words deserted me. Her plea had been too eloquent; she deserved a considered reply. No, she deserved poetry.

'Antonio. Say something.'

What might be between us.

She stood before me, eyes wide, waiting. She'd had the courage to speak her mind, the strength to ask her question. And I had no reply.

'Luisa –' I took a breath, and did my best, as messy as it was. 'If *not hurting* you is all, then you demand too little. I want you to be the happiest woman that ever lived. And your trust… a gift beyond measure. I'll protect it with my life. And as for what might be between us…'

What could I say? I stepped closer, and the moonlight revealed her face – not all at once but a piece at a time: the curve of her cheek, the softness of her brow, the dent at the centre of her top lip, a small scar along her jaw. Things I should have noticed before and hadn't. A strand of hair had fallen over her eye, and I moved it aside with two fingers. My hand didn't want to retreat. My thumb found her lower lip. Soft, it was, delicate. Her breath caught; I heard it.

'Say my name again, Luisa.'

She could have laughed – I would have, or made some joke to deflect awkwardness. But she didn't.

'Antonio.'

I leaned in. Not fast. I hadn't planned it, and I wouldn't snatch at it. I didn't know what I was doing, but at the same time I had no choice. I brushed my mouth against hers. Barely a touch, it could have been spun from air, but I felt it everywhere.

We both drew back. A shared breath.

Then she kissed me, and I kissed her back, and there was nothing delicate about it. Nor careful. Oranges, and messed up hair. Harsh breath. Searching mouths. Hungry bodies. Honesty, certainty, and trust.

What might be between us?

It was never in question.

Luisa

It was a strange thing to wish for Enzo's slow recovery. But as long as he lingered in convalescence, Antonio and I lived in a stolen world. By day, I was Marguerite's houseguest; by night, I slipped away to the orange grove.

It happened one of those nights, with the moon weaving faded patterns on the ground beneath the branches. Antonio leaned back against a tree. I lay on a makeshift blanket – his jacket, my shawl – with my head on his lap.

'I'm not sure oranges will ever taste the same again,' I said.

He peeled away pith with his fingernails, separating delicate lace, then bit half a segment and popped the other half into my mouth. I grabbed his hand and licked his fingers to catch the juice.

'*Caspita.* I cannot promise to behave if you do that again.'

Ha. An invitation. So I did it again. He chuckled and slipped down beside me. His mouth tasted of oranges.

'Luisa,' he whispered, his voice softer than his touch.

'Yes?'

He lifted his head, puzzled. 'Did I say that out loud?' A lock of his hair fell forward where it had escaped from its queue.

By way of answer, I touched his mouth. And by way of reply he nipped at my thumb.

'Ouch. Why did you do that?' It didn't hurt.

'No idea,' he said, and kissed the spot, then my palm, then moved his mouth to my chin, down to the hollow between my collarbones. Where he stopped, as though listening, or tasting.

Enough, I dipped my mouth to his and wound my hand in his hair, and something in me tipped from pleasure to want – a sort of rushing heat. New. There was nothing playful about the way we moved now, we matched touch for touch, and demand for demand. He rolled his body onto mine; stretched, shifted and settled; it felt inevitable.

He checked us, drawing back to watch me, a sudden studious interest in my face; his own all angles and shadows. His hand moved against my ribs, thumb whispering against silk then resting. 'I can feel your heart,' he said. He grinned and tapped out its beat with his fingers. 'Have you been running?'

'No. I'm being seduced under a tree.'

He dropped his head against my neck, his breath hot on my skin. Several seconds passed. Then he shifted back onto the ground. And if he meant it as some new kind of game, it didn't amuse me one bit.

'Antonio?'

He lay on his side, his head propped on one hand, looking utterly relaxed, but for the quick rise and fall of his chest. 'We might go too far.'

I looked up at the stars in the gap between the branches and chose my words carefully. 'Non è possible.' Italian, to be sure he understood.

He didn't move, just studied my face.

I sat and unhooked my chaqueta, then set to work unlacing my stays with slow, methodical movements, relishing my freed breath, the air ruffling my chemise, and its cool touch on my skin.

His eyes never left mine. The moment hovered, delicate as a soap bubble. I thought he might say something. When he didn't, I lost my nerve. My fingers stopped; the laces trailing between them.

Then he gave a quiet laugh – not amused, incredulous – and reached for me.

That's how it happened. Not in grandeur, with fine wine and a serenading musical ensemble. Just two people in an orange grove, under a watching sky.

It didn't feel like a mistake.

Shadows From the Past

3 Aug 1756

It still doesn't feel like a mistake. That's the thing of it. My memories aren't painted in favour; they aren't naïve dreams – at least I don't believe so. They're clear and vivid, close enough to touch. Perhaps that's the unforgivable nature of deceit.

I'll not think of him. Of *either* of them, Antonio or Rafael.

For the first time in days, I wake with a clear mind and only mild aches. I cross to the window and open the shutters to meet morning. The sun spills red and orange across the sky, gilding the rooftops and setting the sea aflame.

Marta must have been nearby; listening for movement. 'Good morning, Señorita. How are you today?'

'I'm fine, Marta, just fine. How are you?'

'I am happy when you are.'

On impulse, I kiss her, and Marta stiffens, eyeing me, confused.

'The blue, with my best ribbons, I would look well for the guests today.'

It's relief I see in her smile. Once dressed, I stop at the looking-glass. Composed, polished. If I act it, I'll feel it. I draw a deep breath and step into the day.

I've barely set foot in my office when Mama sweeps in upon me. 'Luisa! We were not expecting you yet, how was the Collserola? The wedding is almost upon us. You should see my dress, it is divine, it will be featured in *Le Mercure Galant*, only a few days until our final fittings.' She snatches a breath. 'Have you given any thought to your wig? Mine has silver stars and a little bell – it will be a first! It is good you are back; we have been so busy. Señora Cadiz told all her friends about us and now we have bookings into next season – every room! And the accounts are behind, I am quite rushed off my feet, you will need to hire a new manager, for after you are wed. Marta… is all well? Did Luisa and Rafael behave respectably? The chaperone never rests, they say…'

'Sí, Señora. Don Delmau is a perfect gentleman. The house is immense, practically a palace!'

I let Mama witter on and Marta deflect her questions, while I leaf through paperwork, waiting for her to run out of breath. Finally, she leaves me in peace. She was not exaggerating; the accounts are a mess. I lay receipts across my desk – Mama has thrown them into a box – and set about entering details into the ledger. So engrossed am I that I don't hear the knock or notice the door opening, and I jump as Gabriel appears before me.

'Señorita, there is a man who seeks an audience.'

'As you can see –' I wave a hand over the papers. '– I'm busy. Tell him to return tomorrow. Better still, next week.'

'If you please, he came every day while you were away. He says there is no more time.'

I set the quill down, eyes lingering on the ledger. 'Who is he?'

'His name is Signor Enzo Gallo, from Genoa.'

Enzo.

June 1754

Journey's end. We rounded the last bend, and all that remained of our four-day journey was this straight track, stretching towards Casa de Spinelli – my mother's family home growing larger with each bump and rattle.

Antonio drove the two-horse berline we hired in Sant Cugat. I sat beside him, and Enzo – still not completely recovered from his injuries – had passed the journey inside the carriage.

'You haven't spoken for an hour, Antonio.'

He turned to me. 'Do you feel it?'

Although I'd told myself otherwise, I'd been feeling *it* all morning. *Foreboding.* I slid my fingers over his on the reins, seeking warmth.

'Luisa, I'll give up this debt if you ask me to.'

Why should he? The estate before us, and every property my family owned in Spain, had started with a loan that was never repaid.

'I'll speak for you. There should be a settlement.'

'If there's trouble for you, I'll walk away.'

'Try it,' I laughed. 'I'll follow.'

He called the horses to a halt. Behind us, Enzo leaned forward, puzzled. Antonio paid his friend no mind. He took my hands.

'Luisa.' He looked down at our entwined fingers, sighed. 'I wish –' Then his eyes twinkled, my amusing *galante* pushing away melancholy, as usual. 'I wish I could spend my life in an orange grove with you. I don't have to do this. I'm serious. I'll find work, make a living in a way that doesn't offend your family.'

'Why should it offend my family to pay a debt?'

'Why should I pursue a century-old debt? What right have I?'

'Is something wrong?' Enzo called.

'Momento,' Antonio replied, his eyes never leaving mine.

I smoothed the furrow between his eyebrows with my thumb. 'Worry does not suit you. What's the worst that can happen?'

He caught my hand and kissed the inside of my wrist. I leaned forward, brushing my mouth against his, nibbling at his lower lip until I felt his mouth smile against mine.

'*Caspita*, Luisa!' He pulled back, eyes dancing.

'If you two don't mind,' Enzo called.

I kept my eyes on Antonio, but gestured with my chin at the road ahead. 'Let's put this behind us.'

He gripped the reins, then hesitated, turning to me once more. 'Whatever happens, Luisa. Te amo.'

They must have seen or heard our approach, because when we pulled up at the end of the long track, we had quite the welcoming committee: Uncle Alejo, his wife Isabella, my cousins Ambrogio, Elena and Clara; all of whom I was thrilled to see. But my heart sank into my stomach when I saw who stood alongside them. My parents.

My father's face glowed so red, it resembled a tomato bulging above his white silk scarf. I smelled trouble as surely as I smelled Mama's rosewater. A storm brewed, the huge presence looming behind the assembled group left me in no doubt of that. He glowered at us, intimidating in his purple-trimmed mozetta with the vulgar crucifix resting against the barrel of his chest. Why had Don Fausto come?

I gripped Antonio's arm; he placed his hand over mine.

Father couldn't wait. He reached us before we had even climbed down from the carriage – eyes blazing, brow furrowed with deep, angry creases. I might have recognised his violent intent if I'd been able to credit it. Antonio, with his back to Father as he helped me alight, didn't see him coming. There's nothing chivalrous about striking a man on his unguarded side, and the way Father set upon my lover was more beast than caballero.

An actual fight between the two wouldn't end well for my father. But this was no fight. Antonio kept his hands by his side.

My father struck him once, hard against the side of his head. A second blow snapped his jaw upward. A third, to his left side, sent him staggering back against the carriage.

'Papa!' I threw myself between them, and his flying hand caught the side of my head. Stars danced. I stumbled. I didn't cry out; it didn't hurt, just left me with a numb sort of surprise that wasn't even really surprise. More like disappointment. And embarrassment – that my father should expose us this way.

Antonio scooped me to his side, which seemed to enrage Father more, but what else would he do? My lover had my father by his collar – lips flat, jaw tight – holding him at arm's length. As for Father. Ludicrous. Apparently unable to decide whether to wrench free or attack, he wriggled and swore, all the while throwing fists into the space between them.

Thank goodness for Cousin Ambrogio. He heaved Father away, to his wife. And Mother? She screamed and flailed her abanico against her husband in a sort of helpless reprimand. Not to be outdone, Aunt Isabella used hers to fan herself, gasping, 'Oh my heavens, oh my heavens.' When that failed to gain her any attention, she collapsed to the ground, her daughters crowding around her, cooing.

All this over a debt.

'Luisa?' Antonio touched the side of my head, where my father's flying fist had landed. A trickle of blood ran from one side of his nose.

I placed my hand over his. 'This is ridiculous.'

'I couldn't agree more, cousin.' Ambrogio handed Antonio a handkerchief, then placed an arm around my shoulders and kissed my temple. 'It's splendid to see you, but I didn't expect such an exciting arrival.'

He'd grown up considerably since I'd last seen him. Back then he'd been seventeen – and a young seventeen at that. In five years, he'd matured, filled out. He'd become a man of presence.

'Ambrogio, you look so well. May I introduce Antonio Albrono? Antonio, this is my cousin, Ambrogio Spinelli.'

The two men lowered their heads in a semi-bow; all very proper except for Antonio holding the cloth to his bleeding nose. I stifled a laugh at their formality. They must have caught it because they grinned too. We all turned to watch the rest. I hoped we could move the situation along, restore civility, but that hope was short-lived. Mother continued reprimanding Father, who glowered at Antonio, clenching and unclenching his fists by his side. Even as I watched, he took another step forward, until Uncle Alejo caught his arm and stepped across him.

'Don Albrono. I think your business is with me. Shall we go inside where we can talk?'

'Not without me,' said Father, puffing his chest out.

Antonio's patience apparently knew no limits; he didn't react. Not towards Father in any case. The good-humoured lines around his eyes re-appeared. He greeted Uncle Alejo with a polite bow of his head and followed him.

Ambrogio, however, had clearly lost patience with Father's belligerence. 'This is *not* how the Spinelli family conducts its affairs. Uncle Gonzalo, from what you have told us, Don Albrono's claim is with the Spinelli family. Unless you can be civil, you won't help the discussion.'

'I am Alejo's *guardian*.' My father made no secret of his anger at what he must have seen as impertinence from the next generation.

'With respect, Uncle, my father is long past his majority.' Ambrogio's quip was obviously intended to release tension, and it worked. Although I suspect by embarrassing instead of amusing.

'Come, let's go inside.' Ambrogio ushered us all up the steps.

Father appeared at my side. 'Luisa. It was an accident. Did I hurt you?' A somewhat belated recognition of his actions, and as for *did he hurt me…* where would I begin? He locked me in my room, met us with contempt, and behaved like a *matón*.

'Antonio is my guest,' I said, 'What must he think of us?'

'Your guest?' My mother said from behind me.

I stopped. 'Sí, Mama. My *guest*.' I picked up my skirt and entered the house, followed by my mother, her family, and last of all, Father and Don Fausto.

It was half an hour before Uncle Alejo emerged with Antonio. Half an hour in which we ate tortas and drank chocolate, breaking the thick silence with the clinking of cups and every now and again the scrape of a fork on a plate. Ambrogio made a token attempt at conversation, but it soon became apparent that every question touched on a sensitive matter that threatened to break the fragile peace.

'How was your journey, Luisa?'

'It was pleasant. Enzo and Antonio were excellent company and took good care of me.'

'Why don't you tell Ambrogio how you ran away with Antonio, Luisa?' said father.

'Why don't you tell everyone how you locked me up?' I fired back.

'I don't think accusations are helpful.' Ambrogio said.

'Luisa is not at fault,' said Don Fausto. His show of support astonished me, but it didn't last. 'It is clear this *Don* Albrono seduced her and spirited her away.'

I don't know how I kept my temper; I spoke through gritted teeth. 'I'm a grown woman, Don Fausto. I make my own choices.'

He took a sip of his chocolate, eyes glittering above his cup.

'Gonzalo, your hand looks painful.' Mama turned to Isabel. 'Perhaps a poultice for the swelling?'

Isabel peered at the hand. 'Sí, I'll see if we have some arnica, or perhaps rosemary.'

She stepped to the wall to ring a bell. Antonio had been bleeding from the nose after Father's blows, yet here they were fussing over his assailant. Ambrogio caught my eye, a downward twitch of his mouth offering sympathy.

A servant entered. Not, as I expected, to take Isabel's instruction, but to summon the men into a meeting. I stood with them.

'Luisa, this does not concern you,' said Father.

'I'd appreciate Luisa joining,' said Ambrogio.

Father gave him a hard stare, but conceded when Ambrogio returned it. I nodded *gracias* at my cousin.

We sat in mismatched chairs in Uncle Alejos's study: damask, leather, and velvet – old, new and re-upholstered. Don Fausto opted to stand, framed against the window, stiff-backed, a man above such indulgence as sitting.

Enzo kept tugging at his scarf. Ambrogio sat beside me, an ankle resting on his knee, drumming fingers against his thigh. Father perched on the edge of his seat, hands clasped, thumbs pressed together, their knuckles white. Opposite me, Antonio sat still but for his thumb – idly turning the ring on his small finger.

'I think we all understand the matter at hand.' Uncle Alejo began speaking from behind his desk. 'The Albrono claim.'

'I have papers pertaining to the debt,' said Enzo, reaching for his satchel.

'I don't doubt their validity,' said Uncle Alejo, waving his hand, dismissing the lawyer before he'd even begun.

Enzo blinked. He would have been expecting to argue his case, had no doubt been rehearsing the position for weeks, months even.

A movement from Father caught my eye: a shift of his chin. Don Fausto nodded. My stomach tightened.

'I think we can save ourselves some time.' Don Fausto fixed his stare on Antonio, eyes beady, cold. 'Don Albrono, I am not sure if you are familiar with the laws of Spain?'

Antonio said nothing, simply watched the cleric – my self-proclaimed *uncle* – waiting.

Don Fausto stretched his neck, drawing from his endless supply of self-importance. 'Spain is governed by the laws of the Crown and of the Holy Office of the Inquisition, the latter embodied in twenty-eight Articles of Faith.'

Now Antonio narrowed his eyes. I probably did the same. How could this be relevant?

'Under Article Ten, persons guilty of heresy and apostasy shall lose their property.' He looked at Enzo. 'Did you study these Articles when you took it upon yourself to come to Spain with your legal claim, Señor Gallo?'

Enzo said nothing. The air tightened.

Fausto slowed, pressing each syllable into the space between us. 'The definition of property, of course, includes inheritance. And debts.'

I shifted in my seat, suddenly restless. 'Why are you telling us this, Don Fausto?'

He inclined his head. 'Thank you for asking, Luisa.' He turned back to Antonio. 'Don Albrono, your grandfather, Alessandro Albrono, was a heretic. Convicted by the Inquisition in Seville in 1704. Not quite fifty years ago.' He let that hang for a few seconds, plainly enjoying himself. 'Whatever debt *might* have been owed, is void.'

Antonio inclined his head, outwardly relaxed. I ground my teeth at Don Fausto's sneer and Father's equally smug countenance.

'Thank you for explaining,' Antonio said.

'De nada, Don Albrono. I hope we can let this matter rest now.'

'I'd no idea,' said Antonio.

'A shameful history. If the Albronos were a Spanish family, they would no longer enjoy the privileges of nobility.'

Such an insult to Antonio's name. But his expression gave nothing away.

'Do you have proof?' Enzo asked – ever the lawyer.

'Sí,' said Don Fausto, and went to his bag, from which he produced a roll of cloth tied with string. Inside was a roll of paper; he unrolled it. 'As soon as I learned of your arrival, Don Albrono, I took steps to retrieve this document: the decree of excommunication.'

I'd never seen such a document before. The paper smelled of dust and something sour, and although the ink had faded and edges begun to crumble, the writing and signatures remained clear. He placed it on the table, and Enzo stepped over to study it. Uncle Alejo handed him a magnifying glass.

Was this what Father and Don Fausto had been talking about in his study? He must have moved fast to recover a document such as this from archives in Seville, or did he keep his own copy? And why would he?

So many questions, and not just from me. Enzo frowned over it, a finger tracing each line, eyes following.

'This document is dated seventeen hundred and four.'

'Sí.' Don Fausto kept his eyes on Antonio, a smile playing on his mouth.

'Alessandro Albrono died in the year seventeen hundred,' said Enzo. He really was a marvel.

But his point didn't faze Don Fausto. 'Under the provisions of Article Twenty, the deceased may be proceeded upon.'

'My grandfather was condemned after he died?' said Antonio. 'How did he displease the Inquisition so?'

And how convenient it wiped out a debt.

'That would have been a matter for the Seville Tribunal.'

Enzo continued frowning at the document, then looked at Uncle Alejo.

'If I may ask, Don Spinelli, have there been any other claims on this debt? Girolamo Albrono, perhaps?'

Uncle Alejo shook his head, but my father interjected. 'Girolamo Albrono learned the same truth we're sharing with you.'

'That's news to me,' my uncle said.

'I dealt with it, Alejo,' replied Father, 'Girolamo Albrono saw the futility of the claim.'

Something in the glance he exchanged with Don Fausto turned my stomach. I tried to catch Antonio's eye, but he too was watching my father, his expression taut.

'I think this concludes our business.' Father said, 'I understand this is disappointing for you, Don Albrono. A matter of law, nothing personal.'

I couldn't, and will never, understand what passed between Antonio and my father in that long, unblinking look.

It fell to Ambrogio to break the impasse. 'It does seem harsh that the sins of an ancestor have such repercussions,' he said.

'The past casts long shadows. Now and then we feel their chill,' replied Fausto in a slow, deep voice. Never one to let a profound sentiment go begging.

'Don Albrono, I hope you will join us for dinner tonight? There is no reason we cannot be amicable,' offered Uncle Alejo.

'Thank you, Don Spinelli. It would be a pleasure.'

He didn't make it to dinner. Nor, for that matter, did I.

Once I'd changed – thanks to Elena's wardrobe – I sent word to his room, letting him know I'd be at the stable.

I found him in his shirtsleeves, cuffs rolled back, tending to the horses – running his hands over their hides, checking for sores. I lingered in the doorway, so absorbed in watching him I almost felt disappointed when he noticed me. But then his face lit up, and I couldn't help but smile back.

'You look well for a disappointed man.'

'How can I be disappointed, with you before me?'

I went to him.

'Luisa, I'm no great prospect as it stands,' he said. 'I'll understand if I'm not enough.'

I feigned a thoughtful expression. 'Will we have enough for an orange grove?'

He laughed. 'I'll *plant* an orange grove for you.'

I pressed my face against his chest and inhaled – linen, salt and sunlight – so familiar as to be part of me. 'What next, Antonio?'

'Enzo is thinking to go to Seville. He's curious about this posthumous trial Don Fausto spoke of.'

'Seville is a long way.'

'Sí, a month of riding.'

A month, each way. My heart sank. But Antonio was in Spain for a reason, and it wasn't for me to stand in his way. I'd just have to wait. I touched his face. 'I'm sorry about my father; did he hurt you?'

He laughed. 'He hits like a girl.'

'I hit *well*.'

'I don't doubt it. But then, you're not a girl.'

'What am I?'

He didn't answer.

'Let's get away from here,' I said.

'Where shall we go?'

'Seville?'

'I want to be worthy of you.'

'I want to be worthy of *you*. Antonio.'

His smile widened. 'Say my name again, Luisa.'

'Antonio.' I laughed.

He kissed me like he meant it.

I thought he did.

Vengeance is His

June 1754

Perhaps more time planning and less time kissing would have served us better. Had I known we were entering our final moments together, I'd have made the plan firm, inscribed it on parchment, and had Enzo notarise it. As it was, we only got as far as agreeing Luisa would return home with her family and I'd go with Enzo to Seville to discover more about the heresy charge. What did I hope to achieve? I'd some idea I needed to earn my place in the world before I could deserve a woman such as Luisa. For all our talk of living in an orange grove, she deserved better. She still does.

Of course, her father found us in the stable. To spare her another scene, I had to leave. We'd write, we said, and determine our future once cooler heads prevailed.

We were ready within the hour; Enzo and I. Packs loaded onto two mares kindly supplied by Ambrogio. No sign of Luisa. There would be no goodbye – her father had seen to it.

But Enzo interrupted our departure, patting his coat. 'My satchel. It's in the study.'

I offered to fetch it; didn't need him to ask. She was somewhere inside the house.

But I didn't see her. The corridors were empty, just me and my footsteps, echoing the point: I'd outstayed my welcome. A line of Marquéses and their noble relations peered down from their portraits. Unmistakably family: same bone structures, same pointed chins, same full mouths, and echoes of Luisa's eyes – weak imitations.

A particular painting piqued my curiosity, of a man that could be Alejo, but for his archbishop's robes. White lace cuffs and collar, clean as fresh snow, peeking from violet damask brocade, shimmering with gold thread. And that crucifix – heavy, glittering with rubies, vulgar. *Luca Spinelli,* the name engraved on the frame. Hadn't Enzo mentioned him?

I knew where to go. The study. But the door was closed, and on the other side, voices: Fausto and Gonzalo. Now what?

There's only one thing worse than making a hasty retreat from a confrontation, and that's returning to collect something you forgot. And what did etiquette dictate about entering a room where the man inside had punched me in the face once and had to be restrained from doing it a second time? A polite knock would be absurd, but walking in would be confrontational. Again, for Luisa's sake, I chose appeasement. I raised my hand to knock:

'It's done, at least.'

'I'd have preferred not to use the decree again.'

'He should have been killed on the road.'

Not very Christian. Luisa must have told them about the attack.

'I'm as disappointed as you, Gonzalo. They've never let me down before.'

'Three against two left too much to chance, even if one was a lawyer.'

I threw the door open.

The two men jumped to their feet – Gonzalo's brandy sloshed onto the floor. They'd been sitting there, casually discussing my murder, the way two men might talk about silk prices. I'd swallowed every insult that day, clenched my jaw and fists for Luisa's sake. But now, my restraint snapped like an overstretched tether. The only question was whom to strike first.

When I stepped towards Gonzalo, he cringed into his scarf. I picked him up by the front of his waistcoat and slammed him against the wall, gratified to feel him shaking under my fingers. I lifted him onto his toes and was wondering what to do with him when Fausto spoke behind me.

'Think of Luisa.'

Damn the man.

I opened my hands, dropped him. At first, his knees gave way but he pulled himself up. I wasn't done. I made a show of straightening his vest and leaned my face into his. 'How would Luisa feel if she knew you tried to kill me?' I bared my teeth. He whimpered – actually *whimpered* – then bolted for the door. Leaving me alone with Fausto. Some friend.

I faced the Inquisidor; he stood tall, raised his chin.

'I suggest you leave, *Don* Albrono, as we agreed. There is nothing for you here. You're lucky to leave with your life.'

I lowered my eyes to his crucifix, then back to his lifeless eyes. 'What's your interest here, Don Fausto? Why does an Inquisidor creep around the Spinellis like a beggar after scraps?'

He clamped his lips together.

'You'd murder for them. Interesting.'

'I suggest you leave.'

'Is it money?'

I stepped closer. I knew the danger, antagonising an Inquisidor, but anger does things to a man's mind, and I had good reason to be angry.

'Is it Luisa? I've seen the way you look at her. Not very holy.'

'You'd better stop talking,' he said through clenched teeth.

'Or what? Will you have me killed? You already tried that.'

He grew, expanded his chest, fluffed out his feathers, extended his talons. I should have stopped. I went too far, but anger is a reckless master. I leaned my face into his.

'What are you hiding, you old buzzard?'

When he raised his hand to strike, I shoved him. For such a large man he went down easily. As he flew backwards in a mess of limbs, I caught a glimpse of his skinny white shins. I spared him a little dignity. I didn't stay to watch.

4 August 1756

My memories hold nothing more; I may as well open my eyes and face whatever waits.

It must be afternoon because the sun has moved out of the line of the window; the beam of light that marked the morning has gone. Although perhaps I confuse this cell with the one before.

A presence, a scent, a shift by the door, shared air. My senses prickle. Fausto. How long has he been here?

'Don Albrono. Will you clear your conscience?'

The chair seems far too small for him, and I tilt my head to check the legs are holding up to the task.

'Confess and ask for mercy.'

Does he take me for a fool?

He presses. 'Is there anything you wish to say?'

'No.'

'Your situation is serious. You must understand that.'

I make a show of looking around. 'I have an idea.'

He shakes his head; his expression arranged into one of infinite sadness. 'This is nothing.'

'Doctor Balleza has explained. And I've seen for myself what the Holy Office does to its victims.'

'Victims? Respect would serve you better.'

'When is my trial?'

'Tomorrow.'

So, the wait is over. Terror snatches at my skin, teeth clamping everywhere at once. I take a breath.

'Ask for mercy, Don Albrono.'

'And then what?'

He says nothing. His robes are tented over his knees, and he sits with his feet planted flat, like he's about to rise.

'What do you want, Don Fausto?'

'To save your soul.' Glib. His eyelids flicker; my guess is he wants to believe it.

'Admirable. What about your own?'

'That's between me and my Lord.' He fiddles with his cuff, catches me noticing and curls his fingers into his lap.

'*Our* Lord,' I say.

'Of course. And my calling is to lead you back to Him.'

I'd swear he believes it. This man who sent assassins after me and put Enzo into the infirmary.

We watch each other, wary. He moves his mouth as though chewing gristle that won't break down.

'Do you want to find God again?' he asks.

'Are you a godly man?' I ask.

'I try,' he says. 'I offer my deeds up, every day.'

The taste in my mouth is a real thing – something like acid, mixed with rot; I spit into the straw by my cot – I have to – and wipe my mouth on the back of my hand.

He watches, jerking his chin slightly at my movement. 'Showing God your contempt…'

'Will you pray with me?' I say.

'You have had my friar for that. I am here so you might confess and ask for mercy.'

'And then will I receive mercy?'

'Your soul might.'

There it is. Fausto's bargain. No bargain at all. Just a man come to gloat. 'You taunt me. We both know how this ends.'

His cheeks pinken. He's a child.

'I take no pleasure; my concern is for your everlasting life.'

I give him silence.

'You will suffer.'

I already know this and, although I'm not prepared, I'll not let him see my fear.

'You might die.'

'We all die,' I say, holding his gaze.

He stands. Takes a single step towards me.

'Luisa Navas has forgotten you.'

My skin goes cold. I feel it first behind my ears, then down the back of my neck. My mind had known of course, and my gut. It's my heart we'd not managed to convince.

'She's to marry Rafael Delmau. They are the talk of the city.'

Jesu… My mouth opens, but no sound comes – only a wheezing cough, like he'd struck me in the chest.

My fingers claw the blanket. His eyes follow the movement, and he starts a smile, then catches it and corrects.

'He will give her what you never could.'

'If she's happy, then so am I.' The words fall out like they never belonged in the first place – like a mouthful of grit. I know he can see the pain in me, and I no longer care.

He walks over to my cot, and bends forward at the waist, bringing his face close to mine. So close we could kiss. 'You might be strapped to el potro at the moment they exchange vows.'

His words slip in like poison; the venom knows where to go.

He leaves me like that. Broken before my trial has even begun.

Part Three - Exurge Domine et Judica Causam Tuam

Arise Oh Lord, and Judge Thy Cause

Articles of Faith for Conduct of Activities of the Inquisition of Spain. Issued by Tomás Torquemada to the General Assembly of Inquisidors, Seville, 1474.

Article XIV
If any guilty of heresy, shall deny and persist in his denial until sentence is passed, although he asserts that he is a Catholic Christian, the Inquisidors must declare him an impenitent heretic and sentence him accordingly, for juridically the crime is proved, and by refusing to confess his error the convict does not permit the Church to absolve him and use him mercifully.

Article XXV
Inquisidors and assessors and other officers of the Inquisition, must excuse themselves from receiving gifts from any who may have come to have affairs with the Inquisition, or from others on their behalf; under pain of excommunication, of being deprived of office and compelled to make restitution and repay to twice the value of what they may have received.

First Audience

Lorenzo had never seen a room like it. Its power lay in its simplicity. A ceiling that soared, its sweep broken only by concentric arches, hovering as if suspended by the hand of God Himself, and plain windows through which sunlight poured, casting beams that pooled on the oak table at the centre.

The table had been built for forty, yet was so dwarfed by the vast cavern it might have been a tavern bench – no, a raft unmoored in an ocean of stone. He studied the six men clustered with him around one end. Each with a solemn and essential role.

At the head, as presiding judge and highest-ranking member, perched Don Fausto. His status afforded him the grandest chair – carved with a crucifix that rose high from its back, creating the strange effect of appearing to sprout from the top of the Primer Inquisidor's head.

To Fausto's left sat the Second Inquisidor: Don Manuel de Soler y Montana. He had a high forehead, jutting orbital sockets, and silver hair so thick that every time he moved his head, his zucchetto took a moment to follow.

The Prosecutor, Don Joseu de Montejo y Anieva, to the right of Fausto – Lorenzo's left – would take the most outwardly active role in these audiences. A rotund man with a weak chin, pronounced philtrum, and fleshy lower lip, he would lead the examination. It required skill: probing, teasing out the unsaid, and drawing the defendant into unwitting admissions. Not unlike Lorenzo's role. Except where the confessor worked in private, between audiences, the prosecutor performed before the judges.

Opposite Lorenzo, and the only familiar face, was Friar Augustin, chair of the committee of Valencian theologians who had conducted the Calification. He, like Lorenzo, was acclimatising to this new Tribunal; settling his gaze on one man, then another, and every now and again on a window or carved detail around a door.

At least Augustin had no direct line of sight to Tomás Boxo. Lorenzo recognised his name from the arrest warrant and at first had been concerned Fausto had appointed him as second Calificador without so much as a theological title to his name. Yet now, upon seeing him, such concerns faded in the face of a far more striking impression: the man had the largest head Lorenzo had ever seen. Add to that his red face, and Lorenzo had to force his gaze onto the table for fear of being caught staring.

He wished Don Joseph de Vallera, the final member of the group, would stop fidgeting. A fussy man with fine black hair slicked back with pomade and brushed into a curl at the centre of his narrow forehead, he never sat still for a moment. He picked up his quill, shuffled his papers, moved them, replaced them, leaned back, leaned forward again… a constant distraction. How would Lorenzo endure it? Still, he respected him, the secretary, or rather the position he held. For without meticulous records, the Holy Office of the Inquisition of Spain would be nothing more than men passing judgment on other men.

Fausto had decreed no clerical witnesses were to attend, so, apart from the seven officials, the only other men present were two armed familiars: Rafel and Raymundo – men of rough countenance who might have been brothers. They flanked the door through which the defendant would enter and leave, feet planted apart, broad chests thrust out, chins tucked in.

Lorenzo tried to swallow and gulped air. He should have taken refreshment during the last break. Since then, he had spent an hour presenting evidence and then endured a further forty minutes on the Calification – a formality that might have taken ten had the Primer Inquisidor not seized the opportunity for a lecture, expounding upon their sacred duty to lean towards guilt. '*Better to convict an innocent man than risk acquitting a guilty one. For suffering on earth will be rewarded in heaven.*' As if they needed reminding of such a basic tenet.

'Is he fit to stand trial?' A routine question, Joseu directed it at Lorenzo, in his capacity as Physician.

'Sí.'

'Good.' Joseu turned to the familiars. 'Admit the defendant.'

Raymundo straightened, and Rafel barked a command into the space between them. It bounced along the corridor and faded. Minutes passed. A jug of water appeared. Mugs. Blessed relief. Lorenzo stole a glance at Fausto. The Primer Inquisidor watched the doorway, the tip of his tongue resting on his lower lip, like a man anticipating the plato principal at a society banquet.

Boots clumped, chains dragged, distant at first, drawing closer, then impossibly loud. The prison party rounded the door: five heads, Don Albrono among them – a glimpse, a shadow. A guard walked at the front; his tabard embroidered with the insignia of the Inquisition – red on grey – two guards flanked the wraith, and a final guard brought up the rear. They marched to a brutal rhythm. Between their boots, snatches of bare feet, finding the floor, losing it, trailing, recovering, filthy, smearing the stone.

They dragged him to the foot of the table, and Lorenzo saw. A man so wasted that when the guards released him, he pitched sideways, knees buckling, and for a moment, it seemed he would crumple to the ground. Yet he didn't fall.

Don Albrono pressed his hands to the table, bunched his shoulders, drew a shuddering breath through gritted teeth, and locked his elbows.

Lorenzo didn't need his medical training to know the Primer Inquisidor had cut the prisoner's rations again; his shirt was a slack sail suspended from the mast of his collarbones, skin stretched translucent over edges so sharp they transported Lorenzo back to his anatomy classes – bones and sinew. Yet the prisoner's eyes… focused, intelligent, watching.

Lorenzo considered himself immune to silent challenge, a master of the heavy pause, but when that gaze settled on him it took all his willpower to remain still. A shift of his thigh would unstick that patch of wool… the smallest shoulder-roll would loosen the seam bunched into his armpit… No. He set himself rigid. Procedure, not emotion.

And procedure wouldn't be served by a defendant that collapsed before he completed his own defence. He cleared his throat and called to the familiars. 'A chair.'

Fausto's gaze swung towards him so fast it sliced air.

Tell me, Doctor Balleza, does it strike you Don Fausto has an unseemly enthusiasm to see me damaged?

Lorenzo batted away the memory and answered Fausto's unspoken question. 'The defendant is weak.'

Fausto swept a half-lidded gaze over Don Albrono. Lorenzo followed, seeing through his eyes. *Defendant.* The lowest status affordable to man, lower even than the convicted, for at least they have confessed.

But this man, Don Albrono, he met Fausto as an equal – an impossible thing, given his degraded state, yet there it was.

And so, under the jurisdiction of six officials of the Tribunal of the Holy Office of the Inquisition in Barcelona, recorded by a notary of the same city, the trial of Don Antonio Albrono began.

'Please tell the court your name, birthplace, age, occupation, and the date of your imprisonment.' Joseu stood behind his seat, next to the table, peering down at his papers, his chin sinking into his jowls.

The defendant splayed his fingers in front of him on the polished wood, paused as if counting them, then raised his head and spoke in a low, clear voice. 'Antonio Albrono. Born in the city of Genoa, I'm thirty-one, a soldier in the infantry regiment of Asturias, company of Don Jorge Duran. I was arrested on the tenth day of last month.'

'Provide the names of your family.'

'My mother is Isabella Albrono, born Isabella Lanzi, now living in Vienna. My father was Giorgio Albrono. He died in battle in the year seventeen hundred and forty-four, alongside my uncle, Girolamo.' The defendant's condition had done nothing to affect the clarity of his thoughts. 'I have an aunt, Gulia, still living, another uncle, Giacomo, still living. And another, Luigi, the head of the family, still living. My grandfather was Alessandro Albrono. He died in the year seventeen hundred.'

'Have any of your relatives or ancestors ever been prosecuted, imprisoned, or put under penance by the Holy Office of the Inquisition?'

Silence. With excruciating slowness, Don Albrono turned his head toward Fausto, lifted his chin and waited. Lorenzo waited, too. For what he didn't know. Fausto narrowed his eyes.

Don Albrono directed a small nod at Lorenzo, at *him*, then replied in a voice so clear it echoed against the walls, bounced from the ceiling:

'No person in my family. Not my parents, not my uncles, not *my grandfather* –' he raised his brow, '– has ever been prosecuted, imprisoned, or put under penance by the Holy Office of the Inquisition.'

Fausto set his face. A stone carving, but for a tightening in his cheek.

'I am not the first of my family to be pronounced a heretic in Spain.' Why did Don Albrono now lay down contradictory words, in the manner of a man throwing a gauntlet at the Inquisidor's feet? What had changed? Joseph wrote fast, and Lorenzo afforded him a nod of approval – an anomaly on record.

'Can you read or write and have you studied science?' asked Joseu, glancing between Don Albrono and Fausto as if wondering whom to direct the questions at.

'I read and write in Italian, German and Spanish. I learned from Doctor Francisco Labatra in Vienna, and studied grammar at the Colegio de los Praxistas, also in Vienna.'

He did not once shift his stare from Fausto, and the Inquisidor met it, his face still but for a slight and intermittent widening at the tip of his nostrils – a predator seeking scent.

'Are you a baptised and confirmed Christian? Have you heard Mass, confessed, and communed, at such times as the Church directed?'

'Sí,' the defendant said, 'the last time I confessed was to Father Tomás, a barefoot friar of the Convent of the Holy Trinity. I partook of the sacrament there, in the city of Valencia.'

Finally, Don Albrono looked away from Fausto. Lorenzo could have sworn his own collar loosened; certainly his breath came a little easier.

Joseu launched into the standard tests of faith, a formality in all trials. Routine. Yet here, many a prisoner unwittingly doomed his own defence. For that reason, seven faces turned to Don Albrono and seven pairs of eyes squinted, hanging onto his every word. By contrast, directly in Lorenzo's line of vision, over by the door, Rafel's eyes drooped and his head sagged. Lorenzo supposed sleeping upright to be a necessary skill for men whose profession involved standing around listening to matters they did not understand.

At Joseu's behest, Don Albrono recited the *Pater Noster, Ave Maria,* and *Credo* flawlessly in a language not his own. He answered every question well. Too well. Joseph scratched his notes. Don Albrono was not going to be able to argue ignorance.

'What were the primary events of your life?' Joseu moved down his list, reading from the paper before him without so much as glancing at the defendant.

'I was born in Genoa. Moved to Vienna as a child when my father took up a commission there.' Don Albrono studied the wood grain. 'When my father died, I joined the infantry and rose to command a sección. When I was twenty-eight, the regiment disbanded, and I returned to Genoa to re-acquaint myself with my uncle Luigi. He passed to me the responsibility of securing a family debt in Spain.' Don Albrono flicked his gaze up – toward Fausto – before returning it to the table. 'I sailed to Barcelona, proceeded to Bellvís, from there to Seville, by way of Granada and Málaga.'

At some point, Don Albrono had begun to shiver – so faint at first, Lorenzo wouldn't have been able to say when he began. Tremors had spread from hands to arms then shoulders. He snapped his mouth shut when his voice started to betray him too. Then he exhaled slowly through his nose and resumed. 'I didn't resolve the debt, so I enlisted in the infantry regiment of Asturias. We deployed along the coast of Spain, latterly in Valencia, before proceeding to Reus, where I was arrested.'

He had answered impressively considering his condition. Lorenzo took a gulp of water.

A cough broke the silence. Don Manuel peered at the defendant from under his jutting brow. 'I have a question.' He waited, as if for permission, then when none came he pressed on. 'I struggle to understand why a noble Albrono would not be a commissioned officer.'

Being pedantic, Lorenzo considered that a statement, not a question. Still, a valid point. He should have thought of it himself; raised it during interrogation. Heat crept up his neck, and he looked at Fausto. But once again, the Inquisidor's eyes were locked on the defendant.

As for Don Albrono. He tipped his head back and regarded Manuel as if deciding whether to answer. As if the choice were his. 'The manner of my father's death didn't sit well with La Famiglia Albrono,' he said. 'They disowned him – us – for his part in the failed raid at Velletri.' He picked at his thumb, frowning. 'I suppose he was on the wrong side.'

'The Habsburg "*side*"?' Manuel jumped in.

Don Albrono raised his eyes, searched his questioner's face, hairline to chin, before answering very simply, 'The *losing* side.'

Over by the door, Rafel and Raymundo exchanged covert smiles. In three words, the defendant had just distilled the fickleness of modern war. Bourbon, Habsburg, what difference did it make? A single family, allies one moment, enemies the next.

'So, your father was an enemy of Spain,' pronounced Don Fausto, barely concealing his delight.

The defendant shifted his gaze towards him – slow, insolent – he closed his mouth and blinked, just once.

Silence stretched again. Manuel nodded at Joseu, satisfied. The prosecutor gathered himself with a small shake of his jowls and picked up where he left off. 'Do you know, or suspect, the cause of your imprisonment?'

Lorenzo didn't understand why he felt compelled to nod when the defendant looked at him, but nod he did, and Don Albrono commenced his defence.

'I have thought about it, and I suppose it was on account of an act I performed to discover a thief in my sección.'

Joseu waited. The officials straightened. The familiars tensed. The arches above seemed to expand like ribs against an indrawn breath.

'In Valencia, some items were stolen: shirts, stockings, some coins. I offered to discover the thief, using trickery. I assembled the soldiers in a dark room, and informed them they must each dip a finger into a cup of water, and that the water would blacken the finger of the thief. I showed them the clear water, then secretly tipped ink into the cup while they were distracted with the extinguishing of candles. The thief withheld his finger… the only man unmarked.' A casual recounting, an indifferent tone, mocking the gravity of the proceedings.

No. Don Albrono would not be here if the charges were trivial. Had Lorenzo himself not taken the depositions?

'Is that everything?' asked Joseu, glancing from defendant to Fausto and back.

'Sí.' A nod.

'Don Albrono,' Manuel interjected, his voice deep, resonant. 'A man would not be arrested without reliable information he had done something contrary to Holy Mother Church.'

'I feel compelled to disagree,' Don Albrono fired back.

Boxo's face turned puce, Manuel's brow lifted. Raymundo and Rafel exchanged a look. As for Fausto. He turned his gaze on the defendant and smirked, slow and deliberate. Not an accident. Not imagined. He'd caught the scent.

The defendant kept his eyes fixed on his questioner, Joseu. Every so often, his eyelids flickered; he battled an unseen discomfort.

Joseu reached for his water. He cleared his throat. 'Who conspired in this act?'

The defendant opened his mouth to answer and took a breath instead, releasing it slowly through his nose.

'Who conspired in this act?' The prosecutor repeated.

'It hardly bore conspiracy.'

'Who was involved?'

'Define "*involved*".'

'Who knowingly partook of this act?'

'Nobody.'

'What about the men of your sección?'

'They follow orders.'

'Whose orders?'

'Mine, as cabo.'

'With whom did you discuss your intentions?'

'All those present were there unwittingly.'

Thrust, parry. Thrust, parry.

'Who indulged in the telling of it?'

'I don't recall anyone did.'

'I must remind you, Don Albrono, we have written depositions.'

'Then why are you asking me?'

One of the familiars stifled a snort. Judging by the Primer Inquisidor's glower, that man would be looking for work tomorrow.

'In the name of God our Lord and his glorious and blessed Mother our Lady the Virgin Mary, I exhort you to bethink yourself and confess the whole truth in relation to this matter. If you do so, justice will be executed with brevity and mercy.'

'I have stated the truth.' The defendant clenched his jaw, presumably at some unseen pain.

Silence fell hard, and lingered until broken by the prosecutor. 'I have no more questions, Su Excelencia.'

'Very well.' Fausto turned to the secretary, Joseph. 'Read the defendant's declarations back to him.'

Don Albrono confirmed – with a silent nod – his declarations to be true and signed accordingly. Fausto ordered that he be remanded pending the second audience.

Lorenzo watched him shuffle away, dragging his chains. He rested his hand over the place where his stomach burned, telling himself his unease was indigestion; that there was nothing about this case that might disrupt his carefully curated sense of order.

Not My Advocate

Antonio had no measure of time in that first session. He endured it with concentration clouded by hunger and a piercing pain that began in his temples, sending needles into the back of his skull. How had the world become so small that six or seven well-fed men weighed a prank in a cellar against his life?

Afterwards, they took him from the Grand Hall, along a corridor normally reserved for Inquisition staff and servants. The guards kept their tight formation, their pace unforgiving. When he stumbled, they didn't slow; they dragged him, his feet trailing. Their relentless momentum – guards and sorry prisoner – might have been the Inquisition itself. Nothing must impede its progress. Not a trip or a stumble, not his feet grasping at stone, not even the jagged edges of a floor slabs when it tore away a toenail.

When two caretakers working on torch brackets stared, Antonio stretched his face away. They belonged to a different world.

Near the top of the stone staircase leading down to the cells, it came. A voice he knew, shattering the silence, ringing off the walls.

'Antonio!'

No. Not here. If only he could fold in on himself and vanish.

'Espere. Por favor. In the name of Don Fausto.' The bad Spanish. The tap of shoes. The shiny buckles. *Enzo.*

The guards planted their soles as a single precise unit. Antonio pushed the balls of his feet against the stone, willing them on. His left ankle gave way, twisting in the cuff, metal biting cold into his skin.

'I would speak with the prisoner,' said Enzo.

'Who are you? Why do you use the name of the Primer Inquisidor?' The first guard positioned himself between them. Good, all the better to hide behind.

Antonio stared at the floor. Blood smeared his foot, its source clear – a nail hung half-detached from its bed.

'I'm the defendant's advocate. He's entitled to confer with me.'

Enzo, no.

A guard shifted to one side. Antonio twisted toward the wall, but not fast enough. Not before he saw his friend, immaculate in his plain grey waistcoat, brass buttons, white stock. Enzo's clean-shaven face was lined with worry.

'Antonio?'

'¡Vámonos!' He yanked his shoulders, willing the guards forward. A rectangular space beckoned where flagstones gave way to stairs. Beyond lay the refuge of his cell, but he might as well have been tugging at a dry-docked frigate. The guards tightened their grip, fingers biting. One of them – possibly the most senior – narrowed his eyes at the lawyer.

'You can see my client is not of sound mind,' said Enzo. 'Allow me time with him.'

He had no choice. Antonio faced his friend. And recoiled. Enzo. So neat, so measured, showed him what he'd become. Not deliberately, he would never do that, but in his reflex. His eyebrows flew up; his mouth dropped open. He composed his features, but the blow had already landed. 'Allow me to defend you.'

No words. He could only stare.

'Antonio?'

He forced a reply, hoarse to his own ears. 'You don't know what that means.'

'I do.' Enzo said. 'I understand the risks.'

'Is this man your advocate, or not?' The guard rolled his eyes. *Here we go again, another troublesome prisoner.*

The lawyer was either stupid or unimaginably brave, arguing to stand beside him, and Antonio would never have taken him for the former. He reached, straining against the guard, catching Enzo's fingers.

'You'd do it for me,' Enzo said.

Antonio shook his head. 'No. I wouldn't.' He dropped his friend's hand and turned away, neck then body. 'He's not my advocate. Take me back to my cell.'

He Suffers

Nothing could have prepared him. Enzo had barely recognised him. The guards hadn't needed to break stride when he stumbled. They hadn't even broken a sweat.

Antonio might die.

It had occurred to him before, of course it had, but Enzo had only allowed it as a thought, a problem to solve, not a loss he might actually have to carry. Antonio was indestructible. He'd seen off three assassins with nothing but quick-thinking. He took each day as a fresh gift, shrugging off loss, refusing to dwell.

Antonio was dying.

That was the truth of it. And now, admitting it, the path ahead blurred. His breaths came shorter and shorter. Good thing it was an easy route from the Inquisition prison to the Posada del Marqués.

The front door flew open before he'd finished climbing the steps. Luisa ushered him upstairs into her office, where she insisted he sit even though she herself didn't. She paced, twisting her hands, her face pale and tight. *What have you learned? Did you see him? Is he strong? What are the charges? What is his condition? Will you defend him?* Question upon question, each pressing him lower into the upholstery.

Luisa stopped mid-flow. 'Forgive me, Enzo. I'm beside myself. But you're tired, let me get you something to drink.'

'My well-being isn't what concerns me.'

'You saw him?'

'They were bringing him back from a hearing.'

Luisa dropped to her knees so their eyes were level, and took his hands. When she spoke, it was in Italian. 'Dimmi.' *Tell me.*

Enzo swallowed. 'He suffers.'

'What do you mean?' She shook his hands.

He didn't reply because he couldn't. Where would he begin, and what good would it do?

'Did you speak to him?' Luisa's voice was rising.

He nodded. 'They were taking him to his cell. He won't accept my advocacy. He's still Antonio. Still a stubborn bastard… forgive me.'

She rocked back on her heels. Not for his profanity – they'd spent days together on the road; she was no wilting flower – but for his news. There she was: a lady of La Ribera, the daughter of a Spinelli, sitting on the floor like a maid about her scrubbing, looking at him as though he knew what to do.

His place wasn't to ask, but then her place wasn't on the floor. For that matter, Antonio's place wasn't in prison. Nothing made sense anymore. Reality could be like that – merciless and incomprehensible. So, he asked what he probably shouldn't.

'You still love him?'

She closed her eyes, swallowed. 'Of course.' Then she pressed her lips together, as though she'd said too much.

Then what had separated them? It wasn't a poetic, abstract question. He wasn't a romantic; he was a lawyer. And here was another anomaly. And in his experience, anomalies tended to join together into a story, always, in the end.

But all that – their misery, her confession – was batted aside by a voice from the doorway.

'Yet you're marrying Rafael Delmau in a few days.'

Familiar, lofty as ever, he didn't need to look but did anyway.

Gonzalo Navas: curled wig, powdered cheeks, velvet waistcoat embroidered with gold silk swirls, face like he'd bitten into a cutlet and found it rancid.

Luisa scrambled to her feet. 'You were listening.'

'Sí.' Not an apology. A flat fact.

'Rafael and I had a disagreement. We're spending time apart.' Luisa folded her arms, watching her father stride across the study.

'So your mother tells me. I'll talk to Don Delmau. The wedding will proceed.'

'It's not your decision, Papa.'

'All of Barcelona knows you stayed with him at La Collserolla.' By now Gonzalo was standing behind the desk, making a show of examining documents: lifting and replacing them, frowning here and there.

Luisa watched him, mouth clamped shut. *She has a lawyer's instincts*, thought Enzo. She knew when to argue, and when to let the other party finish a performance; to run out of fakery. Then she struck.

'Papa. Antonio is in the Inquisition prison. Please, will you speak to Don Fausto?'

How anyone could refuse Luisa was beyond Enzo.

But Gonzalo threw her a look, then went back to his papers. 'No. What would I say? *Please overlook the heresy on this occasion; my daughter has… flexible… notions on virtue.*'

Sometimes, this being one of them, Enzo wished he had Antonio's talent with his fists. Then again, now was not the moment to open a new battlefront. One day though… he allowed himself the vision of the vicious bastard knocked flat on his arse.

He hadn't finished. Gonzalo dropped the paper, rounded the desk and leaned against it. 'Is this why you and Rafael have fallen out? Past misjudgements? More fool you for telling him.'

He'd meant to cut her down. Far from it, she grew taller – so it seemed.

'Always so quick to judge, Papa. If you won't do something, I will.'

'You'll have nothing more to do with Albrono,' he said. 'I forbid it. You'll marry Rafael.' He took a step towards her.

Lay a finger on her… Enzo thought. Lawyer or no, he'd take his chances.

But Gonzalo might have sensed something, because he glanced at Enzo and changed course; moved instead to the door.

She ignored him. 'Señor Gallo, will you join me, so we may talk privately?'

'Luisa, do you hear me?'

She stepped past her father.

Enzo followed, because what else would he do?

Gonzalo moved to block him. Enzo squared his shoulders. Every fibre of him begged to lunge at the man – though it might be a comical scrap if it came to it.

Instead, he simply said, 'Discúlpeme, Señor Navas,' and turned sideways to slip past him through the door.

'Where are we going, Señorita?'

'I have no idea, Enzo. Actually, yes, I do. Marta!'

As Long as We Live

With Marta and Enzo scurrying alongside, Luisa marched all the way to Rafael's house on Carrer Ample. She'd no idea what drew her there. Not true. She knew exactly: she needed someone who cared, with the compassion to help and the intelligence to see how. With every click of her heel, her father's words rang in her mind: *I forbid it… You'll marry Rafael…* To the devil with him. She'd given Enzo and Marta no explanation, but it would have to wait. Her throat was too tight to speak.

A servant must have seen them coming, because the door swung open as they arrived. And there was Rafael, striding into the entrance hall, bringing sunshine, and embracing her so hard he might crush her ribs.

'I missed you,' he said.

Marta and Enzo hovered, their questions unspoken, and Luisa knew well enough that she and Rafael were not acting like a couple in the midst of a *disagreement.*

'Rafael, this is my friend, Enzo Gallo. I…' Luisa trailed off. What could she say? What help did she expect? She looked from Enzo to Marta. 'Will you excuse us for now?'

'Alves,' Rafael said, turning to the mayordomo standing discreetly by the wall, his blue silk uniform almost blending with the damask wallpaper, 'will you show Señor Gallo and Señorita Bosch to the library?'

Alone in the salon, he sat beside her on the chaise. 'I thought I'd lost you.'

'We promised otherwise, didn't we?' She ran a fingertip over his manicured fingernails.

'Have you forgiven me?' he asked.

'It is what it is,' she said.

He looked down at their hands, then up again.

'So, what brings you here, looking so sad?' He eased back in his seat.

She told him everything. The whole truth: Antonio, the debt, the decree, their estrangement, his refusal to accept his lawyer's help… her own recounting drove it all home anew. Exhausting.

'So, Antonio is the man who came between us?'

'One of them.'

He gave a wry smile at her jab, then rubbed his mouth. 'There is a bigger matter here, a man's life.'

It might have been easy in that moment to surrender to grief or terror. She'd already clung for days to the edge of that particular precipice, one finger loosening at a time. But Antonio lived, and as *Cervantes* had once said – according to her childhood tutor – *'As long as we live, so long let us hope.'*

As for Rafael, he rested his head on the seatback, gazing at the ceiling. 'Will your father not intervene for your sake?'

She shook her head. 'If only. He has influence with Don Fausto. He could end this in a heartbeat.'

'So…?'

'Antonio riles him. Father attacked him in Bellvís. Imagine it, Rafael, my father throwing punches like a brawling thug, drunk in a tavern. All over a debt! A debt easily dismissed.'

'Hmm. Too easily. The decree was convenient, was it not?'

'I thought so at the time.' Luisa waved her hand. 'Let's get Enzo. The issue is how to defend a man who won't accept a defence.'

Rafael went to fetch Enzo and Marta while Luisa waited. Outside, wheels trundled and faded. A dog yapped. Steps – inside now. And voices, muffled, words blending: Enzo's soft staccato, Rafael's low reply, and someone else. '*D'accord…*'

Really?

Given their awkward – to say the least – last meeting, how was she to feel upon seeing Jean-Pierre? No use looking at Rafael; he simply raised his eyebrows, and she knew what that meant. Hadn't he already said it? *There is a bigger matter here, a man's life.* Still, he could have warned her.

As for the Frenchman, he took a step toward her, stopped, then opted to lean against a bookcase, one foot swung over the other.

'I thought you'd left,' she said.

'Oui, and I returned.' Simple as that.

Marta caught her eye, her expression a question too complicated to answer.

Rafael re-took his seat. 'Enzo, Luisa has told me everything, and that Antonio refuses your advocacy.'

'That's right,' said the lawyer. He'd taken up a position before the fireplace, hands clasped loosely in front.

'I'm thinking to appeal to Don Fausto,' said Luisa. 'He *is* the Inquisition – here in any case. It's just that I don't know if he'll listen. He was so unpleasant to Antonio when they met.'

'More than unpleasant,' said Enzo. 'Hostile.'

Jean-Pierre sank into a tall-backed seat. He crossed a foot over his knee and settled back to listen, rubbing the buckle of his shoe with his thumb.

'My father was the worse,' said Luisa. 'He attacked Antonio like an animal. Don Fausto was haughty and insulting.'

'Hostile.' Enzo said, then: 'There was an altercation in the study.'

'Altercation?' Her voice, but outside her.

'Involving Don Fausto.' Enzo looked away just a little too fast.

'And my father.' She didn't wait for a reply, didn't need to. 'What was it about?'

Enzo winced. Looked at his feet, at Rafael, at the chandelier. Swung his hands behind his back. 'They threatened him.' His cheeks pinkened.

Not a lie, she knew that – Enzo lacked the guile for it. But not the whole truth either. She searched her memory. Her father had hidden himself away after Antonio left, and Don Fausto had left that same afternoon.

'What are you not telling us?' asked Rafael.

The lawyer muttered something under his breath, then looked at Luisa. 'Antonio heard them talking. They would harm him sooner than have their secret exposed – whatever that secret is.'

A shadow hovered just outside her vision; a spectre. She knew its name: *Verdad.* Truth.

'Dangerous,' said Jean-Pierre. 'An Inquisidor with a secret.'

'That was two years ago; Antonio vanished from our lives,' said Luisa.

But Rafael scrutinised Enzo, as though his face wore answers written just a little too fine to discern. 'What happened after Bellvís?'

'We rode twenty-six days to Seville to discover more about the decree, to seek knowledge of the charge – I thought it would shed light on this *secret*.' replied Enzo. 'There I remained for two months. I found nothing, ran out of funds and returned to Genoa to resume my work. Antonio chose to stay.' He glanced at Luisa.

'Decree? Charge?' Jean-Pierre dropped his foot to the floor.

Enzo began reciting in that precise, measured cadence that must be part of a lawyer's training.

'The decree concerned Antonio's grandfather, Alessandro. He was head of La Famiglia in Genoa until he aligned himself with Spain and was exiled. He moved to Seville. Don Fausto told us he was found guilty of heresy there, in the year seventeen hundred and four. Four years after his death.'

'Posthumous.' said Rafael.

Jean-Pierre leaned forward, elbows on the armrests, fingers steepled against his mouth.

'In such cases the family of the accused may defend such a charge,' said Rafael, 'though at no small risk to themselves.'

'And as I said. I found nothing.' Enzo let that land, then went on. 'That is the strange thing. None of his family – neither the Genoan nor the Spanish lines – know anything about a charge. Or a decree for that matter.'

'There is a Spanish line?' asked Luisa.

'We stayed with his granddaughter Lucretia. It struck us as odd that a man who was supposedly ex-communicated had passed on such a large estate. It should not be possible in Spain.'

No, it should not, thought Luisa. Spain's heresy laws were clear on the matter.

'You found nothing,' said Rafael. 'That is something.'

'The decree is a fake,' said Jean-Pierre, leaning back and resuming his crossed-leg position.

'There is no evidence, only a lack of evidence. And circumstantial at that. One cannot prove a negative,' said Enzo.

The door creaked open, and two servants entered, carrying trays laden with steaming hot chocolate and sugar-dusted pastries. Luisa declined – couldn't contemplate a morsel. She noticed Enzo passed, too. They both waited for the clinking of plates and cups to subside.

'You saw this decree?' asked Rafael, over the rim of his cup.

'Signed by the Inquisidor General himself,' said Enzo.

'But nobody knew of it, and his family went on to inherit,' said Rafael, placing his cup onto the saucer on his lap.

'Because it is a *fake*,' said Jean-Pierre once again, through a mouthful of pastry. He swallowed. 'We can talk all day about "*circumstantial*," but frankly, that only serves to obscure the obvious. There is no other explanation that makes any sense. Either the entire Albrono family and the authorities in Seville suffered a collective memory loss, or somebody forged a document.'

'It's an anomaly,' said Enzo.

More slurping and clinking.

'Luisa,' said Rafael. 'Why would your father be so concerned with Antonio's claim that he raced to Bellvis? He's not a Spinelli.'

Indeed. She had no answer.

'I wondered the same,' Enzo said. 'Here's the thing. There was a prior claim. Antonio's uncle, Girolamo raised it thirty or so years ago with the last Marqués – Carlos Spinelli. It came to nothing, presumably because of this decree. What's interesting is that, shortly after the claim was rebutted, Carlos promoted Gonzalo Navas from secretary to Protector Designate. A huge leap in fortune, by any measure. When Carlos died the following year, Gonzalo came into his position, and considerable wealth.'

'Et voilà,' Jean-Pierre said, his tone flat. 'We humans can be so tedious. So predictable.'

Enzo talked of her father, yet Luisa felt detached. As though overhearing a conversation through walls, from another room, about other men – dishonourable men at that. What was it they'd said that night? *this needs to end, for good this time… We might be undone.* She felt sick.

'If the heresy conviction was real, if the decree was real, the law would take its course,' Enzo said. 'No need for Gonzalo or Fausto to get involved, rush to Bellvis, make threats…'

And there it is. Somewhere, on the edge of the outer reach of her consciousness, warm fingers closed over hers, and though she knew them to be Rafael's, she couldn't respond; her own felt useless – ornamental.

Jean-Pierre spoke in his infuriating, *everything's-a-joke* tone. 'He doth protest too much, methinks.'

She'd no idea what he meant; no one did, judging by everyone's puzzled expression.

'Shakespeare.' He grinned. 'The guilty expose themselves in their efforts to prove their innocence.'

'Precisely,' Enzo said.

'This picture's missing something.' Rafael stared into his cup, and for a second Luisa wondered if he was talking about something he saw in its depths. 'Everything makes sense, but for one thing.'

He looked at Jean-Pierre. They spoke together. '*What was in it for Fausto*?'

Good question.

'Perhaps Don Carlos inserted something in his will for Fausto too,' said Enzo.

'Men do terrible things for money.' Jean-Pierre frowned at his plate, rearranging crumbs with his fingertips. Then lifted his eyes, trapping her. 'You know him, Luisa. Is it money? What does this Don Fausto value above everything else?'

Therein lay the answer, she knew. And from the silence that hung thick as syrup, so did their companions.

But as fascinating as these insights were, what use were they?

'So what?' Rafael might have heard her thought. 'How does this help?'

Jean-Pierre studied the wall opposite his seat, as if the answer lay in the silk birds etched on the wallpaper. 'Luisa, you are right; you must appeal to Fausto.'

'And say what?' Everything that had just been said now convinced her otherwise.

'Lean on your relationship; ask him to show mercy.'

'Beg?'

He met her gaze. 'Oui.'

'What will that achieve?' His logic eluded her.

'Oh, he will not relent, but with clever questions, which I know you are capable of, you may discover his motivation.'

Enzo's face lit up. 'If it's possible to prove Don Fausto has reason to *want* Antonio convicted,' he said, 'he's not impartial; there is a possibility of a mistrial.'

'You're thinking like Europeans,' Rafael said. 'The Inquisition doesn't yield to such rational ideas as *impartiality*.'

'Then we shall have to make it,' Luisa said. 'I will speak to Don Fausto. I'll beg. I'll tell him Antonio is no threat, that he's dropped his claim and his interest in me. And whatever his reply, we'll learn something.'

'Shall I accompany you?' asked Rafael.

'May I?' Jean-Pierre fixed his beautiful, watchful eyes on hers. 'S'il vous plaît, Luisa.'

Jean-Pierre. The exasperating, arrogant, all-knowing fly-by-night who treated life as a game, and had used her marriage for target practice. Who'd inserted himself into her choices, her plans, her *life*, and now wished to insert himself into her efforts to prevent a miscarriage of justice. As though *he* might be the difference. As though he wouldn't be insufferably smug if he were.

There is a bigger matter here, a man's life.

She couldn't think of anyone better.

Benedic Nos, Pater Caelestis

Antonio sat in his usual position at the end of his cot with his feet drawn in, arms resting on his knees. The guards had left him in shackles and chains – easier to move him that way. Every so often he slid a thumb under one of his cuffs to separate metal from flesh, even though the action only served to move the bite to another patch of skin.

How many days had passed? He'd made a nineteenth mark on the wall, but that had been in his old cell, before he collapsed. Perhaps they'd moved him so they might watch over him more closely, or maybe to be nearer to the trial hall. What purpose guessing? Antonio existed within the decisions the Inquisition made for him until the day when the Inquisition decided he should not exist anymore.

Seeing Enzo, clean and well-dressed in the powdered wig about which he'd once teased him, had been like gazing into a form of mirror. One that showed him what he'd become through everything he'd lost. He didn't want human contact; he could tolerate only the anonymity of the walls, the guards and the silence.

Except for Juan. He took solace in the company of the young friar who appeared in his cell from time to time. Sometimes Antonio wondered if he'd invented him, created a comforting illusion, an imaginary companion. Or perhaps Juan had come from beyond the grave, a benevolent spectre. But no, Juan existed. He suspected the friar had been assigned to keep him just on the right side of the line between despair and madness, fit for trial. The Inquisition didn't do kindness for its own sake; it measured every action in its relentless, methodical march toward purification through penitence.

Still, he appreciated him. There was no pattern to Juan's visits: sometimes the friar came when the sliver of sky behind Antonio's window shimmered blue, other times when it had darkened to slate, and occasionally he was simply there when Antonio woke, leaving him to wonder how the guard had opened the heavy iron door without rousing him. And on the last few visits, Antonio had coaxed him into speaking. Conversation, a treasure beyond price.

As if summoned by his thoughts, a key scraped in the lock, and the friar slipped in. He took his usual seat, hands tucked into his sleeves, feet flat on the ground, watching – like he always did, just watching.

'Juan.'

When the guard's footsteps had faded, the friar reached into his sleeve and took out a parcel, then dragged his chair to the cot.

Antonio smelled it first, and saliva burst into his mouth. His fingers shook trying to unfold the linen fast enough. *Need* growled and rumbled under his ribs.

Cheese: sweating, white flesh yellowing and cracking towards its grainy rind. A wedge no wider than his finger at its thickest, nothing to the living, everything to the dying. The cloth pooled in his lap, revealing a corner of bread – a still life painting wet from the artist's brush.

A skin of water.

He snatched the cheese to his mouth, fingers pressing into its soft flesh, grease sliding against skin…

But Juan tugged at his sleeve. 'Give thanks, Antonio.'

Give thanks? To whom? To Juan? He blinked, but the friar had moved his hands into a position of prayer and began in Latin: '*Benedic nos, Pater caelestis, et haec alimenta quae de tua largitate sumus sumpturi. Per Christum Dominum nostrum. Amen.*'

'Amen,' said Antonio. 'May a starving man eat now?' He smiled at the devout friar to show he meant no harm.

Juan nodded.

Antonio set about the food. With every mouthful, warmth trickled back into his limbs. 'Thank you. Juan.'

They watched each other, boy and man, the space between them narrowing. Friar and soldier.

'You need to stay strong,' said Juan.

Of course. Food prolonged torment.

Now it sat heavy in his gut. The Inquisition didn't offer solace; it weighed souls, measured life, and provided only the nourishment necessary to meet its prescribed outcome. No more, no less.

'You were ordered to.' Not a question, a flat acknowledgement. After all, what right had he to expect anything more from a lad barely old enough to exist within the machine, let alone stand up to it? For a prisoner.

But Juan jerked his head up, widened his eyes. 'No. Señor, no –' His voice wavered, then cracked. '– I would be punished.'

Shame crawled over Antonio. Now he'd hurt him. He reached for Juan's arm, but the chain stirred. A clink, metal against metal. Look here: a blackened, broken nail, and here: dirt etched into the creases of his skin. He snatched back his hand; dropped it to his lap. 'Forgive me, Juan.' Inadequate.

Juan unstopped the water pouch, gestured with it. 'You should drink.'

He took it, watching Juan's face even as he tipped the contents back into his mouth. The first gulp hit his throat with delicious shock. The next unfurled cool relief into his chest and stomach, stretching through his limbs like liquid silk. He lowered the pouch. 'I don't deserve you, Juan.'

The friar shrugged. 'And yet…' a smile played at the edges of his mouth.

Had he just made a jest? The moment settled; Juan toyed with the sleeve of his cassock.

'Who would punish you?' He'd said the wrong thing.

Juan stood. Antonio reached out again, and this time – chains be damned – grasped the rough hem of his sleeve. 'Juan?'

The friar blinked, quivered, a bird in a snare.

'Fausto?'

Juan sank back down, fixing his gaze on the wall at the end of the cot.

'Juan?'

The friar did turn to him then, and in his face, Antonio saw a flicker of something he didn't understand: a hunted pain. 'Don Fausto is not a man of God.' Antonio only just caught the words, so quietly did Juan utter them.

'¿Qué te pasa?' Once again, a language he spoke fluently felt brand new.

'He wears godly robes over an ungodly heart.'

'How would you know his heart?'

Juan lowered his head, thin neck folding so far his chin almost touched his chest. He twisted his hands, flexed whitening thumbs, rubbing at his skin as if washing himself.

A chill settled under Antonio's skin, reaching for his bones. 'You are afraid of him,' he muttered.

'¡Por supuesto! *Everybody* is.' Juan jerked his head up, eyes flaring, lips trembling.

Such anger, so sudden. A thread come loose at the edge of a scarf; Antonio wanted to tug at it, but doing so might unravel the whole. The silence stretched until it became so thin it had to break. 'Does he hurt you, Juan?'

Torment crossed the friar's face.

'Does he… misuse you?' he barely recognised his own voice, thick, quiet.

Juan jerked upright, strode to the door and banged on it, forehead resting against the heavy wood, shutting Antonio out.

'Juan…?'

The friar pressed his hand against the door alongside his head.

Antonio had never felt so useless.

Boots, keys jangling, the grinding of the lock and the creak of heavy iron swinging on tired hinges. Juan left him alone. Antonio glimpsed the corridor outside and envied the guard his freedom to come and go. He didn't envy the friar. For Juan was as much a prisoner as he.

Get Thee Behind Me, Satan

Odd that Luisa had been to the Plaça del Rei so many times yet had never really seen it. Odder still, she'd once sat feet from this spot, in another calesa with Antonio on their impromptu tour of the city, and now she was here to beg for his life.

The square, framed by solid and functional buildings, heaved with officials going to and from Inquisition business: scriveners and archivists, priests and scholars… all moving shoulder to shoulder under the watchtower and the spire of the Chapel of Santa Àgata – both looming heavenward like sentinels appointed by Torquemada himself.

'Here we are.' Jean-Pierre halted their mare at the foot of the wide steps beneath the arched entrance of the Grand Hall. A guard stepped forward, his tunic bearing the embroidered insignia of the Inquisition: the cross and olive branch. He gave no other hint of having noticed them; his eyes remained fixed ahead, his expression impassive.

Now the task was upon her, Luisa's feet didn't want to move. Her legs felt strange, somehow loose, as though they would crumple if she asked them to bear her weight. She searched Jean-Pierre's face for something, anything, an expression of wisdom to reassure her.

'Attends-moi ici. Waiting is forbidden, but I will drive back around.'

It would have to do. She swallowed hard. 'D'accord. Merci, Jean-Pierre.'

Then he caught her hand, low on the seat so nobody could see. 'Courage, Luisa.'

It worked. She raised her chin and climbed down from the calesa, tugging the hem of her chaqueta into place.

'Can I help you, Señorita?'

The guard stood like a block of stone between Luisa and the iron-reinforced portal. From behind came the snap of leather, and a sharp *Allez!* She was alone.

'I have an audience with Don Fausto.'

'Do you have an appointment?'

'Sí... No... I'm Luisa Navas. I believe he will see me. I'm his... niece.'

The guard gave her a hard stare, then shoved at the door. Hinges groaned, cool air swallowed her, and the door thudded closed with ominous finality. She was in the Palace of the Inquisition; a vestibule bathed in welcoming light. Such criminal deceit.

'Wait here.' He disappeared through a door.

As a child, she'd developed a method for controlling anxiety, for when her father turned his temper on her: counting heartbeats. She did so now, gripping her left wrist with her right hand, pressing her thumb to her pulse. A hundred and twelve, she reached, then the guard returned and gestured for her to enter.

It was a grand chamber with stone arches suspending an impossibly high ceiling and a huge oak table stretched down its centre. The tap of her own footsteps unnerved her as she approached the end of the table, so she lifted her heels to walk on her toes. The light. The way dust danced in the rays from the plain window set high in the wall. It should have been an uplifting space. Yet these walls... what secrets had they witnessed? What judgements? This floor... who had stepped here?

Marking the stone beneath her shoes, a smudge of dirt unlocked a memory. Not hers, yet hers. Chains against stone.

Suffering, hunger, fatigue, and something else: anger. Good. Be angry, Antonio. Anger sustains.

A side door swung open, and Don Fausto moved towards her in his long black robe. He made no sound; he seemed to *glide,* a movement so unnatural her stomach rose to her throat.

He wrapped her in his arms. The weight of him. The smell: incense and sweat – a wall of flesh and power. Beyond him, a young friar took a seat by the door, presumably an attendant. She caught his eye, then he looked away, fixing his stare on the opposite wall.

She took a breath and peeled away, affecting reluctance by forcing her hands to linger on his sleeves. 'Uncle, thank you for seeing me. I'm sorry for appearing without warning. I have become so disorganised I hardly recognise myself! I hope you are well.'

He beamed. 'I have no complaints. But you are radiant! As you should be, of course. A bride! I remember holding you as a baby. How time passes.'

Luisa doubted very much she looked '*radiant*' given her sleepless nights. The man merely spouted clichés. Had Don Fausto ever made a true observation about another person in his entire self-absorbed life? As for the wedding… for the purposes of this conversation, she would go along with it.

'Indeed. The day is near.'

'Are you happy, muchacha?' That sickening endearment.

Luisa forced a smile. 'I've never been happier.'

'I am glad. He is the right match for you.'

'I know.' Luisa swallowed. 'Which brings me to the reason for my visit.'

'Oh?'

He narrowed his eyes, cast his face in stone. How many defendants had been on the receiving end of that expression? Whether it was nerves or instinct, she veered off course. 'Are you still able to perform the ceremony? It would mean so much to me.'

'Of course. You are as a niece to me. No. More. A daughter.'

Luisa beamed. 'Perfect. I owe you so much; I will never forget your guidance – how you've tried to save me from my own mistakes.' *Too clumsy?*

Apparently not. 'Sí. I would not allow you to make a bad choice, mi niña.'

She ignored the crawling on her skin. 'Uncle. I know what you are thinking of when you say "*bad choice*". I cannot pretend I don't know of his trial. He's here, is he not?'

Don Fausto held her in his stare, his mouth a flat line, thin, almost purple.

'He fooled me, Uncle. It is difficult to forgive him, even though I know in your wisdom you would tell me our faith requires it.'

He inclined his head, and his mouth drew perilously close to touching her forehead. *Dios mío, please don't ask me to submit to physical affection.*

She fought the urge to lean away and slid her hands down his arms to grasp his hands, like a loving daughter. 'Is he in a great deal of trouble?' She peered up at him through her eyelashes.

'Luisa, you know I cannot talk about the details of a case.'

'Of course, Uncle. I just… I cannot bear to think of any unpleasantness at the same time as my wedding. Has he… did he… insult the faith?'

He pushed his lower lip out.

'It does not surprise me.' She nodded. 'Sometimes when we talked, he… well, he gave me the impression he didn't understand our Holy Mother Church here in Spain.'

He barked an abrupt sound that might have been a laugh. 'That makes no sense, Luisa. God is the same in every country. And so is a man's soul.'

'Of course, what I mean to say is, sometimes in the way of expressing ourselves, we could open ourselves up to misinterpretation in another language.' Luisa talked for the sake of it, throwing words the way a fisher casts bait, hoping to pull in something of value.

'This is not a matter of *misinterpretation;* to practice sorcery is to commune with the devil.'

Sorcery. Luisa's hand flew to her throat and she tried to disguise it, brushing her hair behind her ear. 'Was it the same with his grandfather? It must be the nature of the Albrono family.'

He shrugged, and when his shoulders dropped, his mozzetta stayed stubbornly raised over his shoulders. 'I do not know the details of that case.'

'But you had the decree of excommunication. So, you must have spoken to the Seville Tribunal at some point?'

She'd gone too far. He pulled his hands from hers so fast, hers remained suspended. 'Luisa, why are you prying?'

'Of course I'm interested, Uncle. I narrowly avoided his charms thanks to you. I cannot pretend this case does not fascinate me.'

'It is an unseemly interest. You would serve God and your new husband better if you concentrated on your wedding and your wifely duties.'

Luisa lowered her head and accepted the reprimand. She made her voice small. 'You are right, Uncle.' She lifted her eyes to his again. 'Promise me when I'm married you will still be my spiritual guide?'

He softened. 'Of course.'

'Uncle. May I ask one thing as a wedding gift?'

'Sí?'

She pressed the words, firm and deliberate, into the space between them, along with a silent prayer. 'Mercy for Antonio.'

'Why?' Flung back before her last syllable finished echoing.

'Because I prayed.' *Would this work?* 'And God told me to forgive. What better way than to plead for him?'

He folded his chin into its loose layers, and tilted his head, like a bird spotting a morsel, no, like he was seeing her for the first time. An utterance now, while he weighed her request, might tilt him calamitously, so she tightened her mouth to contain the pleas queuing behind her teeth.

And it came. Redemption, with a lifting at the corners of his mouth, a smoothing of brow.

'You've always been a remarkable child. Where most seek forgiveness for their own sins, you rise higher. To seek forgiveness for a man that sinned against you –' Did his eyes moisten? 'My child, you melt my heart. Grace, is what it is. God sees.'

She could fall to her knees, clutch his skirts and thank him. She could weep. But his decision hung too fragile, and – thinking on it – his words too loaded. She reached for him, for certainty, for persuasion – in case he needed more. But he stepped away, turned, and for a second sunlight bathed his face, his eyes softened to gold, rimmed pink for lack of sleep, or age. Just a tired old man.

With heavy steps he walked to the head of the table and stood behind a chair – one from which a wooden crucifix emerged, elegantly carved from a single piece of wood. He grasped the sides and looked down the length of the table – at what only he knew. Then he looked at her.

'What is mercy, Luisa?'

'I…'

Let him go, she wanted to say. *Unlock his chains. Let him breathe the same air as any citizen; walk the same streets. For the love of God let him be.*

But the way Fausto watched, unblinking, mouth piling left and then right like her old tutor waiting for her to finish her multiplications: seven lots of eight is fifty-six, that's a golden star. There was more at stake now than stars. A man's life. Antonio. 'I suppose it's compassion, forgiveness –'

He finished for her. '– for a man who has sinned. Isn't that all any of us want: to be shown forgiveness and compassion when we sin?' His teeth flashed; a smile of sorts. 'Don't be afraid. I'm not testing you.'

The floor softened.

'*Agite paenitentiam, ut peccata vestra deleantur*. Acts: Chapter three. Verse nineteen. Penance so that sins may be blotted out.' He tightened his fingers on the wood, then abruptly let go, dropping one hand to his side and draping the other over the chair back. 'You have my word. I shall guide him through penance so that his sins might be blotted out.'

'Thank you, uncle.' Why did she feel like a mouse between a cat's paws?

'There is no greater mercy than to lead a lost soul back to God.' On he went.

She steadied herself with a hand against the nearest chair. 'Will he be released? After penance?'

'That's not for me to decide,' said Fausto. 'The Holy Inquisition deals in souls, not bodies.'

'I don't understand,' she said. Not quite true, she simply didn't want to.

'Luisa, when you offer up your forgiveness, when you pray for mercy, do you pray for his body or his soul?'

'I…' she couldn't feel her hands anymore, nor her feet. 'I pray that he repents, so that the Holy Office sees fit to forgive and he might lead a good life.'

His head dropped as though his neck had failed him. He stood like that – sagging like a man who'd been struck – then after several long moments raised his chin once more. Forced it. As though it hurt. Wearily, he lifted his hand – wrist still lolling on the chair's back – and pointed, no, jabbed.

'Get thee behind me, Satan.' Almost under his breath, he spoke. Exhausted, tired of the fight. 'I will not save a body so you might take a soul.'

She swallowed a whimper. That finger, his words, their target. He meant her.

'Muchacha –' A different tone, sing-song, parent to infant.

She was Satan. She was erring child. He was God's messenger, and she'd be whatever he chose to name her. Inquisidor first, uncle second. Had she thought he'd set her above his judgement? There was life or death in that stare, at the end of his pointing finger. For a wild moment – a feral, self-preserving compulsion – she almost let him be right. If she surrendered to the name he gave her, maybe he would overlook her presumption.

'Satan tempts you. Can you feel him?'

Could she? Were they Satan's ice-cold fingers tugging her scalp? Or was he the cold serpent sliding down her spine? She shut her eyes; if only she could as easily shut out his words.

'Cast him out.' He didn't shout. Worse, he implored in a voice thick with what might be tears.

Cast him out.

Just words. She didn't have to believe him. She could choose not to. *Look at him*, she thought. *Drunk on self-regard, puffed out like a rock-dwelling toad.* More fool her, thinking she'd influenced his lust for cruelty. He'd built a theological fortress around his agenda, a structure so impenetrable perhaps even he no longer knew his own motives.

He was right about one thing: Satan did tempt her. But he didn't have horns and hooves. He wore embroidered vestments and a crucifix worth a thousand reales.

She tore her eyes away to the blue beyond the windows. Those lines of light spilling from heaven had as much chance of cleansing this unholy place as her lace handkerchief of mopping a butcher's floor. And what did he make of it, the friar sitting silently in the shadows, with his lips pressed flat?

There he stood. Fausto. At the end of the table, watching, so he might terrify her into conceding an innocent man should die for his vanity.

'Leave here, Luisa,' he said. 'Spend tonight on your knees praying God will light your path. Banish the devil.

Let Don Fausto follow his master into hell. As long as he presided over this trial, Antonio was doomed. It had always been so.

With the terms of the battle now clear, she dipped into a respectful curtsy and – despite his eyes burning into her back – found the strength to make a composed exit from the hall.

Pray Together

Outside she found no sign of Jean-Pierre, and as she tarried at the steps, her steadiness fractured. How she wanted to sink to the stone. She'd draw strength from its cool, solid permanence. If she could borrow a few moments – that's all it would take – her breath would steady, her thighs stop trembling, her heart stop skittering like a moth in a jar.

But women of note do not sit around on steps. Not unless they want to become the talk of the city. Not unless they want to be moved on like a ragged street pedlar by that guard. The one glowering at her. The one stepping her way.

One of the chapel's tall wooden doors stood ajar – an invitation. She accepted.

It was another world. One where light stopped at the windows to don robes of red, blue and amber, before sweeping its hues across the ancient walls. Drawn by an invisible force, she moved to the front – to a slab draped in cloth of gold. The same compelling force beckoned her to a seat in the first row of pews. And there she sat, clasping her hands, staring at a wooden Jesus taut with agony upon the crucifix rising above the altar.

She'd come seeking peace, and sure enough, the silence set to work untangling her emotions. Eventually, a prayer came, a single, simple mantra: 'Bring him out. Body *and* soul.' Not one for another. Don Fausto could keep that sick premise. Both.

Out there, the world squared up against itself, pugnacious, defensive, men's agendas jostling for primacy. In here, it set its own pace. The chapel was imperturbable. The stone was already soaked in the breath of ancestors – kings and commoners alike, and still had capacity for centuries more. Ancient prayers blended with new like songs sung by the same choir. So she added hers. And she sent soaring into the arches all those questions that she'd let chew at the substance of her thoughts: *Does he suffer? Will he live? Will I fail? Will they arrest us? What of Rafael and Jean-Pierre?* She sent them up with the incense and smoke threading from the candles, because the chapel could carry them and a thousand more, whereas they'd swallow her mind in three easy bites if she tried to hold them a minute longer.

And she needed her mind. She needed it for the question that mattered, one that actually might make a difference: What shall I do next?

With lighter limbs and easier breath, she rose. Jean-Pierre would be waiting. She made the sign of the cross, bobbed her head, turned away. And almost collided with a boy.

'Oh' her heel caught an altar step, the world tilted, one arm wheeled behind her, the other snatched for balance, at the boy's sleeve, at air, because he'd jerked away.

She didn't fall. Almost did. Teetered. But the world righted, all without clutching his arm, and that was for the better. Women and monks did not touch.

How had he arrived so silently? He wore the once-white robes of the Dominican order and stood as unimposing as a shadow, with his hands folded into his sleeves. His unlined face was passive; his shiny dark hair lay flat on his forehead and around his face – a dark halo around a stubbled tonsure. This close, she could see dirt in the seams of his robe and grease on his nose. And she recognised him.

'You were with Don Fausto?'

'Shall we pray together?' He stepped past her to the altar, crossing himself. Luisa followed, returning to her seat while he knelt on the first of the three stone steps. They both faced the front of the chapel – just two people seeking divine guidance.

He spoke first, his voice low. 'You are Luisa Navas.'

It didn't seem to be a question. Instead, Luisa asked her own, addressing it to the altar cloth. 'Who are you?'

'Juan. I am Don Fausto's attendant.'

'You followed me?'

'Sí.' He might have been sixteen.

'Why?'

He snatched a glance in her direction, then returned his gaze to the crucifix above the altar, clasping his hands tighter. 'It is my job to watch over the prisoner.'

'Antonio?' She could barely breathe.

'Sí.'

'How is he?'

'He suffers.'

Those words again. 'What does that mean?'

Juan dipped his head, resting his forehead on his clasped hands, closing his eyes. She realised she might frighten him away, this boy who was her only connection to Antonio, yet she'd so many questions…

'When will his trial be settled?' she whispered.

'The second session is tomorrow. After that, it depends.'

'On what?'

Juan didn't reply. She studied his profile; the small bump at the bridge of his nose, the curve of his lashes resting against his cheek, the point of his Adam's apple so sharp it might break his skin.

'On what does it depend, Juan?'

'If he confesses and shows remorse, to the satisfaction of Don Fausto.' He spoke the next words in a rush, almost hissing them. 'Which is impossible, because Don Fausto seeks to entrap him.'

The crack in his demeanour broke a wall between them. 'What do you mean? Juan? Why are you telling me this?'

'I do not know what to do.'

Lifting his head once more, clasping his hands under his chin, Juan gazed into the eyes of the suffering Messiah. And the wooden figure hung sightless, sculpted and painted – after all – by human hands.

They were the only people in the chapel, but borrowing time. She moved beside him. A single tear glistened on his cheek. Powerless, all she could do was look up at the Christ-figure, wondering what he saw.

'Can you help me, Juan?'

'How?'

'I don't know. Meet me where we can talk more easily?'

He stared for several long seconds, hands clasped so tight his knuckles shone white. 'Don Fausto will be occupied with the session tomorrow from the hour of eleven.' His voice carried that strange warbling quality that occurs between boy- and manhood. 'I'll meet you at noon in the cloister of the Monastery of Sant Pau del Camp. It has a garden for visitors.'

Footsteps behind, and Luisa looked over her shoulder. A stocky, middle-aged man bustled about at the far end of the chapel, wearing the black cassock of a verger. He carried a pile of papers, hymn sheets perhaps, and began to distribute them at the end of each row of pews. He threw Luisa a benign smile. They'd run out of time. She rushed out the words that mattered most. 'Tell Antonio to have faith. Tell him… my heart is constant. Tell him…'

But Juan's wide eyes darted behind her. A rustle of papers. The verger had drawn close. She snapped her mouth closed and rose to her feet, addressing Juan in a clear, even tone. 'Thank you for your advice; I'll pray on it.'

Luisa faced the altar, backed away several steps with her head bowed, crossed herself, with a reverence she meant with all her heart, then took her leave, nodding at the verger as she passed.

Emerging from the chapel, she spotted Jean-Pierre and, for the first time since leaving that terrible hall, the air tasted sweet. He leapt from his seat to help her up, casting an apologetic glance at the guard who had taken a few steps toward him.

The calesa tilted one way as she climbed onto the seat, then the other as he joined her.

'Don Fausto won't be swayed,' she said. 'He's resolute.'

Although they'd expected as much, his face fell.

'But we have an ally – his attendant, Juan. We meet him tomorrow at noon.'

Second Audience

Antonio didn't know he slept until he woke with an intake of breath that raked through his throat and set him coughing razors. Fragments of a dream persisted behind his eyelids. Two crows, two rats, and two dormice, seated at a table: *'Bethink yourself and confess.'* At the head of the table perched a buzzard, tearing at something with a blood-red beak; glistening red tendrils looped to the fleshy object trapped under its talons.

He blinked away the lingering images. Dawn's light crawled past the bars of his window, lethargic, as if it had somewhere better to be.

Once again, he bade good morning to his constant companion, hunger. The food Juan had brought him had stirred the beast in his stomach.

Bethink yourself and confess, one of the dormice had said. To what? It was not courage, or even stubbornness preventing him; it was ignorance. If he thought he could save himself by confessing to be a… a *toad,* he would do so.

His legs protested as he straightened them, stiff from too many hours hunched in the same position. A lifetime ago he'd had the discipline to exercise; now it was not a matter of discipline but energy. The shackles grew heavier by the day. When he moved, his left knee clicked so loud the sound bounced off the walls, sending a fresh jab of pain through the joint. Even the task of using the soil bucket left him collapsed on the cot praying for his world to cease spinning. What had become of him? No longer a man but a series of thoughts anchored to a broken body.

Footsteps. The lock scraped, and his jailer swam into view. The same fellow, solid but slack-cheeked, with breeches slung low. As usual, the guard kept his eyes on his work, and away from Antonio. No matter, only one thing interested him. Food.

Yet the jailer brought none. He exchanged used bucket for empty, and left. Antonio had not even the strength for disbelief. The door clanged shut, leaving the hunger beast shrieking and clawing.

The morning crawled; the rectangle of light brightened to cerulean, heat rose, and the air became thick enough to chew. Antonio scraped the stone next to his cot using the edge of one of the irons in his chain. He preferred it to thinking. He'd completed the first line of his initial – a swirling *A* that would have earned him an excellent grade from his calligraphy professor – and had begun rubbing dust away with his thumb, when his cell door swung open for the second time.

No greeting was needed between Antonio and Juan. An odd relationship, it existed beyond the bounds of normal human interactions. For what man in the real world finds himself dehumanised, in extremis, and forced to depend upon the care of a boy? And what boy conducts himself with such quiet grace that he restores dignity to that man?

Juan brought his chair close to the cot and drew out another food parcel – just bread this time – and another skin of water that could have been the finest wine. Antonio held the last of it back, tipping it onto his face and into his dry eyes. For a few seconds, the sensation brought him something close to joy. 'Juan, gracias.'

'I do not have long. Escúcheme.' Juan spoke in a fast whisper. 'Señorita Navas appealed to Don Fausto on your behalf.'

Luisa. A burning in his chest, stealing his breath. She existed only in his imagination, yet the young friar dropped her name as if she were a living, breathing person.

'He will not be deterred,' The friar said.

'And… Luisa?' Antonio didn't know what he asked, only that he wanted Juan to keep talking of her, to keep making her real.

'I followed her to the chapel, and we talked. She gave me a message for you. "*Tell him to have faith. Tell him my heart is constant.*"'

Antonio moved his tongue over each syllable. Each stirred a small flame, but like burning scraps of parchment, they flared then burnt out. Leaving ashes.

'Is that all?' He searched Juan's face. 'Fausto told me she's to marry.'

'Sí, he will officiate.'

It was true. But then, why should she not?

Juan lowered his voice further. 'I will meet with her again today.'

'Why? What will it achieve?'

'No sé. But she asked me, and Don Fausto will be at your audience, so…'

So many thoughts crashed down that the cell itself might have collapsed. Luisa involved herself. She was determined. He remembered how she'd defied her father, riding after him. But La Inquisición was not her father, and – *Dio* – it didn't spare women. Catalina's face swam before him, drawn and haunted. He saw her teetering on the wall of the Puente de Serranos, staring at the rocks below, her shift blowing against jagged bones.

He scrambled to his feet, chains and all, pulling Juan up with him. 'No. Listen to me. Don't involve her. Tell her… tell her I'm set against her.' His throat caught. Who did he think he was fooling? He collapsed onto the cot, dragging fingernails across his scalp. Juan sank beside him and waited, his hands flat on his knees.

Finally, he lifted his head. 'Tell her I won't have it. No, she won't be told –' A dry laugh escaped. '– If soldiers had spine like hers nobody would dare start a war.' He exhaled. 'Tell her I'll find my own way. I'm happy knowing she thrives, and I wish her nothing but joy in her marriage.'

He couldn't read Juan's expression; he could only hope. The boy dipped his head, slow as a man five times his age, and with a final squeeze of his wrist, a look back over his shoulder, left him alone once more.

The seconds and minutes dragged, probably into hours, and Antonio emptied his thoughts sufficiently to begin carving in the wall once again. He'd begun a fourth letter when the door swung open for the third time that day.

The same two guards escorted him, their faces blank as usual, ignoring Antonio's nods of recognition. This time, somehow, he kept pace. He'd be damned if he let them drag him into the hall for the entertainment of the pious menagerie from his dream.

There they were, watching him, their faces arranged into the same sanctimonious masks. The hairy Inquisidor Don Manuel and the soft-faced prosecutor, Don Joseu. The two monks whose names he didn't know, Doctor Balleza of course, neatly turned out as usual, and the man with hair that appeared to have been slicked down by the same ink he used to scribble his notes.

And of course, proud, at the head of the table, the black beads of his buzzard eyes following Antonio above his smug, smirking beak, sat Don Fausto. So familiar that for a second Antonio's disconnected mind entertained the notion of greeting him. Instead, he narrowed his eyes, bringing Fausto into sharp focus, blurring everything and everyone else, because they didn't matter.

In seeing him thus, Antonio was confronted anew with the helpless horror of the imbalance in power between them. Because Fausto regarded him as a cruel child might examine an insect; wondering whether to flatten it under his boot, or first – one by one – tear off its limbs. But Antonio wouldn't lower his eyes, wouldn't give Fausto the satisfaction of his fear, despite what that took.

After the usual administrative pronouncements, the prosecutor came to the business of the day:

'Do you remember anything additional relating to your previous evidence, which you are bound to divulge according to your oath?'

'No.'

'In the last audience, you were exhorted in the name of God, our Lord, and the Holy Mother Church to confess the whole truth in relation to this matter, so your trial should be despatched with all brevity and mercy. Have you considered this exhortation?'

'I have.'

'And do you have anything to add?' Don Joseu peered at him over his paper.

Antonio appraised each man in turn and found nothing. The eyes of the elderly monk were just a little narrower than those of his colleagues. Doctor Balleza had a crease at the bridge of his nose that he'd never seen before. He might as well have been trying to interpret the thoughts of the creatures from his dream. 'I have described the events in full and to the best of my recollection.'

'Who else was involved?'

'I acted on my own initiative.'

'Don Albrono, I would remind you there are several witness statements, all of which are consistent, all of which present a grave case. Bethink yourself.'

'I'm at a loss. What do you seek from me?'

'The *truth*. Don Albrono.' Fausto rose to his feet; he pitched his voice half an octave lower than normal – an affected, deep rumble.

'I have given you the truth, to the best of my recollection. If I have offended Our Lord, I offer my penitence, unreservedly. If there is some detail I have forgotten, I offer penitence likewise. But I can only repent that which I have done, or that which I recall. I cannot guess that to which you allude, and I cannot lie.'

He pleaded, and he knew it. He appealed to the others… perhaps the curious monk, or the puzzled doctor? But when he looked into their faces for a flicker of something, of *reasonableness*, he found only a detached blankness. This was all in the course of a day's work for these men.

Of course, not for Fausto. He thumped the table. '*Some detail?* If you consider heresy to be *some detail,* then what value your penitence?'

Antonio sagged under the weight of his intransigence. Why defend himself? The Inquisidor would pick apart his words and find new fault at every step. And the rest nodded along – as one in their indignation of the immense magnitude of Antonio's sin.

'Do you have anything to add?' the prosecutor said.

'I have spoken the truth according to my oath.'

As required, Antonio signed the record of his evidence, stealing a look at Don Fausto as he did so. The Primer Inquisidor smiled at the paper Antonio had just signed. And he knew. Whatever trap Fausto had set; he'd stepped into it. But then, there could have been no other outcome. He was in a deadly game where only his opponent knew the rules.

The Elegant Way

Ten minutes early, Jean-Pierre and Luisa strolled around the cloister. The air pressed like a damp cloth but the blue sky promised any storm was still days away.

'I hope it doesn't rain on your wedding, Luisa.'

She fanned her abanico against the side of her neck, to no effect; stray hair clung to her skin – a maddening itch. 'We haven't said we're going ahead with it,' she said.

'But all your "*good reasons*", is it not a fait accompli?' Jean-Pierre walked ahead, examining the shrubs, every now and again trailing a finger over the delicate petals of a rose.

They did have *good reasons*. She and Rafael had talked about it into the night, after her father had visited and as much as demanded Rafael make an honest woman of her. Reason to rebel in that alone, but it would be a hollow victory. In point of fact, the incident showed what rebellion would cost. Whereas Rafael would set her free, her father would continue to rule her. Freedom would mean she could continue to manage El Marqués, or another hotel, go into business, study, or see the world. The point was the choice. And – just perhaps – with her marriage, her father would no longer consider Antonio a threat. Maybe he'd persuade Fausto to lift his foot from his throat. And the marriage would clear a path for Rafael and Jean-Pierre. Because who would suspect a respectable married man?

They'd explained all this to Jean-Pierre over breakfast. All these '*good reasons*.'

He'd listened in silence, then dropped his napkin onto the table and taken his leave.

'This concerns you, too,' Rafael had said.

Then he'd turned. He'd turned and fixed an empty, unintelligible gaze upon Rafael. 'Nice of you to decide this *concerns me too*, after you weighed it all up without me. Better to be an afterthought than nothing. This time anyway.'

'We haven't made a decision,' Rafael had said.

'Be sure to let me know when you have,' said Jean-Pierre, and stalked out.

They'd ridden here in silence when they should have been discussing the real issue, the reason they'd come here, and she resented him for that. He might have a fair grievance; given time to think on it, she'd likely concede it. But that was the point – they didn't have time.

'You know, the marriage won't be valid anyway,' he said.

'How so?'

'There's the matter of consummation.' He paused to inhale from a milk-white bloom, closing his eyes against its perfume.

Luisa brought her abanico around to her face to conceal the heat rising there. 'How crass!'

He shrugged. 'It is a fact.' He dropped the rose and resumed walking; hands loosely clasped behind his back.

This wasn't about not being consulted. She stopped in her tracks. Jean-Pierre continued a few steps then must have noticed, because he turned to face her, an implausible smile playing about his mouth.

'Qu' est-ce qu' il y a?'

'Do you mind?'

His smile fell. He stepped closer, his voice little more than breath. 'Oui, I mind. I mind that something you have as a right, an expectation, is judged unnatural for me. I would absolutely mind him standing before God and witnesses, and making vows to you that belong to me.' He reached out and tucked a strand of her hair behind her ear, an oddly absent gesture, as if she were one of the roses they'd just passed, as if by feigning indifference he might feel it. 'I know your *good reasons.* Moreover, I expect them to prevail, because reason should. But – and though I don't recognize myself in saying it – perhaps, on this occasion, I'm not inclined towards reason. It's too cruel a master.'

She watched the elegant line of his back as he began walking again, then scurried to catch up. 'I'm sorry, Jean-Pierre. I didn't think.'

'Ce n'est rien.'

It was not nothing though, Luisa knew. She tried to think of something to say, but words deserted her.

He hadn't finished. 'What about Antonio?'

What about him? 'He moved on. The miracle of his release, if we manage it, will be enough for me.'

'Vraiment?'

'Vraiment.' *Truly.* Luisa told herself she believed it, but by his raised eyebrows, she knew Jean-Pierre wasn't going to even try.

By now they'd completed another circuit of the cloister, and run out of conversation. The harder Luisa searched for words to break the tension, the further apart they became. Where was Juan? He must be ten minutes over time now.

As if summoned by her thought, the young monk appeared beneath a cluster of olive trees. He wore a black cappa over his white cassock, hiding his face in the shadows of its hood, so at first Luisa didn't recognise him. When she did, she tugged on Jean-Pierre's arm.

Juan led them into the building, down a corridor and out to the exterior wall of the monastery. A few more steps led them to a single-storey structure with limestone walls and a tiled roof: a small room or a large storage cupboard. Wooden floorboards creaked under their feet, and a large spider, startled by the light, scurried into a crevice between two sacks. Just as well they'd not brought Enzo and Rafael; the three of them barely had room to stand.

'Juan, how are you?' asked Luisa.

He removed his hood to reveal his smooth young face, and it struck Luisa once more how childlike he appeared.

'This is a friend, Jean-Pierre.'

The friar ignored him. 'I saw Don Albrono this morning. I gave him your message.'

'What does he say? Is he…' she had been about to ask if he was well, but what a banal question that would be.

'He asks you not to involve yourself. He wishes you happiness in your marriage.'

She checked Juan's face for a joke, as if the friar had the capacity for mirth. 'He was the same with Enzo, refusing help.'

'He said he will find his own way.'

'And how is that going?' said Jean-Pierre.

Juan might have noticed his sarcasm – he surely did – but chose a straight reply. 'It's going badly.'

'He fears for Luisa,' said Jean-Pierre.

'He said –' A small and remarkable smile touched Juan's mouth. '– "If soldiers had spine like hers nobody would dare start a war."'

Jean-Pierre laughed then; a thunderclap in the tiny space, cut off as fast as it began. 'And you thought he'd forgotten you.'

'Never mind what he says,' said Luisa. 'Juan, we think Don Fausto has a personal interest, and so should not judge Antonio's case.'

'He hates him, that's plain to see,' said Juan. 'Why?'

'A good question,' said Jean-Pierre. 'Antonio represented his family's claim to a debt owed by the Spinelli family.'

'My family,' Luisa interrupted.

Jean-Pierre ignored her. 'Don Fausto went to unusual lengths to block the claim. It has a stink of self-interest about it.'

Juan's eyes darted between them. 'He *is* partial. He rode four days to Valencia to bring the case under his jurisdiction. He argued for a *de vehementi* case. Of course I lack his experience, but the theologians of Valencia had already judged it *de levi*.'

'What does it mean?' Jean-Pierre asked.

'He raised a light sin to a grave sin,' said Luisa.

'Oui, I understand Latin, *Luisa*. I meant, what does it mean for Antonio?'

She gave him a withering look.

'It means if found guilty he will be abandoned to the secular arm,' said Juan.

'But that's good, is it not? It would get him out of the clutches of the Inquisition,' said Jean-Pierre.

'No,' Juan said. 'It is a formality for capital offences. The Church cannot shed blood, so the prisoner is abandoned to the secular authorities for the sentence to be carried out.'

'It means death,' whispered Luisa.

'And godly men clean their hands. Like Pilate.' Jean-Pierre glared at Juan. 'How do you tolerate such hypocrisy?'

Luisa opened her mouth to protest. But Juan answered, his voice threadbare.

'I cannot. My master is an unholy man, cruel…'

Luisa barely dared to breathe, afraid even the softest sound might send Juan back into himself.

Jean-Pierre, meanwhile, watched Juan, his expression quiet but weighted.

Juan changed direction. 'Don Fausto has intervened with Don Antonio's conditions, his rations…'

'He suffers.' She echoed Juan's own words, and Enzo's.

'Señorita, I am tasked with keeping him as close to death as possible while still fit for trial. Those were my master's exact instructions.'

Luisa's legs sagged; she reached behind for something to lean against, fingers finding coarse sack.

'I cheat; I bring him bread and water, but if my actions were discovered… I think he would be in more danger.'

'And so would you,' said Luisa.

'Why do you take the risk?' asked Jean-Pierre. 'Why are you here?'

Juan swallowed, a dry gulping sound. 'I have recently become a friar. Don Fausto prefers a novice. He has set his sights on –' The way Juan's lips twisted, Luisa thought he might break down. But he raised clenched fists to his chest and spoke through gritted teeth. 'He has set his sights on my brother.'

'Dieu…' Jean-Pierre said quietly.

'Gregor always followed me,' said Juan. 'As children, we talked about dedicating ourselves to God. Now look where I have led him.'

Jean-Pierre had paled. 'Entiendo, Juan,' he whispered.

Luisa didn't understand what Juan had just shared, but saw why nobody would want their brother to fall into the clutches of a corrupt and vicious master. 'Juan, if we could prove your master's judgement is partial, there might be a mistrial, an opportunity for a more objective hearing.'

'The Inquisition will never be lenient,' said the friar. 'But as long as a prisoner confesses, he will not be executed for a *de levi* sin.'

'Then that must be our goal,' said Jean-Pierre. 'C'est simple. Fausto must be removed from the case.'

'How?' Juan had begun scratching at his sleeve, and now he did it so hard Luisa wanted to reach out and stop him lest he break a nail.

'There are two methods: elegant or inelegant. We need to prove Don Fausto is not impartial. We believe he used a forged document – a falsified decree of excommunication against one Alessandro Albrono. If we exposed such a fraud, then –'

'Then he would be discredited,' finished Juan.

'Oui. Elegant, no?' Jean-Pierre folded his arms.

Juan tucked his hands back into his sleeves – mirroring Jean-Pierre's posture – and delivered his considered opinion. 'Sí.'

'Do you have access to his documents?' Jean-Pierre asked.

'His office. Some in his room. But even if you had this decree, what would you do with it?' Juan began scratching at his sleeve again.

'There must be someone we can speak to. Even the suspicion of partiality should place a question over the trial,' said Jean-Pierre.

'Doctor Balleza. He does not work for Don Fausto, so perhaps is less afraid of him.' Juan's gaze darted to the door, as if the Inquisidor might suddenly burst in on them.

'D'accord. Will you look for the document?'

'He might catch me.' Juan stopped scratching one arm and began kneading both, comforting himself.

'He won't catch you on the ninth day of this month,' said Luisa.

Both turned towards her.

'Not if he's officiating at my wedding.' She offered a tight smile.

Placing credit where it belongs, Jean-Pierre showed no emotion, perhaps a slight widening of his eyes, and even that she might have imagined – it's often the case that we see what we expect.

As for Juan, his expression softened, his shoulders dropped. And that settled the matter.

'Tres bien,' said Jean-Pierre. 'I'll meet you in two days, Juan. While Don Fausto joins Luisa and my friend in holy matrimony, you and I will see what we can find to discredit him.'

After they'd parted company with Juan, they walked back to where they'd left the calesa, a thousand thoughts swirling in Luisa's mind.

Jean-Pierre stared at the path, and she touched his arm, seeking to break the miserable spell stretching between them. His gaze flicked to hers, then rested there. Those eyes as unfathomable as the ocean they'd stolen their colour from.

'I had to,' she said.

He resumed looking ahead. 'Oui.'

They walked a few more steps.

'I'm sorry –'

He cut her off. 'You are ruthless, Luisa.'

Behind her eyes, she felt that treacherous, hot prickle, and willed it back. Repeating herself was, it seemed, all she could manage. 'I'm sorry –'

He held up a hand. 'Non. I cannot fault you.' He chuckled under his breath. 'This Antonio must be everything to you, that you fight so dirty.'

They reached the calesa, and upon seeing them, their mare began twitching and snorting, as though she'd been bored.

'Can we do this, Jean-Pierre?'

He considered, then delivered his verdict. 'Oui.'

They climbed onto the seat; she took the reins. 'What if we fail?'

He fixed his gaze on the track ahead, face blank, voice steady. 'Then it will have to be the inelegant way.'

'So, it's not just I who is prepared to fight dirty.'

He gave no answer. The mare snorted again, impatient. She flicked the reins, and they rode on; the breeze cooling their faces.

What lay ahead wouldn't be elegant, no matter how it played out. Luisa knew it, and she was fairly sure Jean-Pierre did too.

Matters of Procedure

For Fausto, the second audience had been like a bowl of migas: quick and satisfying. Too quick. He lingered after the prisoner had been led away, thinking upon another soul too ungrateful to grasp salvation when it's offered.

Unfortunately, Balleza spoiled his meditations, returning with his *matters of procedure.*

'Make it quick, Doctor Balleza. Unlike you, I have more than one matter requiring my attention.'

'Discúlpeme, Su Excelencia,' Balleza said, 'just a couple of anomalies.'

Fausto's jaw ached.

Oblivious, Balleza turned the pages of his journal with slow precision. 'The Calification.' He peered at an underlined note. 'It currently lists the suspicion as *de vehementi*, which is appropriate given our discussions when you came to Valencia. However, it does not align with the documented Calification from May seventeenth.'

Fausto forced his mouth into a smile. 'Valencia had overly lenient Calificadores. Friar Francisco, wasn't it?'

'Sí,' Balleza confirmed with a single sharp nod, 'and he has been removed from his position.'

'Then what troubles you?' Fausto sharpened his voice.

Balleza blinked. 'The official record. We will need to convene a session, so we might update it. Before the next audience.'

'Then do so.'

'It will require four Calificadores, but we only have two at present.'

'That's not a problem. I will supply two loyal and learned friars.'

Balleza's brow lifted, the closest he came to an expression. 'Shall I schedule the session this week, then? It will mean delaying the third audience until the twelfth or even the thirteenth.'

'No later than the twelfth.' Fausto pressed a hand against his temples; a pulse throbbed there. 'This case has dragged on long enough. Deliver the revised Calification to me the day before.'

'Of course.' Balleza hesitated, shuffling through his pages with more of that meticulous diligence that made Fausto want to snatch the notebook and hurl it down the table. 'There is a second matter.'

Fausto's fingers drummed a slow rhythm on the table.

Balleza continued unfazed. He had flicked to another page in his infernal notebook. From where Fausto sat, he could see more of the same handwriting – neat, orderly, like the bureaucrat who wrote it.

'In my first interview with the defendant, he informed me he was not the first member of his family to be prosecuted by the Inquisition.'

Fausto's pulse leaped, and he closed his eyes to compose himself. 'You must be mistaken, Doctor Balleza. We covered this in the course of the first audience.'

'Indeed. I thought so, and in their replies, the other Tribunals confirmed as much. But I checked my notes from my first interview, and the defendant clearly stated there was a prior guilty verdict.'

'That is indeed strange.' Fausto swallowed dry air.

'I wonder if he should be questioned further on the matter, and if we should check again with the relevant Tribunals.'

'I don't see what purpose it would serve other than bureaucratic. It will have no bearing on the current crimes.'

'Sí. But procedures require clarity on this matter.'

'Thank you for bringing it to my attention. My judgement is that it is irrelevant to the case; there is no reason to delay in respect of this detail.'

'It would be a simple matter to –'

'With respect, Doctor Balleza. You are in *my* Tribunal now. I don't know how you run things in Valencia; painfully slowly, I imagine, given your obsession with *procedure*. I cannot imagine the unnecessary suffering you inflict on your prisoners with delay upon delay. You may pursue this '*anomaly*' to your heart's content once justice has been served, but you will not delay my case over it. That is my decision.'

'But –'

'That will be all. Doctor Balleza.'

Fausto fixed the physician-confessor in his well-practised glare until he had collected his bag, quill, ink, and ridiculous notebook and risen from his seat. He watched him to the door, his heels rhythmic on the polished flagstones. And he watched him leave the hall, closing the door behind him with a controlled thud. Only then did he allow his tension to unravel, standing, leaning over the table, knuckles pressing into the wood, and staring down the length of the polished surface to the spot where the defendant had stood.

Don Albrono. He'd questioned Fausto, mocked him, pushed him to the ground, shown him contempt and walked away. He had thought to place his undeserving hands on his beloved niece Luisa, and threaten his own reputation.

He should have ordered five assassins, not three.

Until Death Do Us Part

Luisa

Despite her mother's ambitions, Rafael and Luisa had chosen an intimate ceremony in one of the chapels of the Monastery de Pedralbes, on the outskirts of the city. It was family members only inside the chapel, with a small reception to follow in the courtyard. Guests had been notified that the happy couple had opted for a simple occasion. However, they came from that section of society that had never had to reconcile the terms '*noble wedding*' and '*modest*'. And so, a quiet courtyard, normally filled with birdsong, prayer, and nuns in plain robes, transformed into a hub of exclamations, laughter, towering wigs and skirts wide as bookcases.

Luisa took a breath, inhaling lavender and rosemary. Perhaps a kind nun had thought to calm her nerves by placing the herbs in bundles around the vestibule. Did she really mean to vow before God and their families that she would dedicate her life to a man to whom she could never be a wife?

She peeped around the garlanded entrance, down the length of the aisle, past the ivory roses tied to the ends of the pews. Mama sat conspicuously adorned beside cousin Ambrogio in the family's designated row. None of the other Spinellis were present. Alejo had fallen ill, so his wife and daughters had remained in Bellvís to take care of him.

On the opposite side of the chapel were the Delmau family pews. There sat Rafael's father, Ramon, frail and stooped, his wife

Gabriela settling him into his seat. Soon she would take her leave of him; as *madrina,* she would walk down the aisle with Luisa and her father.

Rafael sat alone in the front pew. How handsome he looked, and how vulnerable for such a confident man, gazing at the cross above the altar. *Look around, Rafael. Look at me.* Just one glance, she needed. So she might decide: marry or run. Like a game of primero: take another card or stick with her hand? *Voy o paso? Look at me, Rafael.*

He couldn't possibly have heard her, yet he turned. Her hand – moving under its own will – found the black cuarzo pendant at her throat; the first gift he'd given her. His gaze flicked to the stone, and his face lit up. Her doubts evaporated. *Voy.*

Her father stood in the entrance to the vestibule, his new silver-grey wig sitting prim over his powdered face. It was no choice. Not really. Papa or Rafael. Oppression or freedom. *Voy. Voy every time.*

The first bass notes of Pachelbel's Canon in D interrupted the rumble of muted chat, and were soon overlaid by the charming melodies and harmonies of cello and violins. Luisa looked up at the string ensemble perched in the mezzanine and took a breath. '*This is really happening.*' For once, she appreciated her father's hard presence. The strength of his grip on her arm reminded her what she was escaping. Gabriela Delmau held her other arm, her touch gentle, eyes warm – the same eyes as her son.

By the time she arrived at his side, Rafael was all she saw, even with the towering Don Fausto standing over them, booming his holy exhortations.

Rafael cast his eyes down the length of her gown, and Luisa grinned with him. The silk was exquisite – ivory threaded with gold – but the structure parodied the shape of a woman with its broad skirt and its long corset pushing her hips downwards while crushing her ribs. The only part she'd chosen herself was the sky-blue mantilla, and her mother had even ruined that by insisting on pinning it against an ornate tiara encrusted with gemstones as big as eggs – a Spinelli family heirloom.

With Don Fausto distracted by his own marvellousness, Rafael dipped his head and mouthed the words she needed to hear: '*Te quiero.*' His thumb grazed the back of her hand. She squeezed his fingers.

Jean-Pierre

Most of Jean-Pierre's acquaintances would describe him as a man of light beliefs – a free soul who charmed his way through life, seeking joy, and avoiding commitment. Only those closest knew the truth. When it came to principles, he could be as zealous as any man of the church. He wholeheartedly believed in compassion, reason, and equality – the opposite of the reactionary dogma of the Inquisition. And his contempt wasn't only ideological. It was personal. Jean-Pierre knew that in the eyes of the Inquisition, he and Rafael were as guilty as any heretic. If the wrong person ever discovered their secret, Don Fausto would see them burned at the stake together; and he would do so with such impunity he would enjoy a fine dinner after. With such motivations, it had been inevitable Jean-Pierre Vauvignarde would commit himself to the cause of Don Albrono in his struggle against the Holy Office.

He waited as planned, in the alleyway behind the prison – an inhospitable space, meant for deliveries and removals, reeking of the drains carrying waste from the complex. Alone with his thoughts, he placed a palm on the cold rough stone and looked up. And up. For the wall stretched high, impenetrable, blocking light and warmth. It left only a sliver of blue sky blinking above – apologetic, like someone who knows they're intruding but has no place else to go. How sorry, the souls rotting inside, close yet unreachable. How fared Antonio? A man he'd never met, but who had begun to occupy his thoughts. What if it were Rafael trapped inside? Unthinkable. He couldn't carry such a thing. Yet Luisa had to. What a triumph it would be if they succeeded.

But he wasn't naïve. Who had ever won an argument with the Inquisition? Its power loomed unyielding, like this stone wall.

Juan arrived with a bundle wrapped in linen.

'What is this?'

'Señor, you cannot enter the Palau dressed like that.'

He supposed he was somewhat conspicuous; a French gentleman in fine taupe breeches and waistcoat. But this, really? 'Tu es sérieux?' He wrinkled his nose, fending off a sneeze.

'Sí. Vite.' A good effort, Juan's French.

He gave himself up to the disguise: white cassock – not too clean, from the mud about its hem, and the mouldering sweat seeping from its coarse weave – scapular, hood, leather belt, rosary beads, and a woollen cap to hide his lack of a tonsure.

He followed Juan around the side of the complex, to the courtyard, and through an arched double doorway.

'His office is on the principal floor. Do not speak,' Juan said.

As if he needed telling not to reveal French-accented Spanish while disguised as a Catalan monk.

They made their way to a mezzanine overlooking an airy, light-filled atrium, then turned right, through a door, along a short corridor to another door: stained oak, carved with intertwining branches and leaves – Fausto's office. Juan produced a key from the purse at his belt. Once inside he locked them in.

Away from prying eyes, he relaxed. They had time; they knew what they were searching for; surely this would be straightforward.

Not so. They rifled through every drawer, box, shelf, and chest, taking pains to replace every document as they found it. There were transcripts of trials held in this very complex. And lists – so many lists – of heretics proved and suspected, their families and associates. Given the sheer number, Jean-Pierre doubted any man, woman, or even child could wander Barcelona free from Fausto's watchful eye. He looked for '*Delmau*'; absent. Thank God.

And there were ledgers. There must have been thousands of pages listing the values of assets seized from individuals deemed '*heretics*', '*conversos*', '*masons*', and '*sodomites*'. Easy to see how the Inquisition made its money, and looking at the opulent office, with its mahogany desk and polished floor, they'd put it to use.

They scoured and searched. Looking for a decision against Alessandro Albrono here among hundreds – maybe thousands – of records was no small task. But they finished. Jean-Pierre sat in Fausto's leather-upholstered chair, feet up on the polished mahogany desk, surveying the room. 'It's not here, is it Juan?'

'No.'

'What now?'

'He keeps some papers in his room.'

Jean-Pierre looked out of the window. The sun had dropped; the afternoon marched on. But the wedding celebrations were scheduled to last all afternoon, and the monastery was forty minutes away by carriage. They had time.

Luisa

At the Monastery de Pedralbes, the bride and groom completed the *lazo* – whereby Gabriela and Papa placed a fine lace ivory mantilla over their shoulders, followed by the long rosary, crossed in the centre in the shape of an eight, joining the pair together. Fausto muttered his blessing while the couple bowed their heads.

Next came silent reflection on the duties of religion and marriage. Luisa slid into her own thoughts: *What's Antonio doing? Is he afraid? In pain? What of Jean-Pierre and Juan? Have they found the document? What next if they have? What of Enzo? It's been two days…* Rafael reached for her hand.

The string ensemble struck the first joyous notes of a concerto by Corelli – Mama had done a fine job with the music selection – and the couple paraded down the aisle, guests spilling from their pews behind them. The chapel doors were thrown open, and a page in velvet breeches jumped to attention, cleared his throat and announced:

'Señor y Señora Rafael Delmau.'

There followed exclamations, and a whoosh of skirts as guests crowded around, taking turns to wish them felicitations, prosperity… and children. Marguerite bore her away, but the two friends had barely exchanged kisses before Mama tugged her the other way to greet her cousin.

'Luisa, you are so beautiful, I'm happy for you,' said Ambrogio. 'The Spinellis send their affection. They would have loved to be here.'

'How is Uncle Alejo?'

His smile fell. 'He ails –'

'You must meet Luisa's husband,' interrupted her mother, flapping her fan against her neck to relieve the heat blooming from all her bustling around. 'Where is he? Don't move.'

She floated off once more.

'Are you happy?' he asked.

'Sí, Rafael is a wonderful man.'

'It's been a while, hasn't it? Since that strange incident in Bellvís.' He leaned his face towards hers and whispered. 'Please don't think me indiscreet, but I thought you and… what was his name?'

'Antonio,' whispered Luisa.

'Yes. I thought you had an understanding.'

She and Ambrogio had grown up together, knew each other's childhood secrets, and had always been able to broach subjects others would find intrusive. But now words failed her. She looked down, then at his face again, then behind him. Odd to find herself wishing her mother would return.

'I can see I overstepped; forgive me.'

'No, really, I… it's too big a subject for here.'

'But you're happy?'

How to answer that? She looked away, over to where Señor Despujols guffawed at some witticism by Señorita Goytisola, who must have purchased her wig from the same peluquera as her mother. 'Sí. I'm happy. There are complications. But then life can be hard. You know that only too well, with your father so ill. How are *you*, Ambrogio?'

Instead of answering her question, he searched her face, eyes narrowed. She knew him, and she knew he'd seen through her evasion. His next words confirmed it. 'Your face is too thin.'

There it was, the Spinelli bluntness. She made a point of widening her eyes. 'Ha! You aren't looking so handsome yourself.'

But he was not so easily deflected. 'What is it?'

At any other time, she would have appreciated him, but in this moment, she could do without the questions. And thank goodness, here came Rafael. She beamed, knowing full well her smile was a little too wide.

'Ambrogio, may I introduce my husband, Rafael Delmau. Rafael, this is Ambrogio Spinelli. He's here representing his father, the Marqués de Bellvís.' She nudged his arm. 'And of course he's here because he's my favourite cousin.'

'A good recovery,' said Ambrogio. And the conversation moved on to safer topics: where did she and Rafael meet? When might they visit Bellvís?

Like any meeting at a wedding reception, theirs didn't last long. Señor Cardona dragged Ambrogio away – the silk merchant had long wanted to make a business proposition to the Spinellis – and for the first time that day, Luisa and Rafael were alone.

'Señora Delmau, how do you feel?' Rafael said.

She dropped her forehead onto his chest. 'Free. When can we leave?'

'Soon.' He lifted her hand and kissed it, for the benefit of watchers. 'Once politeness has been served.'

'And to keep Don Fausto from returning to the Palau.' Luisa looked toward the chapel.

But she didn't see him.

Nor did she spy him in the courtyard.

'Rafael, where is Don Fausto?' A hot, molten weight settled in her stomach.

He dashed into the chapel.

'Mama.' Luisa snatched at her mother as she glided past in the direction of Doña Xifres.

'Luisa. Señora Delmau does not grab people's arms.'

Rafael reappeared. 'He's not here.'

'Mama, where is Don Fausto?'

'He left. He's a busy man. Excuse me, I promised Dolores some time. We have her daughter's Presentación en Sociedad to plan.'

Rafael's face had taken on the colour of cold embers. 'Jean-Pierre –'

'– y Juan,' Luisa finished.

They walked with mounting urgency, and on the other side of the courtyard gate, having deflected well-wishers along the way, they ran. A driver dozed across the seat in the back of the foremost calesa. Rafael startled him awake by shaking his foot. The fellow scrambled up, wiped his chin with his sleeve and patted at his hair with a spit-coated palm. *Never mind your hair…* Luisa unloosed a dappled mare from the hitching post and Rafael secured the harness himself while the bewildered fellow fumbled with the traces, mumbling apologies. When he went to climb onto the driver's perch, Rafael took his arm gently and guided him down. In a flurry of dust and with a clatter of hooves, they set off, leaving the driver watching after them with his hat askew.

Juan

Juan led Jean-Pierre up a narrow staircase to Don Fausto's quarters. This particular staircase did not officially belong to his master, but as nobody else had rooms nearby, it might as well have been a private wing. Please, God, may Gregor never have to climb these steps.

It was the work of a moment to unlock the door and push it open. Dread pressed his chest, and at first his legs locked, refusing him entry. Then Jean-Pierre's hand landed warm on his shoulder. The touch propelled him on. 'It's dark, I'll light some candles – he will expect that in any case.'

Juan set about the task, using a taper to catch a flame from the wall sconce in the stairwell outside. He talked as he worked. 'He keeps some private documents in the bureau; the key is underneath that tankard. There is a chest in the foot-space. After that… there is nowhere else.'

They got to work. Quiet but for papers rustling, drawers sliding, and every now and again a '*hmm*' or disappointed sigh.

Finally, Jean-Pierre, rummaging through the chest, whistled through his teeth. 'Letters addressed to Luisa Navas.'

Juan peered over his shoulder. 'Sí. I did not realise there were so many.'

'You knew? Why would he have these?'

'The Inquisition intercepts letters of persons under suspicion.'

'Luisa is under suspicion?'

'Or the person writing to her.'

Jean-Pierre turned one over; the seal had been broken, so he opened it. 'It is from Antonio.'

Juan's skin tightened. 'Oh. I didn't –'

Jean-Pierre started to shove the letters into his satchel, but fear bade Juan snatch at his sleeve. 'Leave some from the top. Or he'll know.'

The Frenchman opened his mouth, then closed it and nodded. He left a handful and took the rest.

They did not find the deed; not in the drawer nor in the chest. Perhaps God never intended them to. 'There is nothing else to be done.' Juan shrugged.

'I *feel* it is here. Are you sure there's nowhere else? Might he have hidden it behind one of these?' Jean-Pierre started slipping books out from a shelf, shaking out their pages, looking underneath.

'I regularly dust those; there's nothing there.'

Jean-Pierre regarded the bookcase. And his face lit up.

'What?'

'That bookcase, those four carved scrolls, it is identical to Rafael's.'

'Perhaps a local furniture-maker. We should go.'

'Oui, perhaps a local, who specialises in –' He started to press the centre of each scroll.

'What are you doing?'

'If there is nothing *in* the bookcase, perhaps we should look –'

Juan jumped back as the bookcase shifted. At first, it seemed to be falling, and panic clutched his chest. But no, it swung vertically, about some hidden hinge.

'– *behind* the bookcase.' Jean-Pierre peered into the dark. 'A hidden space. What have we here?'

Although the discovery excited him, a worm of fear had awakened in the pit of Juan's stomach. If he had to give it a name, it would be *Presagio*. Foreboding. In the courtyard below, a steady flow of people moved across the square, leaving and arriving, all going about their business: nobles, clerics and officials. Two guards crossed together; one barked a laugh and slapped the other on the shoulder.

'Voila!' Jean-Pierre produced two small books, and a wrapped scroll.

He barely spared them a glance. The worm had divided and multiplied; his guts writhed. 'Please. Put them in your bag and let us leave.'

Jean-Pierre must have caught his tone, because his smile dropped, and he moved fast. Too late.

He strode across the courtyard: Don Fausto. Face set, purpose weighing his brow. Everyone out there averted their eyes; they all knew his unpredictable temperament went everywhere with him.

Juan's throat constricted, so when he spoke it was a yelp. 'He comes!'

Jean-Pierre jolted into action, lunging against the open bookshelf. It didn't move. Wouldn't. Juan threw himself beside him, shoulder to wood. Together they grunted and shoved. Still nothing. The harder they tried, the more it resisted.

'Wait, wait, Juan, espera.' Jean-Pierre exhaled, long and slow.

Juan tried to do the same, but his breath came too sharp, too fast. He scrambled to the doorway and peered down the stairs. 'Get *out*. You cannot be here.'

It was part of its genius that the bookshelf only yielded to calm. Jean-Pierre pressed its outer edge; it glided into place and settled with a click. He stepped to the door.

'Go *up* not down, hide behind the bend, I will detain him, then you may slip past.'

The last compassionate touch Juan ever felt was that of Jean-Pierre, squeezing his arm.

As the Frenchman's footsteps faded, the Inquisitor's grew loud. Juan ducked back into the chamber, frantic; nothing must be out of place. He smoothed the bedcover. The door creaked open.

'Juan. You are a little early today.'

'I did not know what time to expect you; I wanted to make sure I had your room prepared.' A poor excuse, but all he had.

'You're flushed.'

'I have been rushing, Su Excelencia. How was the wedding?'

'A beautiful occasion, Juan. A handsome couple. I admit I'm a little proud. I had a hand in the match, after all.'

'I am sure Señorita Navas will always be grateful to you.'

'Señora Delmau, now.'

'Sí.' Juan caught something on the floor at the edge of his sight. A folded paper. They must have dropped one of the letters. He moved, blocking it.

'It is warm in here, have we not agreed you would open the window when you light the candles?'

'I was getting to it.' Juan tried to smile, a rare thing in the presence of Don Fausto.

'Well?'

He couldn't leave his spot in front of the incriminating paper. He thought he might vomit.

'You really do not seem well, Juan. I'll do it.'

Don Fausto's step to the window gave Juan a moment to pick up the letter, but no more. He tucked his hands behind his back just as his master turned back.

If Juan thought Don Fausto wouldn't notice the movement, he misjudged. The Inquisidor's eyes narrowed, looked down Juan's arms, then slid back to his face. 'What have you got behind your back?'

'Su Excelencia, I…' Juan's voice faltered; he swallowed.

'Show me.' He held out his hand. 'Have you been prying?'

Juan did not move. His master had seen through him, had probably suspected him since he'd found him here so early. Don Fausto grabbed his arm and tugged. Juan pulled away; an instinct, no more – nobody resisted the Inquisidor. It was not much of a struggle, and one Juan was about to concede in any case. He'd already begun to formulate his explanation.

But Fausto yanked his arm just a little too hard. Juan lost his balance. As he stumbled, he stretched out his free hand to grab something, anything. A tall candlestick. It teetered. For a moment it seemed to right itself: a taunt – just to show it could, if it wanted.

It didn't want. With infinite slowness, it set off on its graceful, illuminated arc.

It fell against the ancient tapestry stretched across a wall – an exquisite depiction of Christ's sermon on the mount.

Leached of moisture, caked with years of dust, the hanging caught flame with a *whoomp.*

In one moment, fire spilled across its length, and in the next, it surrounded the hill upon which Jesus stood. The Messiah addressed a sea of fire, then in a blink the furnace consumed him too. Flames leapt, licking at the ceiling. A tongue of fire tested the desk, liked it and returned for more.

Juan's fascination snapped into mortal compulsion. Escape.

Master before servant, the Inquisidor reached the door between heartbeats. Gleaming eyes above a slack-mouthed grimace, a creaking lurch of oak blurred into a sweep of black robes, vanishing into the shadows beyond. Juan lunged for the same safety, but his palms struck solid wood, an engraved lamb, the symbol of mercy. A click. Soft. Deadly. He was locked in.

Hell unrolled incandescent red and amber across the ceiling. Papers on the bureau crackled and curled in merry yellow flames. Their glowing embers whirled into the breeze from the window, lifting, spinning, and smouldering where they landed – moths of fire nibbling at the bedspread, their bites trailing smoke that thickened into roiling columns.

Heat tightened his skin, wringing sweat from every pore, transforming his cassock into dragging weight. He sucked in a breath. A mistake. Coughing, gagging, doubled over – *smother it* – he groped for the bedspread; pressed his face into it; dragging air through the cloth. Then with handfuls of the material in his fists, he summoned the Lord's strength and billowed it out before him.

The fire leapt with the joy of release.

No longer a bedcover, but a wall of flame. Bed, drapes, ceiling, an inferno. Smoke coated his mouth and airways, tainted his sweat and tears. Each inhale flayed a new track; each exhale scored deeper. His lungs screamed against their own collapse. *One breath, just one clean breath…* the window.

He slid along the wall towards sunlight. Purity against incandescence. Heaven against hell. The window receded as the edges of his vision faded and compressed. The floorboards met his knees and hands, their melting polish stripping his palms. He hauled thick yet scant air into his throat '*Sancta Mater, ne me deseras.*' One trembling arm after another, he dragged himself to the window, bathing in its light. '*Ego sum lux,*' saith the Lord. He levered himself up against the ledge.

Oh, the relief. Sweet, clean air. He coughed, breathed, coughed again. His eyes stung, his throat caught, his lungs swelled. He came back to life. With life came understanding, and pain. Such pain.

Flames climbed the fabric of his cassock. White, black, transforming to orange, red, yellow and bright… so bright. His eyes hurt, his skin blistered, he beat with his arms and watched in horror as they charred, swelled, split and ignited. His own hands blackening claws before his eyes. '*Jesu miserere mei.*' This was the damnation Don Fausto had warned him about. He had taken the Inquisidor's sins upon his body, and now he took his punishment.

His scream was cut off when his scorched throat could no longer carry his voice. With no other thought than to escape hell, Juan launched himself bodily at the window. Glass splintered, lacerating burned flesh. He breathed again for just a second and it did nothing to relieve his agony. That only ended when he met the slabs of the courtyard. Black.

Jean-Pierre

Nothing out of the ordinary. Not as far as Jean-Pierre was aware. Though he waited where Juan sent him – beyond the turn in the staircase, above and out of sight of the door – nothing gave him cause to think they'd been exposed. All was normal: footsteps, the rattle of the doorknob, *Juan, you are a little early today*, and the door clicked shut.

Anyway, what could Fausto possibly suspect? And if the document in his satchel was what he hoped, then they had achieved their aim. Nevertheless, and just to be certain, he lingered on the stairs: a muffled voice – something about the wedding – polite chat.

They had done it. With his usual light tread, he headed down the stairs, out onto the mezzanine.

'You!'

He froze mid-stride. A man in dark robes, bony face, thick silver hair watched from the opposite corner. He had the imperious voice, stance, and clean starched robes of a cleric of status. Jean-Pierre bowed his head; a hand crept to his hood.

'Is that how a friar conducts himself, running like a child after a ball?'

What *did* friars do? Jean-Pierre had seen enough of them – childhood school and endless obligatory church services. Familiar enough, they were, that he'd have thought he knew how they moved, and how they should reply to a clear reprimand. But now, tested, he feared any response would seem like mockery. All he could think of was to bow his head as low as it would go and clasp his hands as if praying. So that's what he did.

The cleric sighed. 'Silence is it? I suppose there's that. You might think upon a penance whilst you're meditating.' A pause. 'No supper.'

Jean-Pierre lowered his head further. Supplication he could manage, though he longed to flip the fellow's zucchetta off his head into the atrium below.

Silence. He studied the floor. The toe of his boot poked from under the hem of his robe; he shifted to cover it. Should he wait to be dismissed? What *did* friars do? Breathe. *In… un … deux. Out… un … deux.*

'I have an errand for you, a letter for the postmaster.'

He couldn't incline his head any further, so he lifted it, just enough to observe the fellow from under his lashes. The man beckoned, so he set off after him, dread weighting every step.

He needn't have worried. He followed the vicar-priest-cleric – whatever and whoever he was – into a corridor, and an office almost as fine as Fausto's. The man handed him a sealed document. Jean-Pierre slipped it into his satchel, gave him a deep submissive nod – they seemed to do the trick – and was dismissed without another glance.

He descended the final flight of stairs with slow contemplative steps, just in case, and emerged into golden sunlight.

He'd done it. *They'd* done it. He inhaled clean air, blew out a long slow breath and shook out his arms.

As he crossed the courtyard, head down, inconspicuous, a hellish racket stopped him in his tracks.

For the rest of his life, whenever he looked back, he'd remember a premonition: a fraction of the moment before, when the air contracted and blood stopped moving in his veins. At the same time, his future self would know that to be a contrivance, his way of affording gravity to the event. Because the truth is that life's worst moments flow at us from within banality: a scurrying clerk, a chapel bell, a steaming pile of fresh-dropped horse manure, a dropped sheaf of papers, sunlight, a waft of roasting almonds, a couple arguing, a cat hawking up a fur-ball, a splintering crash, a scream. And the world is forever altered. Scarred.

Like everyone else in the square, he turned to face the sound. But whereas everyone else wondered what had shattered the hazy afternoon peace, Jean-Pierre knew.

In Venice, he had once seen a clever magic lantern. On the outside, only a box of wood and brass, but inside, an oil-carrying wick and a curved mirror projected light onto glass slides painted with images. This lantern could layer several slides, creating an illusion of movement, clear yet otherworldly. He processed the trauma of Juan's death in the same way – a series of disjointed images projected through that magic lantern's eye: The monk at the broken window, anguished face framed in fire. The flames themselves, flickering and hungry, reaching outwards. Black smoke trailing skyward. The falling angel engulfed in fire. Dozens of people, emerging from nowhere, beating out flames. And finally, a charred body, shattered against the stone.

Jean-Pierre stepped forward, already knowing but compelled to acknowledge. The gathered onlookers parted for him – a fellow friar. He squatted and looked into the sightless eyes of the boy he'd started to think of as a friend. Blisters marred Juan's face; his lips had all but burned away; as for his ruined torso…

Jean-Pierre covered his own face with an arm to block a smell both familiar and corrupt. He staggered backwards. His thoughts flowed clear, but his body reeled. People crowded in once more, guards barked orders.

And here came Fausto.

He knew him. By the way people parted before him, bowing their heads. By the way he approached – aloof, above acknowledging them. He knew him before he spoke. And when he did, he knew him for his lies.

'But this is my servant.' He looked up. 'That is my room. A fire? How can it be?'

His gaze swept the crowd as he spoke. It landed on Jean-Pierre, lingered briefly, and moved on.

With nothing more to be done, Jean-Pierre turned and walked away.

Perhaps the smoke had affected his vision. It looked like Rafael and Luisa on a calesa approaching the entrance to the square.

But there was nothing wrong with his eyesight. As if the day could become any more unreal, there they were in their wedding finery, driving towards him.

A High Price

Incongruous though he was against the crowds flocking into the square, Luisa hardly noticed the monk walking in the opposite direction – away. Too busy craning her neck towards the source of the rising black plume, she didn't notice when the monk shifted direction, and ran towards their vehicle. She did notice when he vaulted into the back. The wheels lurched, her seat tilted, and she grabbed Rafael's arm.

As for the monk – Jean-Pierre – he uttered a single word. 'Va.' *Go.*

Her husband didn't need to be told twice. He steered the mare into a sharp turn, and the three of them headed for home, their home.

'Where is Juan?' Luisa turned to the Frenchman. His eyes were wide and bottomless, staring in the direction of the square. His face was grey.

'Il est mort.' A whisper so faint she might have misheard. But then Jean-Pierre's face crumpled, and her stomach rolled.

'What did he say?' asked Rafael. 'Where is Juan?'

'I think he said he's dead,' replied Luisa.

She couldn't bring herself to ask more. Jean-Pierre watched the passing streets, but she doubted he saw them. His hands trembled in his lap.

By the time they arrived at the house on Carrer Ample, Jean-Pierre had composed himself enough to remove his disguise, but in the privacy of Rafael's office, he collapsed. He sank into a seat, running his hands through his hair, his legs juddering so hard his feet tapped a fast rhythm on the hardwood floor.

Juan. *Dios mío.*

Luisa did the only useful thing she could manage, and poured a brandy.

Jean-Pierre snatched at it; threw it back. 'I should not have left him. I listened at the door. It was quiet. They were talking – just *talking*.'

'Did Fausto attack him?' Rafael asked.

'Sais pas, from the courtyard I heard a crash. Flames. He fell from the window. Burning. Burned. Excuse me.' He lowered his head between his knees, dragging in one breath after another.

Luisa pressed her hands to her eyes to block out the image.

'Oh,' Rafael said, sinking onto the edge of a seat. 'A boy.'

'We were supposed to detain Fausto,' Luisa said. To her own ears, her voice sounded tight and forced.

'My fault.' Rafael said.

'Juan begged me to move faster,' Jean-Pierre said. 'What kind of man am I to leave him to cover my escape?'

'You said all was quiet,' Rafael said. 'How were you to know?'

'We failed him,' Luisa whispered.

The colours of the room: drapes, wallpaper, even the flowers in the vase on the window-ledge – all bled into grey.

Jean-Pierre retrieved his satchel from where he'd thrown it atop the heap of monk's clothing. 'This is what cost Juan his life.' He pulled out the wrapped scroll and the two ledgers.

With gentle fingers, Rafael opened the scroll.

Such a small document, such a high price.

Yellow and mottled it was, slightly swollen, and soft. But the words lay neat and clear:

> *In Nomine Patris, et Filii, et Spiritus Sancti,*
> *We, the Inquisitors of the Holy Office, find:*
> *Alessandro Albrono, born of Genoa*

guilty of manifest heresy.
We excommunicate and anathematise
Alessandro Albrono
thereby separating him from the communion of the faithful.
Let all true Christians shun his name, for he has been cut off from our Holy Mother Church.
Given on the 4th day of the month of March, in the year of our Lord 1704.
Vidal Marin del Campo,
Inquisidor General del Santo Oficio de la Inquisición.

'Is this the same that Fausto showed you in Bellvís?' Rafael asked.

Luisa nodded. 'Enzo would verify it. My cousin Ambrogio is here in town; he would recognise it too.'

'And these two books are ledgers, records of financial transactions.' Jean-Pierre handed them to Luisa.

She opened one, blowing away dust. She didn't recognise the creditor and debtor, and the dates spanned over two decades. She opened the second book and leafed quickly through it. The last page snagged at her.

'Wait…' A coincidence?

'Do you see something?' Rafael asked.

'Maybe.' Luisa closed the books. 'There's something I need to check. Where's Enzo?'

'I haven't seen him since the day before last,' Rafael said. 'Shall I send Señor Alves to El Marqués to ask after him?'

'Sí. We need his help,' Luisa said.

Rafael stepped out, leaving her with Jean-Pierre. He leaned back against the desk, staring at the floor.

She considered reaching for him, but something held her back. Instead, she fumbled for words to fill the void, to make sense of loss.

'Juan's death has to mean something.'

His head snapped up. 'Spare me your trite sentiment, Luisa.'

She flinched. That glare.

'I only meant –'

He cut her off. 'You reach for cheap words to soothe yourself. Show some respect. Stay with the pain.'

He swung his head away, mouth tight, eyes closed, as though he couldn't bear to look at her, and that, as much as what he'd said, struck clean through her.

But what hurt most was that he was right; that burned in her chest as though she'd swallowed hot stones.

Jean-Pierre's voice cut through her misery. 'Forgive me. Rafael tells me *mon coeur est trop ouvert.* I wear my heart outside.' His expression had softened to concern.

Concern she didn't want. She gave him a curt nod. 'You're right. Stay with the pain.' She swallowed. 'It's just that it hurts so much.'

Jean-Pierre nodded. 'Oui.'

Silence settled; not awkward, but not entirely welcome either. Then he jolted and straightened.

'Luisa. You said… you told me Antonio abandoned you; why do you think that?'

Sometimes, Luisa reflected, talking to Jean-Pierre was like riding a horse too fast; one must grip the reins and go with each swerve or become unseated.

'Did Rafael ever ignore a letter from you? Did he leave you in silence?' she asked.

'Non,' he said. 'He might be busy, distracted, or travelling… but always a letter will come in the end.' He smiled. 'Often, he writes nonsense, and he's no poet. But he writes and I reply.'

'There we are then,' she said.

'Here we are then,' he replied.

Jean-Pierre reached for his satchel, hesitated – as if bracing himself – then, without a word, he tipped its contents onto the desk.

Letters. They spilled out, cascading in a haphazard heap, tumbling onto the polished surface and over each other. Dozens.

Luisa reached for one. The seal had been broken, and she unfolded it, skimming the words within.

Amore mio… Suyo en cuerpo y alma. Yours in body and soul.

She heard him, as if he stood there beside her. She reached for the edge of the table to steady herself but missed.

Arms caught her, traces of smoke, Jean-Pierre.

'Luisa?' Rafael's voice, far away.

What had she done?

The letter slipped from her fingers; her legs crumpled; she sank – seeking emptiness, finding only cold unyielding floor.

To Presume to Question

Barcelona was nothing like Valencia. In Valencia, Lorenzo enjoyed autonomy as a respected official; here, he required Don Fausto's permission for every step. He worked relentlessly on the Albrono case. He had to. A mistake, a slip, a missing or incomplete record, could lead to all manner of diplomatic complications; the prisoner was an Albrono after all. Yet the First Inquisidor complained at every effort. Don Fausto might be confident in his own authority, but without proper procedure, the foundations of the case would crumble.

For instance, the new Calification: Fausto had made the arrangements as agreed; nominated two clerics. But, according to Friar Augustin, they'd signed off the change without reading it, then headed out to lunch.

It would have to do. The third audience was tomorrow.

Fingernails tapped the door; it must be Gregor – the novice friar Don Fausto had assigned to him. Nobody else had such a pointless knock. The boy grieved because his brother had died two days ago. A terrible business – the word was he knocked over a candle while cleaning Don Fausto's room.

'Enter.'

The door opened a crack, then another.

'Come in, I won't bite.'

'A request for an audience, Doctor Balleza.'

'You know I require prior notice.'

The boy looked mortified. 'Sí, they made the appointment yesterday. I forgot to note it in your book.'

More Barcelona ineptness. The sooner Lorenzo got back to Valencia, the better.

'Who is it?' Not that lawyer again – what was his name? Gallo. How many times must he explain? The prisoner didn't want him.

'Don Delmau and his wife.'

'Oh?' He'd never heard of them.

'Shall I show them in?'

'Sí.' He had an hour to spare. Besides, curiosity tugged at him. Apart from Señor Gallo, no civilian had asked to see him in all the weeks he'd been here.

Five minutes later, Lorenzo sat opposite a beautiful young woman and her husband. Affluent, they were, judging by the cut of their clothes. The man insisted on being called Rafael. Most inappropriate. Lorenzo introduced himself as Doctor Balleza.

'How may I be of assistance? I must inform you I am only a visiting confessor so if you have a denunciation, you must register it with the Tribunal Secretary – Don Joseph de Vallera. His office is two doors down.'

'Oh, no,' said Delmau, 'we're aware you are concerned with the Albrono case.'

'That's why we're here,' said his wife.

Such patience – Delmau did not seem to mind his wife finishing his sentence for him. And what interest could this apparently noble couple possibly have in the prisoner languishing in the cells next door?

'Go on,' he said.

'It's sensitive.' Delmau glanced at his wife.

'What you say in here can be just between us, Don Delmau. Please speak freely.'

'It concerns Don Fausto.' Delmau swallowed.

He might well be nervous – introducing the name of probably the most powerful man in the city. Lorenzo waited, giving him space to go on.

'I'm sure he's a noble and godly man, my wife is close to him, has grown up knowing him –' He looked at Señora Delmau. 'However, in this case, he's too close to be impartial. He has a personal interest.'

Sincerity was written all over his face. Right or wrong, Delmau believed his own words.

'I can assure you, Don Delmau, if he had a *personal interest*, Don Fausto would have declared it and recused himself. We have procedures for that very circumstance.'

'I'm sure you do. And his failure to recuse himself makes me fear for a just outcome.' Delmau leaned forward. 'Because there is no question his judgement is compromised.'

Lorenzo straightened his fingers on his chair arms. 'You go too far.' But even as he spoke, the prisoner's own voice echoed in his mind. *Tell me, Doctor Balleza, does it strike you Don Fausto has an unseemly enthusiasm to see me damaged?*

Delmau watched him, silent.

'Suppose you tell me the nature of this personal interest,' said Lorenzo.

What followed was fantastical. A story about an Albrono family claim on a debt owed by the Marqués de Bellvís. Don Fausto having a hand in crushing the claim, using a conviction for heresy against the prisoner's grandfather – one that might have been fraudulent.

Yet even as one chamber of his mind dismissed the tale, Albrono's words echoed in another. *'I am not the first of my family to be pronounced a heretic in Spain.'*

'Where is this deed of excommunication?'

Lorenzo had not expected Delmau to have the document with him, so he flinched when the man handed him a wrapped scroll. He resisted his mounting urgency, and opened it with slow, careful movements.

'Why would Don Fausto have intervened?' Lorenzo scarcely believed he indulged the story, but his profession required him to be curious.

'Difficult to say,' said Señora Delmau. 'The document was first used to deflect a claim brought to my grandfather by Girolamo Albrono. At the time, my father and Don Fausto were friends. My father was thanked by being made Protector until Alejo came of age. Quite how Don Fausto was rewarded we don't know, but I have noticed some financial anomalies in my family's accounts.'

Santa María, Madre de Dios. If this woman was as loyal to her husband as she was to her father, Lorenzo pitied the poor man sitting opposite him. He directed his question at Delmau. 'Why do you believe the deed to have been falsified?'

'Antonio went to Seville, where Don Fausto said the trial was held in seventeen hundred four. He stayed with Luigi's granddaughter – his cousin – Lucretia. She knew nothing of a heresy charge against her grandfather. She had a substantial inheritance through him.' Rafael shrugged. 'Can you make sense of that? Because I cannot.'

Lorenzo opened the document. He read each line, studied the font, the ink, the paper and the remnants of the seal. 'It seems to be genuine. I have seen many of these documents.' He rolled it up and placed it on top of its linen wrapping on his desk. 'More likely the Albronos found a loophole in the inheritance rule; that happens, unfortunately.'

Señora Delmau slumped a little.

'How did you come by this document?' asked Lorenzo

The couple exchanged a look. There was certainly a story here. It was Señora Delmau that answered. 'The friar who died, Juan, he gave it to us. He found it in Don Fausto's room.' She twisted her fingers as she spoke, Lorenzo knew a lie when he saw it.

Sure enough, Delmau, steered the conversation away. 'Have you noticed Don Fausto's treatment of the prisoner is unduly harsh? Was his eagerness to bring the case under his jurisdiction a little unseemly? What about his insistence on it being a *de vehementi* offence?'

Lorenzo jerked back in his seat. 'Who told you these things?'

'The same monk,' Delmau said. 'He saw it, why cannot you?'

Lorenzo was not about to be lectured on how to do his job by a couple of civilians. 'It is obvious someone has been spying on the case and reporting to you. It seems to me it is *you* who has a personal interest.' He shook his head. 'To question the objectivity of the Holy Office is a serious matter. You're fortunate; I promised to keep this conversation inside this room. I am a man of my word, so leave now, and we will say no more on this matter.'

Lorenzo stood. End of meeting. Don Delmau and his presumptuous wife gaped at each other, but rose too. He moved to bustle them along, but Señora Delmau placed a hand on his arm.

'Please think about what we've told you. If the heresy charge existed, surely the Seville Tribunal would confirm it. Don Fausto seems to be the only one with a copy of the decree. He produced it in Bellvís. In front of witnesses. Come to our house, meet with some of them. Give us the opportunity to explain what we know.'

He searched her face – she believed every word of this story. 'Señora Delmau, for your own sake, I advise you not to question the Holy Office of the Inquisition.' He shrugged her hand away. What obsessed her so? Her husband needed to check her. Good luck to him.

'Doctor Balleza,' said Delmau. 'We'll wait for you at our residence on Carrer Ample, at the hour of six, tomorrow evening. We will share what we know, without presumption or accusation. I ask only you weigh the evidence.'

A logical suggestion, man to man. Perhaps he didn't understand the dangerous waters into which he steered.

'I'll think on it,' Lorenzo replied. 'Otherwise, I implore you, for the sake of your new marriage, the lives you have ahead of you, drop this matter.'

After they had gone, he folded himself into the seat behind his desk. He'd seen it too many times to count – well-meaning friends grasping for influence, making final, futile attempts to alter the course of justice. It must be hard, learning someone close has fallen on the wrong side of the faith. Heresy was a selfish master; it trampled all in its path. He rubbed the bridge of his nose and closed his eyes.

A mistake, for now the prisoner appeared behind his eyelids, crouched at the end of his cot, hands draped over his knees, head tipped back, eyes narrowed – either bored or resigned. There was something unsettling about him, a certain composure that bordered on defiance, not even counting the time he had reared up at him over Catalina.

And there was another thing: how did he know of her case? He seemed to possess information he should not. And in that reaction – misguided though it was – there was a certain integrity. Heretic he may be, but Lorenzo couldn't imagine him lying. An honest heretic. Lorenzo laughed quietly, but there was no humour in it.

Tell me, Doctor Balleza, does it strike you Don Fausto has an unseemly enthusiasm to see me damaged? How did he even know Don Fausto?

What was he doing? entertaining fanciful theories. Now. So close to the end. Don Albrono was not the first heretic to be brought to justice, nor would he be the last. This case would soon be over and he could get back to normality.

The rolled-up document still lay on the desk. In their emotional state, the Delmaus must have forgotten it. No matter, he would have it delivered.

'Gregor!'

The boy must have been right outside, for he appeared in an instant, closing the door behind him with a careful click. His eyes were rimmed pink. *Give him some credit*, thought Lorenzo; he grieved but asked for nothing.

'What can I do for you, Doctor?'

Balleza reached for the scroll, but didn't take it. Instead, he dropped his hand onto the table. 'Gregor, I have a task for you, but it must be carried out in absolute secrecy. Can I trust you?'

The Wager

Jaume Soler yanked at his drawers and tightened the string of his breeches around his waist for the third time since arriving on duty. He was getting paunchy. He'd always been a big man, and his job didn't demand enough of him to keep muscle from softening to flab.

He worked shifts in the gloom of the prison corridors. Ironic considering his name. Nine years he'd done this. Nine years of feeding prisoners, clearing their piss and shit, dragging them to justice – whatever form that took – and now and again hauling out their bodies.

This was not the future he'd envisaged as a child growing up. Born in Llorac, a hamlet on the borders of Tarragona, his father had been a farmhand, and he'd have followed suit. It wouldn't have been a bad life; sun on his back, clean dirt under his nails, perhaps a wife, children… But a bad harvest followed by a fire had put his father out of work, and they'd sent Jaume off to Barcelona. An excited youth with naïve expectations, waved off by parents glad of one less mouth to feed.

He'd not been fussy about how he earned his living – hauling cargo at the docks or carcasses at the slaughterhouse; it was all the same. Being a prison guard was easier money. In return for keeping the Inquisition's secrets and turning a blind eye, he earned twice what his best job had paid – more than enough to meet his needs, which were few. A roof over his head, good food in his belly, and enough left over to soak his liver in wine. Now and again, he called upon his landlady, Merce, a widow. For a scarf or a compliment, she would see to his other appetites.

He had a talent for his work. The trick, he found, was to think of prisoners as slabs of meat from his days at the abattoir. Some guards engaged; more fool them, they never lasted. Tuesday evening, he'd encountered an ex-colleague, Gaspar, propping up a doorway, steeped in liquor and his own ordure. At first, Jaume had not recognised the man grasping his sleeve, not until he spoke. Even then, it had taken a moment to place the roughened voice:

'You think you're just following orders?'

Like a dog wanting play, Gaspar wouldn't let go when Jaume shook his arm. He had to stop and peel jagged nails from his sleeve.

'You've a reckoning coming,' Gaspar had said.

He'd left him there, festering. That's where thinking got you. That would never be Jaume Soler. The prisoners were none of his concern; their offences against God and King were between them and their judges.

And the prisoner in cell eight must really have offended. For three days ago, just as he was arriving for his shift, his boss, Ramon, had called him and his three colleagues aside to share the latest from *Upstairs.*

'Per order of the Tribunal, there will be no visits to eight until instructed otherwise.'

'What about water?' asked Benet, his day-shift partner.

Fair question, Jaume thought. Withholding food was routine, but water… best clear up any misunderstanding. This prisoner had danced on the edge of death once already.

'No food. No water. No contact. Entiendo?' Ramon growled.

'You think you're just following orders?' Jaume snuffed out Gaspar's voice in his head, and nodded.

Benet nodded too, as did Esteve and Josep, the night crew.

'Every quarter-hour, strike the door hard three times.'

Josep opened his mouth but snapped it shut when Ramon turned a frown on him. A complaint from the night shift was predictable; their only perk was grabbing an illicit nap.

All four watched Ramon's back as he retreated into the shadows, waiting for his footsteps to fade into silence.

Benet turned wide eyes towards Jaume. 'Why do you suppose…?'

'No idea.' Jaume cut him off. 'Not our business.'

'Mierda,' grumbled Josep.

'Every quarter-hour.' Esteve shook his head.

Benet eyed the door of cell eight, tracking its studded iron bands. Jaume knew what was coming. Sure enough, when Benet turned back, his eyes were gleaming. 'What do you think?' he asked. 'One night, two days?' He answered his own question with a single nod. 'Sí. Tomorrow night.'

They had few enough diversions in this place; betting was one of them, and Jaume held the prison record for this game – guessing how long it would be before a prisoner began banging the door and pleading. It didn't have to be pleading. Shouting or whimpering also counted; the point was *submission.*

'He's already on quarter rations,' said Esteve, lips pursed, 'by tonight. One day.'

Josep eyed Benet, then Esteve. 'Ex-military. He will not fold today. No.' He squinted. 'But he has collapsed once already… this time tomorrow.' He folded his arms. 'Sí. A day and a night.'

Jaume mulled. This one was strong. Not in body; that would be impossible after a few weeks in here. But he had character. He'd never had a prisoner ask his name before, nor thank him for changing his soil bucket. Once, despite Jaume's best efforts, the prisoner had caught his eye, almost had him nodding a greeting, as if they were in a tavern about to share a jug of pansal wine.

He'd never seen him plead. Not when they stopped his food, not even that day he'd collapsed. Oh, he'd made all sorts of sounds

– laughing, groaning, rambling – but not the kind of grovelling that meant victory for *Upstairs*.

And that time he'd lunged at the confessor from Valencia... Jaume had punched him to the ground, where he'd sat, licking blood from his lip, glaring. Secretly though... well, the confessor was a pompous prick; he could think of worse things than letting the prisoner have a second swing.

No, this one would take a while. 'Two days. Two nights.' He nodded, yes, it sounded right. He would crumble. That was never in question. Not with Inquisition prisoners. And yet... a shame.

No. He shook off the thought. *Slabs of meat.*

Benet spat into his palm. 'One real?'

Jaume looked at the door, then spat into his own. 'Make it two.'

They took turns spitting and shaking, then Josep and Esteve headed out into the welcoming sun.

Well, three days and three nights had come and gone, and all four jailers had lost the bet. There had not been the faintest sound from number eight. Not so much as a groan.

'He's either dead or close to it.' Benet chuckled.

Jaume's mouth felt grainy. He spat on the floor.

When his two days, two nights had passed, Jaume had pressed his ear to the keyhole and heard only the rushing of his own heartbeat in his ears. That had been yesterday. Today, still nothing.

Now they had three hours to clean him up and rouse him, for their orders were to make sure he was fit for trial. Fit to be found guilty more like. *Upstairs* liked them this way. Defendants too weak to defend themselves.

Jaume pulled his scarf over his mouth and nose, gesturing for Benet to do the same. He selected the key – smooth from use, cold in his fingers – and slotted it into the lock.

His throat closed. He listened again, willing number eight to make a sound, any sound. The prisoner's silence had a substance all of its own.

He twisted the key.

A silence that taunted.

Twisted again.

He glanced over his shoulder. Benet watched him, wide-eyed over his scarf.

Twist. The lock gave way, grinding out its protest.

His chest tightened. He squared his shoulders.

Stepped inside.

Saw.

Third Audience

Unusually for Lorenzo, he'd not slept. It was the visit from the Delmaus that had done it. Planting doubts when all he wanted was to finish and go home. He glanced at Don Fausto, seated to his left at the head of the table. Never had he seen a man with such zeal for his duties. Then again, was it zeal?

Joseu was speaking – to him. 'Is he fit to stand trial?'

'Sí.' Lorenzo said. He had examined him four days ago. 'Stable since he recovered from his collapse.'

'Admit the defendant.'

Lorenzo was watching Don Fausto as the rasping of chains against stone grew louder, so the first hint he had that something was awry was when Manuel and Boxo both jerked upright in the corner of his vision. He turned to see what they saw. And his breath left his lungs.

A wraith, a spectre, a fragment of a man. Two guards carried him by his armpits; his feet floated over the floor; his head flopped down onto his chest.

'Is he conscious?' asked Manuel.

By way of reply, one of the guards gripped the prisoner by his hair and yanked his head up – a rag doll in the hands of a careless child.

Conscious, yes, barely. Those eyes – sunk deep – shifted between the men at the table, then beyond them to the walls. Sharp bones, deep shadows, sick yellow pallor, cracks around the mouth, dried blood against ash-toned lips. He licked his own. A reflex.

'A chair,' said Fausto.

Apparently, a chair is permissible now, thought Lorenzo.

The defendant was dumped onto a wooden seat and immediately sank sideways. He righted himself with a jolt. His hair clung to his forehead, his camisa to his skin – to the valleys between his ribs. The guards must have doused him.

Don Albrono gripped the edge of the table, set his jaw and lifted his head to face his accusers.

Or rather, he faced the jug on the table. Fixated on it.

Friar Augustin poured a mug of water and walked the length of the table to where Albrono slumped. He even held it to his lips. Lorenzo couldn't tear his eyes from the unprecedented performance.

'I suppose a trial cannot proceed if a defendant cannot speak,' said Fausto, a moment of reasonableness, undone by sarcasm. 'Are we finished pandering to the prisoner now? Or would somebody like to bring him a cushion?'

Albrono took the cup and placed it on the table, settling a steady gaze on Don Fausto. He nodded as if to say, *'I am ready.'*

With a glance at the Primer Inquisidor, Joseu stood and opened proceedings.

'Do you remember anything relating to this affair, which you are bound to divulge according to your oath?'

'No.' Albrono's voice was gravelly, as if dragged from a river bed. He directed his answer at Joseu, crossing his arms over his chest, hunching into himself for warmth, or to stay his trembles.

'In the name of God our Lord and his glorious and blessed Mother, our Lady the Virgin Mary, you have been exhorted to bethink yourself and confess the whole truth in relation to this matter. So that justice may be executed with brevity and mercy. Have you considered this exhortation?'

'I don't know what else to say.' The defendant sank in his seat; his eyelids drooped. Was he about to sleep?

'In that case, I submit the case to Licentiate Don Fausto de Alenya, Inquisidor Fiscal of this Holy Office, so the accusation may be read in keeping with the Calification. Let the defendant be provided with a copy.'

Albrono reached for his water cup again, but missed – or his hand shook too hard – either way it flew from the table, rolling on the floor, spilling its contents. His eyes traced the rivulets of water into the cracks between flagstones, his body shifted towards the cup, and for an insane moment Lorenzo thought he might follow it to the floor. But he splayed both hands on the table, steadying himself; at the same time studying them as if fascinated by his own fingers.

Secretary Joseph placed the defendant's copy of the charges before him, and Albrono whipped his hands back as if the papers might burn him. Then he leaned forward slowly, brow furrowed, squinting at the document in the manner of Lorenzo's professor in the dissecting lab.

'Don Albrono.' Joseu pressed on.

The defendant acknowledged his own name with agonizing lethargy. How tremulously he moved – an elderly man at the frail end of his existence. It seemed an age before he raised his head again, steadying it with a hand either side of his temple.

But now there was nothing lethargic about his eyes. They locked once more onto those of Don Fausto. The next battle in this apparent war between the two men was about to commence.

Judgement

He flew over the spiral track. The die rolled. Let it be a goose, he prayed. Or there, let him land on that square with the apricots, ripe, bursting with juice. Or bacalao. Had he once turned his nose up at bacalao? Look at that moist white flesh.

Thud, thud, thud. Musket fire.

The creature clawed for nourishment in the cavity beneath his ribcage. Dark. Sleep. Black square. Blue square. The die rolled, and he was off again. He soared over an orange grove, and she reached for him, brushing his fingertips.

Another volley. *Bang, bang, bang.*

The door shook in its frame. Thirst. No matter how many times he turned it over, the bowl would always be empty. He felt his lips crack, actually *felt* them split against his own groan, touched blood and licked it off his fingers. *Waste makes want.* Ha! Sleep. Blessed sleep. He closed his eyes even though they were coated inside with sand.

The die rolled, and now he flew over rats, insects, a cell. Yet he prayed to be set down, even there, because he knew. Ahead were worse squares. And the die. It was blank. Had been all along. This was never a game of chance, for when he craned his neck to look up, he was caught in the talons of a bird. A black buzzard. And it would drop him wherever the hell it chose.

Crack, crack, crack. A pistol firing. This time waking was the lesser horror.

Antonio was curled on his cot when they came for him. He didn't notice them enter. The noise at the door was surely more shooting practice. There had been moments when he realised this was a deliberate new torment; he even understood why: Fausto had discovered Juan's deceit with the food and this was his deranged punishment.

He prayed his young friend had not been punished, but a part of his heart had darkened, and he feared he knew why.

By the time they came for him, he'd become thirst and hunger. Nothing else or more. Those monsters had him in their clutches, and he submitted to them willingly. It was not so bad. Death meant fading. Death was a place where, bang and crash as they might, they couldn't stop him sleeping. In an orange grove.

So he raged when they yanked him to his feet, stripped him, soaked him. Then he fell on the water and drank: slime, rust and wood. That was when he met a new monster – one that gripped his innards and forced it all out again in splashes over his cell floor. One of his guards made some kind of a joke to his colleague and laughed at his own wit. The other stepped aside and watched.

They left him with a bundle of clothes. Crawling on all fours, he began the impossible task of retrieving some dignity.

Now here he sat, watching his judges drift in and out of view. Shadows loomed and receded: the ghosts of past prisoners arranged against the back wall in a tiered gallery, their features blending and shifting. He supposed he would soon join their number. They whispered among themselves, comparing experiences, placing bets. A few seemed sympathetic. A couple detached themselves and drifted to him. One righted his shoulders. Another told him to read the paper. Ha! The words would have to stop dancing first.

At the centre of his vision – the only thing that didn't move or recede, but stayed fixed in place at the end of the long length of the table – Fausto, wearing that grotesque idol to vanity, his crucifix. He lifted his document.

Antonio straightened his copy, leaving a bloody fingerprint on its left edge. He regarded his finger, perplexed, then touched his lip. Never mind. Let this blood-stained document be entered into the Tribunal's archives. Fausto was speaking. This was his fate.

> *BY THE AUTHORITY VESTED IN US BY THE HOLY OFFICE OF THE INQUISITION.*
> *'I, the Inquisidor Fiscal, accuse criminally Don Antonio Albrono, a native of the city of Genoa, for this person, being a baptised and confirmed Christian, and not having the fear of God, has committed heavy crimes against our Holy Catholic Faith and Holy Mother Church…'*

Antonio tried to read as Fausto droned, but the letters floated and mixed. He dragged his eyes to watch Fausto's lips, but they made shapes out of step with his words. He was fighting for his life and failing.

Help me. He shaped the plea in his mind, and no sooner had he done so than something touched the back of his neck. A cool hand. A phantom whispered. '*Breathe. Despaci.*' Inhaling hard through his nose, exhaling through his mouth, his heart steadied, and when he dropped his eyes back to the page, his reading matched Fausto's pace.

> *'… and accuse him of the whole, both in general and in particular, as follows:'*

Fausto lowered his paper and nodded to his colleague, the one with the red face. Antonio had never heard him speak before.

'Doctor Boxo. Read the Calification.'

Boxo rose to his feet, lifting his chair to avoid raking its legs on the floor.

> *'One: The defendant, in March of this year, specifically on the date of the holy festival of Domingo de Ramos, and in the company of witnesses who have provided their depositions, declared he was able when anything was stolen, to discover the thief, by the practice of magic.'*

A fist to his chest. *Palm Sunday*. A crackling firepit. A hungry audience. It had not been the trick in the cellar. It had been *talking* about it. The expectant silence, wide eyes wanting a show – ha! A pity they missed the ending.

Doctor Balleza. Antonio tried to catch his eye. Why had he not told him? Antonio wouldn't have denied. Their conversations had been at cross-purposes. But the confessor didn't – or wouldn't – meet his gaze. If he stared any harder at the papers before him, he'd burn a hole in them.

> *'Such a boast, and the date of its occasion, are conformable to an endorsement of the heretical practice of necromancy, and an insult to the sacred ceremonies of the Catholic faith and Holy Mother Church.'*

The prosecutor rose. 'You may answer the charge, Don Albrono.'

Antonio closed his eyes, drawing himself back to that evening, clambering through debris for remnants of memory.

'A trick to uncover a thief. Not magic. Never magic. Ink in a bowl. That man had a purse stolen. I meant no insult to the sacred ceremonies …' He tailed off; knew he was rambling, making little sense. He needed to arrange his words, put them in the right order, not just throw them out and hope.

'*Repent*,' said the ghost by his ear.

And repent. Yes. If that was how to feed this menagerie, then he'd give them all they could eat.

He took a breath.

'The audience present appeared to enjoy the wonderment of the story, and I indulged my own vanity in telling it. I didn't understand it to be evil. And if I offended, I wholeheartedly repent and will learn from my error.'

The gallery murmured among themselves; some nodded. The men at the table read their papers. Balleza still wouldn't meet his eyes. Only Fausto did, and there was no relief to be found there; his eyes were as dead as his soul.

'The audience, Don Albrono?' asked the prosecutor. 'Who was present that – as you say – enjoyed the wonderment of it?'

No. Antonio would not, could not, name other souls for these men to crush. Impossible. They might as well ask him to drink molten lead.

'That I don't recall,' he said.

The shadows shrank against the wall.

> *'Two: Continuing the conversation with the above-mentioned persons, the defendant said he learned from a sorcerer in Vienna. Such learning is conformable to the heretical practice of necromancy, and he should be examined regarding this sorcerer, and regarding other spells he may have learned, may hold in his possession, and, or have practiced.'*

Now the edges of Antonio's vision turned dark again. What could he say to a manufactured charge? He shook his head. The gallery joined in – twisted truth no new thing to them.

'There is no *sorcerer* in Vienna. I had an associate who taught me innocent tricks, child's play. These were amusing diversions, no more.'

'Is that your defence?' asked the prosecutor.

'It's the truth,' replied Antonio.

Silence.

Boxo pressed on:

> *'Three: Being later questioned whether he knew any art relative to winning at games, he went to a man's house and wrote a spell upon a strip of parchment, directing him to wear it upon the little finger of his left hand under a white stone set in a ring. Such a spell is conformable to the heretical practice of necromancy.'*

Antonio touched the dent on his small finger. His mother's ring. '*A charm*,' that man had said. What was his name? Curious, eager. All filth and poverty but for that silver dollar.

A silver dollar.

Christ. How had he not seen it?

A trap.

They'd gossiped, the men in his sección, about the Inquisition's paid informers. And he'd continued blithely on, trusting, thinking himself the cleverer. Thinking he'd been the one with the trick.

He searched for a defence, uttering the only words he could find. 'Not necromancy, just a dishonest man fooling another dishonest man for money, and for that I wholeheartedly repent.'

'Repent, repent,' the gallery echoed, its approval swishing across the walls, soaring into the arched ceiling. Antonio tilted his head to watch.

'And what of the spell, Don Albrono?' asked the hairy Inquisidor.

The spell. Indeed. The words he'd scrawled. Not funny now. Not then, in hindsight. 'There was no spell, just a joke, in German – my second language. "*Du bist ein Narr, dass du das glaubst.*"'

'And what does that mean?' interjected Fausto.

Antonio opened his mouth, and dropped his head. 'It means, "*You are a fool to believe this.*"'

And he had been.

The menagerie exchanged looks.

'Is that your defence?' asked the prosecutor.

'I suppose it is.'

'Will you now name your accomplices? Who was present? Who indulged your heresy?'

This stops with me. He took a breath. 'I had no accomplices. I don't recall who was present. Nobody indulged my… heresy.'

Boxo dropped his papers onto the table, retook his seat.

The prosecutor nodded, satisfied, and turned to address Don Fausto. 'And here rests the case against Don Antonio Albrono.'

Three charges. Not Barbieri who had spoken against him. Not the ruse with the ink. It was *talk of it* that had undone him. That and a silver dollar.

Fausto rose again, swelling, doubling, tripling. Shadows cowered. Antonio hauled shards of breath through a throat that had collapsed to the width of a reed.

'I direct the court to regard the accusations as proved.'

I direct the court? Is this how it worked? The floor beneath Antonio's seat softened and melted.

> *'The defendant has been exhorted to declare the truth and confess his crimes. He has insulted us with a partial confession. Thus, he has rendered himself unworthy of that mercy which the Holy Office extends to those who confess fully and with sincerity.'*

Fausto read from a document. The sentence had already been decided. Of course it had. Antonio had told the truth, offered his repentance, and it was not enough. It was never going to be.

> *'The defendant is therefore subject to the heaviest punishments thereto assigned by the sacred canons, pontifical bulls, common laws, and edicts of this realm. For a punishment to him, and a terror and example to others.'*

The words slammed into him, knocking him against the back of his chair. *A terror and example to others.* What manner of death would it be? He'd toyed with the idea of dying, even convinced himself he sought it, but now, staring into its gaping mouth, he knew with ice-cold clarity, he didn't.

He gripped the edge of the table, but it slipped. No, something pulled him away. He watched his own fingers whiten against the wood. The menagerie swayed and shrank before him. No use fighting it. He let go.

He rose; circling high, watching the curious spectacle below. Pain, hunger, thirst and that indefinable, all-consuming, bone-deep agony he now recognised as a craving for sleep – they all slid away as easily as an overcoat. He laughed at the joy of it. Smiled at the gallery of ghosts. Should he join them now, or wait?

But Fausto was still talking. 'If the court will indulge my compassion, I would give the defendant one more opportunity to repent.'

Antonio sagged back into himself. A reprieve. From Fausto. Who'd have thought? His throat unclenched; breath flowed – sweet, life-giving air.

> *'I therefore decree that, before his body be surrendered to the sentence, the defendant shall be rigorously examined, in accordance with the provisions of Article Fifteen. That is to say, the defendant is to be put to torture, to be continued and repeated till he confess all his crimes and accomplices, and thus preserve his immortal soul. In Nomine Patris, et Filii, et Spiritus Sancti.'*

The shadows rose as one. A single dark wraith circling, wheeling, spiralling along with their moans, shrieks, screams. Wall to wall, ceiling to floor, faster and faster until Antonio was consumed with torment – theirs, his, it was all one.

A single figure rose in the centre of the swirling black. Those blank eyes watched him. The buzzard stretched his talons, poised to tear him apart.

Unseen hands hauled, and the bird squawked. No, it was the screech of his chair. As they dragged him away, he caught papers shuffling, and mumbling. Something about trying the food at the new posada on the seafront. Tears burned, and though he tried to blink them away, one escaped.

The Inquisidor's smirk deepened; his triumph was complete.

There were two squares left: torture, and death.

Antonio allowed his limbs to fold, his body to sag, the room to fade, and submitted.

Article Fifteen

Lorenzo

The case advanced to its relentless conclusion, and Lorenzo ought to have been pleased, but he had lost count of his reservations.

The state of the prisoner.

What had happened since his last examination? Starvation and thirst played their part – that much was obvious – but something else was at work: the way his eyes darted one moment, then drooped the next. Hallucinations, disorientation, lethargy, ill-timed emotions – he had laughed at his judgment – Lorenzo had studied the effects of sleep deprivation, and what he observed confirmed his learning. This prisoner had been weakened for his trial.

The prisoner's defence had not been without merit, even allowing he had not been afforded the usual time to prepare it. If a friar were assigned to advise him, Lorenzo had a strong sense Albrono would submit to penance. But Don Fausto had determined the case as *de vehementi*, *proved*, which meant the only purpose of confession now would be to modify the manner of death.

Irregular. It wouldn't happen in Valencia; Don Ortes and Don Inviola would never pronounce without hearing the defence in full. The three of them were as one in their respect for procedure.

Does it strike you Don Fausto has an unseemly enthusiasm to see me damaged?

'Yes, Don Albrono, it does.' Lorenzo muttered under his breath.

What about the Delmaus and all their talk of Don Fausto being compromised by personal interest? And the things they knew. There had been a spy inside the Tribunal – that alone was cause for concern.

Lorenzo liked order; he couldn't tolerate a puzzle made of so many pieces; especially when each changed shape even while he examined it. He took a sheaf of blank paper from his desk, and a pencil, and started to write his questions – a sheet for each. As he progressed, he laid the papers on the floor, corners touching where there were obvious connections. He needed to move quickly – the prisoner's first Article Fifteen interrogation was scheduled for this afternoon. As attending physician, his job was to declare Antonio fit to undergo its rigours.

Antonio

'*Jesu miserere mei.*' An explosion of agony, unstoppable, full body, inhaling yet suffocating. Antonio inhaled his shriek and flung out his arms to ward off flames. Blinked. His hands floated unmarked, before him – white beneath streaks of dirt. Breath dragged from his lungs emerged clean. For now.

He groaned and threw his head back against the wall. '*... a punishment to him, and a terror and example to others.*' He slammed his head once more, cursing the lack of conviction that stopped him breaking skull against stone. Cursing himself more for falling from his cot to reach the life-giving water in the bucket.

He drank. Sweetness awoke in his veins, prickled under his skin, cleaned his mouth and throat. He heaved into a sitting position, leaning against the wall; drew his knees up, rested his forearms on them, hands dangling between, breathing in the fetid, moist air of his cell. Numb. Now even fear deserted him, and that of itself was a terror.

He stared at his name carved on his cell wall, following its lines and swirls. A feeble monument, as close to a memorial as he would ever have. How would they do it? He didn't want to die. Would he still feel that way when they were stretching him?

The defendant is to be put to rigorous torture.

He flexed his fingers, marvelling at how they still obeyed, how blood still pulsed through his veins. Life clings to its victims long after they beg for release. What would be the limit of his endurance, and why must it be tested?

And after. Would he be burned into ash and bone, or dumped into a pit, his corpse left to rot on top of the city's refuse, along with the nameless, the shamed, and the discarded?

He stretched a trembling hand into the solitary beam that pierced the gloom of his cell, watching the way the light shone through his skin, the framework of bones beneath, ghostly and fragile. Death lurks beneath our skin – how miraculous he'd lived so many days and never understood that before.

The guards had stripped his cell bare, taken his chains, left him with nothing he could use to hasten the conclusion of his torment. The machine of the Inquisition would have the final say.

Clinging to the wall for support, he hauled himself to his feet. His legs wanted to coil like rope, but he would use them while he still could and, shake as they might, they would damn well obey. Arms. Thin, streaked, tissue over bone and wasted muscle. He crossed them over his chest and grasped his shoulders, feeling the bones of his joints. Why had he never appreciated their perfect engineering before? Why now, when they were to be dismantled? He stared at the painted blue sky beyond his window, intolerably near, impossibly far.

When they came for him, he backed away. Struggled when they took his arms, a ripple defying tide. It made no sense.

Outside his cell, they turned him to face a door at the end of the corridor. Had it really been so close all this time? How many times had he looked that way when they brought him back to his cell? He'd had no idea hell was inside.

He couldn't match them; his feet trailed. When an unseen hand opened the door, he tried to plant his soles, to slow his entry, but there was no limit to the guards' strength, and too soon they had him inside, presented to Fausto like an offering. And oh, how he wanted to face him on his feet, but his treacherous legs wouldn't obey; he sank to his knees on the cold damp stone.

Don Fausto towered over him. Next to him stood the secretary; ready to record every utterance, as procedure required. Beyond them, Antonio glimpsed a large man with a pockmarked face, wearing a rough woollen shirt that might once have been white. It was his leather apron that stopped Antonio's breath.

He looked, his breath thinning with every new sight. The ceiling was much higher than that of his own cell, with all manner of manacles and chains suspended from it. Stone surfaces protruded from the walls, and there were devices… he jerked his head away in case he understood their use. The space reeked of damp and human suffering. There were no windows; the only light flickered from candles in sconces along the walls.

He tensed his limbs trying – in vain – to stop them trembling. A hint of perfume drifted to him from Fausto's robes – remnants of incense from his last ceremony. Luisa's wedding? He sank back onto his heels, fixed his eyes on the torn hem of his own shirt, while the secretary recited something in the monotone that procedure demanded.

'Confess all your faults, and what is known to you of the faults of others, Don Albrono.' Fausto's voice boomed with the confidence of the self-righteous.

He tried. In case a shred of mercy existed in the man towering over him, he tried to give him what he wanted. Subjugation. 'I confess in the name of our Holy Mother Church. And in the Name of Our Lord.' A whisper through a constricted larynx.

'To what do you confess?'

'To –' Antonio's mind raced… what were the charges again? 'To insulting the Church, and the Holy Office of the Inquisition, and God.' To his shame, his voice cracked and died.

'Is that all?'

Though he combed his memories, Antonio found nothing. A void.

'What else?'

Perhaps the secretary… 'Will you remind me of the accusation, so I might confess.'

'What truth in that?' said Don Fausto. 'We require your full and honest confession, and the names of your accomplices; the word must be yours.'

'Give me some time to think please, Señor.'

He couldn't fathom Fausto's reaction. His upper lip drew back, baring teeth – an actual snarl. What new crime had he committed?

It was the secretary who answered. Stepping forward, he muttered into Antonio's ear. 'His title is "*Su Excelencia.*"'

'May I have some time to think, Su Excelencia?'

His obsequiousness must have worked, for a smile now played about Fausto's mouth. 'Truth does not require thought, Don Albrono. It is absolute.'

An echo. A conversation from a lifetime ago with Doctor Balleza. He'd believed it then, and still did. Truth *was* absolute. He and Fausto both knew the truth, so why beg? Why hope?

He slipped outside himself. His fate had already been sealed; he was audience, not participant. The Antonio kneeling on the ground fixed his eyes on the gold thread embroidered on Fausto's slippers, and wordlessly lifted his arms to his side, palms upturned.

He gave himself up. For he couldn't entertain both hope and horror; the burden was too much.

But the secretary was saying something to the Inquisidor; the words drifted towards him as he studied a crucifix made from miniature golden stitches painstakingly embroidered into a velvet shoe. 'Su Excelencia, we must wait for Doctor Balleza; Instrucciones forbid us to proceed without medical supervision.'

Fausto tutted. 'I am aware, Joseph.'

Antonio shifted his attention to the brown dirt ingrained in the hem of Fausto's robe.

'Water while we wait. To refresh his memory.'

Rough hands clamped his arms, hauling him to his feet. Air mocked him, caressing his skin as his clothes were torn away. Manacles bit into flesh, reopening wounds, tendons and bones a throbbing tangle. His spine creaked, armpits burned, ribcage stretched his skin drum-tight as they pulled him up. He scrabbled with his toes, searching for purchase – anything to ease his flattened lungs; so he might steal another breath. At the edge of his sight, Fausto's robes swept out of view. Then ice-cold shock, every part of his body – inside his mouth, his throat – all constricting at once, tightening, shrinking against the assault.

He spasmed, jerked and kicked, coughed and retched where the shock of the cold had forced water into airways. His throat burned. His lungs raged. Even as he sought to recover, even as his breath returned, a next dousing. And a next. And more. A jerking, retching creature on the end of a chain, helplessly excoriating his own wrists as he thrashed against each offence.

The torment didn't end with the water. They left him suspended, stretched out, shaking with cold and heaving with eviscerating coughs as his lungs tried to expel the drops that had invaded them. They left him to *bethink himself*, so he might confess.

Lorenzo

Lorenzo had laid out paper trails – a 'Si' and a 'No' branch for each question – each leading to more branches, some doubling back; a tangle transferred from his mind to the floor.

If the heresy charge exists, then why had Seville said otherwise? If it were false, why was there a deed of excommunication? And – Sí or No – why did Don Fausto's keep the decree in his possession?

There existed a barrier: if this thing had been happening, in front of his eyes, and while he had been watching, then everything he stood for – everything he had done in his career – might also be in question.

If only it would all go away. Don Fausto had talked of an anomaly – a clerical error in Seville. But as much as Lorenzo wanted to believe that, his treatment of the prisoner said otherwise.

Lorenzo picked up the scroll, weighed it, passed it from one hand to the other, and back. He had already examined it: ink, words, even the paper itself, every detail, authentic. What impossible devilry it would take to create such a perfect counterfeit.

He unrolled it again, using brass weights at each corner to hold it flat. Leaning over it, hands propped either side, he read each line yet again, with meticulous care. *Give me something.* A spelling mistake, a stray scratch, a blot. But even if he did spot such a thing, so what? Humans erred. The absence of error would be more startling.

He stared until the words took flight from the page and floated. He stared until his head ached. Something. Something tugged at him. A shout from the courtyard outside broke his concentration, and he flicked his gaze irritably towards his window, even though he had no line of sight to the ground. The interruption drew a line under it. He shoved the paperweights aside and began rolling the document.

There. There it was. Lit up. Standing proud of the page. He'd been staring at it all along but only now saw.

He took a breath so deep its sound startled him in the silence, then he exhaled with a simple. 'Oh.'

His mind was clear, perhaps clearer than it had ever been. He held the document aloft. A simple fact. A thing that couldn't be. An unambiguous, inarguable truth. As for the papers he'd spread across the floor, a clear line ran through them now. Tracing the only possible path.

And no, Don Fausto, this was not an anomaly to be pursued once justice has been served. There was a case to be answered. And it stood between the Inquisition and justice.

He had work to do, and so little time.

Outside, the cathedral bell marked the hour. His stomach lurched. He should be in the cells below ground, confirming the prisoner's fitness for what Don Fausto had ordained must follow.

He gathered the papers from the floor, shoved them in his satchel, scrambled his physician's bag together and hurried out of his office, locking the door behind him.

Antonio

At first, the slaps startled him. Not a feeling, but a sensation, his face jerking from side to side, rocking his head on his neck. They dragged him from a velvet cushion of grey, into stark, raw, vibrant pain that began at his throbbing fingers, grew into the furnace of his chest, trembled into his spasming thighs and faded at his cramping calves and feet.

Antonio scrabbled on the floor, an instinct, finding stone with the tips of his longest toes. As he returned to full consciousness, a face breathed hot and sour into his.

Funny. This was the first time he'd looked Fausto full in the face. The additional height afforded to him by the pulley meant he gazed straight into his eyes. He'd been right; even close up, they were the beady, soulless orbs of a buzzard.

A flash of memory, of a dream. And he realised – the thing the buzzard had held in its talons, torn apart with its beak. It had been his own heart.

When they released the tension in his body, his useless limbs crumpled. Fausto's feet drew close.

'Are you ready to confess?'

He tried to nod, but his head wouldn't obey – it hung loose on his neck like a wet cloth. He placed a palm on the damp floor, feeling cold stone, seeking its strength.

'Are you ready to confess?'

'Sí.' But the word stuck, a shard in his throat.

'He's not ready to confess. Prepare *el potro* while we wait for the doctor.'

Hands under his arms, his skin dragging against stone. The ceiling drifted above – a stone arch, another, shadows deepening. The cell tilted into view as they pulled him up. His back grated against metal and wood before they pushed him back onto a table. But not a table.

Everybody knew about the horrors of *el potro*. The rack. Even schoolchildren whispered of it, made a game of it. This was no game. He tried to sit, to push himself away, but infinitely strong hands pressed his shoulders. The man in the leather apron leaned above and over, his face impassive. How could a human do this to a human? They bound his wrists; the loops of rope were ingrained with rust – someone else's suffering. Tension in his legs; ankles encircled hot, tight – then tightened some more, fibres biting skin.

And there he lay, shallow breathing, spine arched, arms over his head, a sacrifice to Fausto's vanity.

'Confess your faults,' said Fausto beside him, 'and what is known to you of the faults of others.'

Catalina peered down at him. A far sweeter sight than the buzzard. She smiled, just as she had when they said goodbye, when he'd believed his feeble care had saved her. The *Holy Inquisition* had put her through this same torture. Bound her fragile wrists like this.

Her cries had echoed off cold stone walls like these. The rage was white hot and glorious. Purifying. He twisted his head towards Fausto.

'Are you ready to confess, so your soul may be saved?' asked the Inquisidor.

'Are you?'

Fausto's eyelids dropped briefly over glossy black spheres before sliding up again. 'Do not test me, Don Albrono.'

Antonio looked up, tracing cracks in the stone arch above. A growth of some sort bloomed from them – some form of algae, perhaps.

'I will have my confession, Don Albrono.'

Catalina's face floated before him. Her lips moved; he squinted to read them. '*Courage.*'

'Begin,' said Fausto.

'Su Excelencia, the medical examination.' A voice, probably the diligent secretary.

Correct, Antonio thought. *Procedures, after all.*

A sigh. 'Confess, and be spared, Don Albrono.'

He opened his eyes. 'You repeat yourself, Su Excelencia.'

'Names.' Fausto looked at leather-apron. The ropes tightened. His shoulder cracked, and, so close to his ear, it sounded like a musket firing – only a warning shot; he was still intact, still had the strength to pull on the rope. He took a deep breath, blowing out in small puffs, ligaments adjusting to the tension.

'Confess.'

Antonio spoke through his clenched jaw, straining his neck to get the words out. 'I will not confess to a man who –' He dragged in a breath. '– takes unholy liberties with novice friars.'

Fausto leapt backwards. One of the guards snickered.

'Begin!' The booming voice filled the chamber.

'Su Excelencia, the Physician –'

'*Verdugo*, if you like your salary, you will begin.'

Antonio squeezed his eyes shut. *Catalina?* But she was gone. The rope tightened, or was it his own body straining against it? Impossible to tell.

'Espere.' *Wait.*

A new voice. Distant. From another world.

'Doctor Balleza. Good of you to join us.'

'Forgive me. I was delayed.'

Balleza's face floated into view. Looking him up and down as if he were a cut of meat. Antonio supposed he was.

'I see you have prepared the prisoner. May I have some time alone to complete my examination?'

'You may complete it now; we will wait.'

Balleza frowned and looked back over his shoulder. He placed his medical bag on the rack next to Antonio's waist, a more ironic mockery of his own profession Antonio couldn't imagine. Cold on his chest and sour breath on his face as Doctor Balleza listened to his heart. Warm fingers on his neck and wrists.

'When did you last evacuate?'

Antonio searched the physician's face for humour.

But Doctor Balleza had finished; he snapped his bag shut and turned away.

'The prisoner is not fit to proceed.'

Antonio gaped, though now he only saw the back of his head, his thin queue trailing beneath his wig, held together by a black ribbon. For once, Antonio found himself grateful for Doctor Balleza's *procedures*. For a short while, sweet relief wrapped him in its embrace.

But he couldn't indulge it. A conversation was taking place outside his line of vision, a power struggle upon which his fate rested.

'Doctor Balleza, you go beyond your authority.'

'I'm doing my job.'

'Three days, Doctor. I expect you to get this prisoner fit in three days. I will see you back here then.'

Three days. Not a reprieve, a delay. To be made whole enough to break. Three days and this would all begin again. The Inquisition stopped for no man.

They took him from the rack and placed him on the filthy ground. He tried to stand, to find something of the man he'd once been, but his legs failed, and his arms with them. He curled into a ball and sobbed, for Catalina, for the man he'd once been, for the life he'd never have.

As a Sister

Luisa patted the spare place on the settee beside her. 'No, Marta, don't leave. We need your wisdom.'

Marta frowned, and Luisa knew why. Her maid believed in social order, especially in front of a guest like Ambrogio Spinelli.

Rafael's mahogany-panelled office was crowded, despite its generous size. Luisa and Marta sat by the window, Rafael behind his desk, while Jean-Pierre occupied a discreet position on a small chair against the far wall. Enzo fidgeted in a tall-backed leather chair. He'd tried his utmost to give it up when Ambrogio arrived – Luisa had the sense he'd rather sit on a spike than in greater comfort than the Marqués-to-be.

Ambrogio, meanwhile, looked perfectly at ease on a plain, hard, wooden chair. His ankle rested on his knee, and he played with the buckle at the hem of his breeches. 'What's the mystery then? Why have you gathered us here?'

'Because there's a slim possibility –' Rafael looked at Luisa. '– that we'll have a visitor at six. We need your help with a complicated matter.'

'Enzo, it's been a few days,' Luisa said.

'I've been at El Marqués, researching.' He widened his eyes. Clever though he may be, he couldn't give a subtle signal if his life depended upon it.

'Wait, secret glances… cousin?' Ambrogio said.

Rafael stepped in. 'An innocent man is awaiting trial in the Inquisition's prison. He may already have been tried.'

'Do I know this man?' Ambrogio asked.

'Sí, a little,' said Luisa. 'Antonio.'

'Uh.' Ambrogio snapped his mouth shut, blinked, then composed himself. 'What did he do?'

'There was talk of a trick he played to expose a thief in his sección,' said Enzo. 'The man must have been bitter at being caught and denounced him.'

'Fffh,' Ambrogio huffed. 'Sadly, I can believe it. But surely, Antonio will be ordered to perform some kind of penance, and that will be that.'

Jean-Pierre laughed quietly. All eyes turned towards him, and he held up his hands. 'Pardon.'

'One would think,' said Rafael. 'But the man presiding over his case bears a grudge. Luisa won the confidence of a young friar. He told us this person, this Inquisidor, has taken measures to secure a death penalty.'

Now it was Ambrogio who laughed. 'You jest.'

'No jest, Señor Spinelli. This spy was a boy. He's dead.' Jean-Pierre's voice, harsh at first, cracked at the last few words.

'Dead? Over this?' Ambrogio stared at Jean-Pierre, as if doing so would make sense of it.

The Frenchman simply watched him back, over his steepled fingers.

Ambrogio swallowed. 'Why would the Inquisidor bear such a grudge?'

'You know him,' Luisa said. 'Don Fausto. As to why, do you recall that day in Bellvís?'

'I remember it well. Don Fausto might be severe, but he's a friend to the Spinellis.'

'Indeed,' said Jean-Pierre, his voice coated in sarcasm. 'There's *nothing* he won't do for them.'

Rafael glared at his lover. 'He took issue with the Albrono claim,' he explained.

'And his means of "*taking issue*" was not entirely legal,' added Enzo.

'Better if you don't know the details. For your protection,' said Luisa, firing warning looks at Enzo and Rafael, and – for good measure – a withering look at Jean-Pierre. 'I simply ask that you bear witness to what happened.'

He stared, open-mouthed, at all of them one by one. 'You're taking on forces too great.'

'An innocent man suffers.' Rafael leaned forward, forearms resting on the desk.

'And you!' Ambrogio snapped. 'You're supposed to protect your wife, not dance her into danger.'

'*Cousin!*' Luisa said. Hot words formed in her throat, but Marta closed a hand over hers. Cool and dry. A flame doused.

'But for Senor Delmau's protection,' said Marta. 'I'd be out of my mind with worry for my mistress. If you think she wouldn't act alone in this, then you don't know her. And that I don't believe.'

She held Ambrogio's gaze, until he dropped it.

'I will protect Luisa, to my last breath,' said Rafael. 'You have my word on that.' He looked at Jean-Pierre as he said it.

'Have you asked your father to intervene?' Ambrogio asked. 'He has Don Fausto's ear.'

Luisa pressed her lips together.

Ambrogio frowned. 'You're not on good terms.'

'He refused. Are you surprised? But I went to Don Fausto myself. I begged.'

'And how did that go?'

'He told me Satan spoke through me. Told me to get on my knees and pray, and concentrate on serving my new husband.'

Ambrogio dropped his foot, leaned forward, and rested his forearms on his knees, staring at the floor. Every now and again he shook his head, and sighed, and gave the odd small laugh.

She waited.

'Luisa.' It was just the two of them. He lifted his head. 'You were such a pest, growing up – in the best possible way – I always knew you'd be a singular woman. I don't understand all this.' He gestured loosely with one hand. 'If I'm to help, I'll have an explanation. That's non-negotiable. I'm not accepting all this "*for your protection*" nonsense.' His eyes softened. 'But you have me at a disadvantage. You are as my sister. If you ask for my help, it's yours. It will always be so.'

Arise, O Lord, and Judge Thy Cause.

Fausto adjusted his mozzetta, flexing his shoulders to stretch the fabric. Perhaps he should start declining dinner invitations; he needed new robes in any case. That fire: *The Lord hath taken away…* As he crossed the courtyard, such thoughts receded, replaced by the growing irritation that was Doctor Balleza. That man would be lucky to keep his position when his superiors in Valencia learned of his behaviour. Interfering with Article Fifteen – an unforgivable overreach, and for nothing. Because today, they would agree the means and timing for *surrendering the prisoner to the secular arm.* The prisoner's soul couldn't be cleansed, but at least Barcelona would be.

A wooden plaque lay over the entrance to the Grand Hall, its message engraved and gilded. Though he'd passed beneath it countless times, today it called:

> *Exurge Domine et Judica Causam Tuam.*
> Arise, O Lord, and Judge Thy Cause.

That flawless cursive. That perfect plea. He ached to reach for it; could already feel the smooth curls and ridges against his fingertips. He curled his fingers at his sides, and entered.

The six were already in place. The infernal Balleza, rigid in his usual spot with his back to the door. Don Joseph perched beside him, quill ready. Beside Joseph, Boxo jabbed the table to emphasise some point or other. Across from them, Joseu conferred with

Manuel, and to Manuel's left sat Friar Augustin, looking as usual as if he didn't know the day of the week.

It was the latter that spotted Fausto. He elbowed Manuel, who froze mid-gesture, which alerted Joseu mid-sentence, leaving his jaw flapping as if its hinge had broken. Laughable really. Boxo and Joseph both turned on cue; the only one not completing the dance was – of course – Balleza, an unmovable square of a back.

Then he noticed they'd been here a while: the half-empty pitcher, the scattered mugs, and – as he approached – the scrawls on Joseph's papers. And that didn't sit right.

'Am I late?' He took his seat.

'No, Su Excelencia,' Manuel said, 'we were continuing a meeting from yesterday.'

'Meeting?'

'Sí.' Manuel's *manzana de Adán* bobbed in his neck. 'A matter has arisen.'

'Yet I was not informed.'

'The matter concerns you.' At first, it seemed Manuel addressed the table – the way he stared at it. Better for him if he did.

Joseph wrote something down. Joseu straightened the edges of his papers. Boxo dropped his hands behind the table. Balleza held him in a cold, steady gaze, and for some reason Fausto's stomach lurched.

'Su Excelencia,' said Manuel, 'irregularities have been brought to our attention –' Beads of sweat glistened at his hairline; he patted his sleeve against them. '– A denunciation.'

Denunciation. The word hovered. Settled. At the edge of Fausto's vision, shadows flickered against the walls. The six at the table watched. Their gaze signalled a new reality; one his skin retracted from – shrinking back against his bones.

'Denunciation against whom?' That wouldn't do – his words all sticky and coated; he cleared his throat.

Manuel found his voice once more. 'You. Su Excelencia.'

The shadows stretched and reached. He hunched forward, away, and forced a low, measured tone. 'To denounce me is to denounce the Holy Office. Witnesses will be examined, perjury exposed and penalties applied according to gravity.' Now conviction strengthened him. He leaned forward in his seat and planted the side of one fist on the table. 'You may rest assured, brothers, there will be consequences.'

The shadows sprang back. He held his position, head thrust forward, locking his gaze onto each man in turn, until one by one, they shrank.

Except Doctor Balleza; he met him with a plain face and vacuous words. 'Indeed, perjury must be exposed and penalties applied according to gravity.'

But they'd met without him; lent credence to the claims; stepped out of line. It could not go unsanctioned.

He sat back. Jesus spoke of one prodigal son. Fausto, it seemed, had been blessed with five. 'You disappoint me, every one of you. Do you think I'm the first Inquisidor to be railed against? Your duty is to stand firm; not indulge.'

He turned the full power of his gaze onto the man he suspected – no, knew – to be the ringleader. 'Doctor Balleza. We have no further need of your services. You will return to Valencia. I am afraid I shall have to prepare a report for your superiors.'

The six watched. Unmoving. Even Joseph stopped writing.

Fausto stretched his neck, loosening his collar where it pinched. 'Shall we return to business, gentlemen? God's work.'

'I am afraid this new matter stands between us and God's work,' said Manuel. He looked at the physician-confessor. 'Doctor Balleza has compiled the charges, so you may answer them and, as you say, demonstrate where perjury has been committed.'

'Charges,' whispered the shadows, growing and reaching once more. Cold; his skin tightened.

The confessor rose, raised his paper – this was happening – and cleared his throat:

> *'Charge One: That Don Fausto acted towards a prisoner of the Holy Office of the Inquisition with partiality, imposing undue harsh conditions, and over-riding the conclusion of the Calification in respect of the gravity of the offence, so an unduly terrible penalty may be imposed.'*

'A jest,' said Fausto. 'Everything I do – every thought, every *waking moment* – is in service of a fallen soul.' He inhaled long and deep.

'Some say they don't deserve it. I say every soul is precious. *Every. Single. Soul.* None shall be abandoned. That is my vow, and to that end I will fight unto my dying breath, even if it means facing the devil himself.

'And know this –' He waggled a finger, lowered his voice. '– the devil is ruthless. Clever. He does not come in flame and fury, wielding a sword or a musket. No. His weapons are *sympathy* and *pity*. He slides into our minds, so we question our cause and methods – though they've been proved for centuries.

'Answer me this: What chance Albrono's soul if we bow to his intransigence? Would you have me offer him my own rooms? Tuck him in bed at night? Bring him chocolate and say, "*Shall I warm your slippers, Señor?*" How would that bring him to God?'

A fine speech. Surely, one of his best – and all without notes. That's conviction for you. And now the six sat as though they'd been turned to stone, jaws agape with awe.

Not awe. Something else. Something wrong.

'I did not mention Albrono,' said Balleza, his voice flat, face unreadable.

Fausto clamped his lips together. He breathed in through his nose, but the air seemed to stop short of his lungs.

'There are witnesses,' said Balleza.

'Who?'

'I am not at liberty to share names. Article Sixteen forbids it.'

'Now he quotes Articles of Faith at me.' Fausto gave a small laugh. 'Need I educate you, Doctor? There is nothing in your *charge* that relates to a crime in the faith.'

'We shall come to that,' said Balleza.

Fausto might have been punched in the chest.

'There is more,' Manuel said. 'And Don Fausto, I have to warn you, you may reply in respect of clarification or in respect of affirming or denying, but do not presume to dismiss a charge without allowing procedure to take its course.'

Manuel warned *him.* Fausto clasped his fingers together, squeezed hard, so the discomfort might override his compulsion to lean forward and box him about his ears.

Balleza raised his paper again:

> *'Two: That Don Fausto kept a fraudulent document in his personal possession. A decree of excommunication against one Alessandro Albrono, dated seventeen hundred and four. Said document being used by the aforementioned to disprove a debt claimed: first by one Girolamo Albrono in the year seventeen hundred twenty-one, and second by one Antonio Albrono in the year seventeen hundred fifty-four.'*

Fraudulent. He dragged in a breath. *Decree.* He held himself still, despite the shadows buffeting him. 'Evidence, Doctor Balleza.' He tried to drum his fingers on the wood of the table, but with his tremor it was more a scrabble. He snatched his hand onto his lap.

'Did you possess such a document?' asked Balleza.

It would have been burned in the fire; all he needed to do was deny. 'I know of no such document.' He tried to fix his gaze on Balleza, but his eyes ached. He rubbed the space between them with his thumb and forefinger.

Balleza reached into the satchel hanging from the back of his chair and removed a cylindrical bundle.

All too familiar. Fausto couldn't feel his toes. He might have been turning to stone from the feet upwards.

With a slow flourish, Balleza unwrapped the package and unfurled the scroll on the table. 'Do you recognise this?'

'No. No… I…' His thoughts, like his words, had splintered into fragments.

'Bethink yourself,' said Balleza.

How?

'*Bethink. Bethink.*' Enough from the shadows! He whirled.

Saw.

A spectral jury – separate forms. But then a single wraith, twisting, rising, falling. He blinked. A jury once more – shadows in rows against the far wall, nodding, whispering behind ghostly hands.

His skin lifted from his bones so horror might settle between – after all, it was part of him now, and had nowhere else to go.

He turned back to his accusers – compulsion, not choice. Augustin stood beside him with a mug of water.

Just as he had for Albrono.

Fausto knocked it to the floor. Large droplets caught the hem of his robe, and along with the clatter – sharp as a slap – pulled him back to himself. A better self. Blood singing, heart strong, head clear. There is no greater purifying force than earned rage.

He fixed each official with a fierce stare, imprinting the moment in his memory. Each would pay. Oh yes, they would pay.

He eyed the paper; its words swimming, familiar, accusing.

Balleza droned on. '… and a witness has testified you stored the document in an alcove behind your bookcase in your private quarters.'

Juan. If only he could burn him a second time.

'There are men at this very moment searching the remains of your room for the space in question. Will they find it?'

A hole in the wall of a burnt-out room. All they had to connect him to the document. He could laugh.

Still the confessor went on. 'Witnesses have testified you produced this very document from about your person, on the estate of El Marqués de Bellvís, two years ago. Is there anything you wish to say to that?'

'No.'

'Did you use this document to protect the Spinelli debt?'

'It is you who claim it.'

'There are eye-witnesses.'

'God help their souls.'

'Indeed.'

Then a new thought struck him, and under the table he curled his fingers, driving crescents of pain into his palms.

Eye-witnesses.

Who would testify against him? Who had been present? That lawyer and Luisa Navas – neither impartial enough to be credible. Gonzalo? Alejo? Never.

But another image: Luisa's wedding, Ambrogio beside her mother, the same Ambrogio that had been in that meeting. And on neither occasion had Fausto seen loyalty in his eyes.

'*Bethink yourself*,' whispered the shadows.

Ambrogio Spinelli had testified against him.

Now that he looked from face to impassive face around that table, something else struck him. Something that stopped his breath.

Each of these men already knew. They would have seen the depositions, the names of the witnesses. He alone had been denied that knowledge. *Procedures*, after all. Who ever won a duel with an invisible foe?

Bethink yourself.

They had him; he could not deny the decree; he must re-direct. He gave a short laugh, intended to appease, to draw them onside. 'Forgive me, I have not been allowed to prepare, and it was a long time ago. I believe I recall…yes… I attended a meeting in Bellvís, and I presented the decree of excommunication when the matter of the debt was raised. I thought to end a troublesome matter.'

Balleza stuck his bottom lip out. 'How do you answer the charge that the document was forged?'

If only those shadows would settle down and let him think. They jostled and shoved, thinned the air, starved his lungs and his mind.

'It is not a forgery,' he said.

'There are no records of a case against Alessandro Albrono in Seville,' said Balleza.

Fausto shrugged. 'Records can be lost,' he forced his face into a smile. 'I cannot answer for an error half a century old. Can any of us?'

'How did you come by the document if Seville had lost it?'

'Let me see. It was many years ago, but I recall I applied to central records, to the Inquisidor General himself, on behalf of the Spinelli family.'

'And you received this document, the decree I mean, directly from Madrid.'

'Sí.'

'So it cannot be a forgery.'

'Impossible. Huh! Unless you mean to imply the Inquisidor General forged it. Perhaps you think we conspired together? Will you be pursuing him next?'

'Please examine the document for our benefit and confirm this is the same.'

Fausto stood; pressed his hands to the table – thank the Lord, his tremor had vanished – and leaned over it, affecting scrutiny. 'This is the document.' He re-took his seat.

'The document that is a genuine decree of excommunication?'

He scowled. 'Are you slow of understanding, Doctor?'

'Discúlpeme. I only ask because this document is a forgery. And since you claim to have received it directly from the Inquisidor General's Office in Madrid, you are – I regret to say – failing in the truth.'

The shadows shrank back as one – a tide receding. Then leapt. Shrieks filled his ears, his mind. They whipped against his skin, clutched his throat, gripped his arms, hauling him to his feet.

Fausto reached for his old friend: anger. 'How dare you, Doctor Balleza? How dare *you*, question *my* integrity? I've indulged you with patience; with more politeness than you deserve. Yet you call me *liar*.'

'Sit down,' said Manuel.

Did he just hear true? From *Manuel*?

Heat surged faster than thought. His muscles coiled, his right arm flew back, and his vision narrowed to a single small target: the space between Manuel's ridiculous, pronounced, perfectly arched eyebrows.

But no matter how hard he strained, his clenched fist stayed locked behind his shoulder. And the source of the restraint?

A guard. His fist clamped over Fausto's wrist.

'Sit down,' Manuel said again.

'Sit down. Sit down. Sit,' echoed the shadows gleefully.

Between Manuel and the guard – and the shadows (though they didn't exist, not really) – Fausto understood his cold choice: comply or lose his dignity. Not that he had any left. He lowered himself into his seat.

'Please read the signature at the bottom of the decree,' Balleza said.

Fausto did. What of it? He licked his lips and coughed to release the words caught in his throat. 'Vidal Marin del Campo.'

'And what was his role?'

'Can you not read for yourself?' He tried to snarl, but his mouth wouldn't obey.

'Indulge me, por favor.'

'Inquisidor General del Santo Oficio de la Inquisición.

'And the date?'

He shook his head. 'I hope there is a point to this. The fourth day of March, seventeen hundred and four.'

'A forgery, no?'

He blinked. The document blurred. What was the confessor getting at?

'It is impossible that this – or any genuine document – would be signed thus.' A single clean vertical line sat between the confessor's eyebrows. Finally, an expression of some sort – though Joseph might have marked it there with his quill.

'Vidal Marin Del Campo was not Inquisidor General in the year seventeen hundred and four. Your forger did not research his dates.'

Oh.

He could deny. He could demand it be checked. But he had an idea it would be pointless.

The other officials watched him. The shadows watched him. They sat at the table now – those shadows – alongside and between the men. He'd never seen the huge table full to capacity before. It looked somehow better. Right. There they sat, nodding like interested delegates at a theological debate. He squeezed his eyes shut. This dream would pass; he had been working too hard.

But no, there they all were when he re-opened his eyes. The cold blank stare of the Inquisition alongside ghosts of the past. And now they judged him.

One last roll of the dice. It was surely a good one. 'Gentlemen.' His own voice let him down, more air than tone, but he pressed on. Seeing a flicker of sympathy on Joseu's features, he directed his words at him. 'Ask yourselves. What would I have to gain from such an act?' He forced reasonableness into his tone. 'Why would I compromise myself on behalf of a third party? A Spinelli?'

'Indeed,' said Balleza. 'A good question, and it troubled me.'

Finally, some sense from the man. Fausto shifted weary eyes in Balleza's direction.

'That brings me to the final charge,' said Balleza:

> *'Three: That the aforementioned committed the above act(s), for personal gain.'*

'What personal gain?' asked Fausto. Though he was beginning to understand Balleza's methods, his thoroughness, his talent for pre-empting and unravelling defence.

'You were rewarded with property.'

'Farcical…'

'And money.'

'Laughable.'

'You became owner of La Posada del Marqués, in Barcelona. Its lands, buildings and revenues,' said Balleza.

Fausto closed his eyes, and rubbed at his jaw, day-old stubble rasping against his palm. 'Evidence…'

'Ledgers recovered from your room show cash transactions into an account – traced to you – that match deficits from the hotel.'

Though the floor beneath his chair had become marsh, and he knew he was sinking, still he argued on. 'Circumstantial.'

'And there is the will of the fourth Marqués, witnessed, signed, and notarised. It is clear on the matter.'

And that's what it took. Every challenge rebutted, every argument cast aside – by fact, by hard evidence, by a relentless bureaucrat who chased the law like a starving hound loosed on a scent.

Fausto slumped. Words gone, lungs empty.

He afforded Balleza a single nod. Of respect. How had he built this case in just a few days?

He followed the line of spectres down the table. They could be anyone – prisoners tend to sameness, when one's been Inquisidor long enough: jagged, collapsed and degraded – nothing men and women.

But Fausto did recognise the friar sitting at the opposite end of the table: with his hands tucked into his sleeves, his straight back, his neat tonsure, and his infinite sadness. He flickered in and out of sight.

Master and servant locked eyes. The friar dipped his chin. No benediction. No salvation. Juan faded. Vanished.

The prosecutor stood, unrolled his paper; already prepared, of course – when were the Inquisition's questions anything but rhetorical?

> *BY THE AUTHORITY VESTED IN US BY THE HOLY OFFICE OF THE INQUISITION.*
> *Don Fausto de Alenya.*
> *A denunciation has been made against you, and witness depositions collected, that place you under suspicion in the faith.*
> *Article Twenty-Five prohibits an Officer of the Inquisition from receiving or benefitting from gifts, under pain of excommunication, being deprived of office and being required to repay twice the value.*
> *How much more grievous such a contravention if said Officer in fact conspired to earn such a gift? This charge alone is enough to bring you before the Holy Office of the Inquisition.*
> *The details of the case will be examined by the correct process of Calification. You have been afforded the unusual privilege of prior knowledge of your charges, owing to your years of service and the esteem in which you have been held.*
> *You will also be afforded the privilege of a closed trial, recognising the potential for damage to the reputation of the Holy Office, of a defendant who is one of our own officials.*
> *As a further privilege, you will be confined to a monastery – yet to be determined – so you do not suffer the depravation or indignity of incarceration. In the meantime, quarters have been identified for you in the Palau. You will be placed under guard.*
> *You are, with immediate effect, relieved of all of your duties.*
> *You are exhorted to bethink yourself and confess the whole truth in relation to this matter. So justice may be executed with brevity and mercy.*
> *In Nomine Patris, et Filii, et Spiritus Sancti,*
> *Nosotros, los Inquisidores del Santo Oficio.*

He had been beaten as soundly as if he had been set upon by six bandoleros, not six bureaucrats of his own Tribunal.

And the worst, the thing that skewered him with humiliation and shattered his mind, was a single word. A word he would spend the next hours, days, and weeks writing in his notebooks, ledgers, and journals. Over and over. A word he would keep writing until he covered every page in Barcelona.

He had sunk to the lowest level possible by his own measure.

Primer Inquisidor no more.

Now: Defendant.

Part Four - Fiat Iustitia

Let Justice Be Done

How Am I to Suffer?

I seal my mouth against the bread and my body rages. My treacherous body. It would have me regain strength for the man in the leather apron. I'll die by my choosing, not for the entertainment of Fausto.

I lie motionless on my side, drifting. Hunger, that gnawing beast, is only still when I am. There's an empty cot beside mine, and a friar in brown robes nearby. He keeps holding a cloth to my mouth, tormenting me with golden, clean honey. Smack my lips and nourishment will find me. It's a new kind of torture; offering nectar to a man set upon starving.

An eternity has passed since they carried me through the rain to this room – a windowless space so devoid of feature that even time is denied entry. Death may take another eternity. Maybe I'm already dead. But no, in my ears rushes the pulse of my own veins and I curse it for not weakening.

Someone is speaking. To me? I close my eyes, drag my arms over my head. I'm no longer here; perhaps he will understand and leave me be. It's Juan's voice; he's come to comfort me as I die. I lower my arms and look.

Even my hearing betrays me. It's the doctor: Balleza. What now? Has he come to enquire after my evacuations again? Cold fingers take my wrist – clean, clipped nails. Yes, Doctor Balleza, I live. What do you want now? A chair scrapes the floor, and his face appears; I close my eyes.

'Don Albrono.'

His voice is gentle. I ignore him.

'Don Albrono.'

I lay still; squeeze my eyes shut.

'Antonio.'

I cannot help but look; he's never used my given name before.

'Antonio. You must not refuse food; your health is in peril.'

Ha, he's here to entertain me. I shut him out.

Hands under my arms – the friar – and I'm hauled into a half-reclined position. Balleza himself plumps a pillow behind me. My head is too heavy for my neck, and I allow it to fall back. Since he's going to such pains, I may as well enjoy his performance.

'Don Albrono, there is a development in your case.'

I'd shrug if I had the strength, as it is I blink.

'Your judgement has been reviewed and reduced. Your punishment will be reduced accordingly.'

An obvious trick. 'No.'

He frowns, then continues. 'You have confessed to the charges of insult to the faith, the Holy Office, the church and its holy sacraments. Your defence against the charge of necromancy is accepted. There will be no more interrogation.'

'Are you lying?' I try for the words, but my mouth is too dry, my tongue too swollen.

He signals for water, and the friar presses the cloth to my mouth. It's a mistake to accept it; the moisture is irresistible. I grab the mug, gulping. The water runs into my throat and down my chin – sweet with honey – and for a moment I close my eyes with the joy of it. When I open them, Balleza is watching, his chin bobbing up and down with small satisfied nods. I settle my head back onto the pillow.

'How am I to suffer?'

'I don't understand,' says Balleza.

'My death. Will it be hard?'

He tucks in his chin. 'No, Don Albrono. You've confessed and offered repentance; you will live. Your sentence is commuted to exile.'

It turns out I'm not resigned after all. If I were, my breath wouldn't have caught; my heart wouldn't have leapt.

Still, I will not believe it. For hope to be crushed once more would be worse than a thousand deaths. Bile rises in my throat.

'A lie.'

'No.'

'Why?'

'Because the Inquisition does not make mistakes.'

I think of Catalina and know for a fact he's wrong.

'I shall return later with the formal judgement.'

I close my eyes, and when I open them, he's gone. Have I been dreaming? A cruel dream if so. But I'm still in this half-reclined position; my head rests on the pillow Balleza placed there. My sentence has been determined. To live.

If You Knew the Woman

I cannot stop my mind racing. Days have passed since we met Doctor Balleza. I hardly sleep; I cannot eat; I push Marta away. We're all on edge – this odd family of Rafael, Jean-Pierre, Marta, Enzo, and me – spending hours talking, turning the matter over: *What if this? What about that*? I'm terrified, not in the way one might claim to be terrified of, say, spiders or an angry dog. No, I've come to know terror, how it sits in the bones, grips the heart and unravels one's very existence. I'm adrift.

Work would be my refuge, but I'll be damned if I lift a single finger to feed Don Fausto's coffers. Almost a decade, nearly ten years I dedicated to managing El Marqués, only to learn every *real* was for *his* account. The very ground beneath my feet always belonged to him.

By day I sit by the window with Antonio's letters stacked beside me. I don't want company, yet they come: Marta, Rafael, Jean-Pierre, Enzo. An endless parade of exhortations: *Eat, Luisa… Rest, Luisa… Drink, Luisa… Walk, Luisa… Talk, Luisa.* But all I want is to trace the lines and curls of his script, to memorise each inkblot. And when I reach the last letter, I turn the stack over and begin again. What cruelty to re-discover him in the shadow of his death.

The heaviest burden is guilt, because I know now, I abandoned him, while he remained steadfast. If he lives to forgive me, I won't let him down again.

I know when the house is silent, Rafael and Jean-Pierre go to each other, and God forgive me, I resent that they have that. I'm ashamed to feel this way and have taken to staring out of the window for long hours, rejecting company, craning my neck for signs of a messenger.

Here comes my father, puffing with strides that his short legs protest. Funny, except his face is crunched in anger. I won't let him see me in any state but composed, so I shove the letters into a drawer, move to the looking-glass above the fireplace and tidy my hair, tucking stray curls into my moño. I will have to do, because voices rise from the hallway, footsteps thump on the stairs, and Señor Alves shows him in. Father is speaking before the door has swung closed.

'What have you done, Luisa?'

'Papa, what a surprise?' I move to kiss him, even though my feet prefer to stay planted.

'Do you know where I've been?' He shoves me away.

'I cannot guess.'

'I've spent this morning being questioned by the *Inquisition*. Insane questions: about your grandfather's will, about your *puto* lover.' Spit flies from his plosive consonant.

He swipes his hat off, twisting it. 'What did you do?'

My heart dares to lift. Might this be Doctor Balleza's doing?

Father stands before me. 'What do you have to say?'

I swallow; step back. 'What happened?'

He looks ready to ignite. 'Don't feign innocence. Who else would have thought of the will?'

'The will?'

'Stolen from my office. Your doing Luisa, don't deny it. And somebody has been to the Inquisition with a story of –'

'What matter if there is nothing to hide?'

For a moment his words vanish, then he begins again, faster, louder. I can smell his breakfast on his breath. 'You couldn't leave the *hijo de puta* alone. What would your husband think if he knew? Do you think of that *coño* when you lie with him?'

'Papa!' I recoil. Such language, such tone. And now I'm backed against the wall. His body, close and warm.

'I've a mind to tell him.' He's getting louder, good, perhaps someone will come.

I want to protect myself, but my arms are pinned between us. I brace, mind emptying, I'm a child once more.

His buttons press against my ribs. 'You are nothing but a *puta* yourself!' His arm flies back, fingers bunched, poised.

I squeeze my eyes shut.

Cool in place of hot. A trace of cologne.

Rafael, but not. Teeth bared, neck corded. He has his hands on my father, *throwing* him, and Father is clambering to his feet, and now I'm afraid of Rafael; no, afraid *for* him, because I don't know what he will do. Actions have consequences; I've never seen this side of him.

I clutch his arm; cry his name.

And now Jean-Pierre appears, fists and jaw clenched. Equal fire. Equal anger. Striding towards my father, who squares up to him, nose to chest.

Dios mío, three angry men. Nothing good can come of this.

'Stop.'

By some miracle, Marta's voice – she doesn't even shout – cuts through Rafael's rage; stops Jean-Pierre in his tracks. The three spring apart.

'If you knew the woman you married, Señor –' Father's words are for Rafael, but he scowls at me, and it should pierce my heart, but somehow does not.

'If *you* knew the woman you raised, you'd be a better man for it.' Rafael shoots back

His words hang in the air. They glare at one another. This could go anywhere.

Father moves first. He shakes out his sleeves; his face is flushed. He seeks to regain dignity, and we must give him some if this confrontation is to end.

Rafael watches, clenching and unclenching his fists.

Jean-Pierre steps to my side; touches my arm.

Papa's gaze swings towards the Frenchman. 'Who is this, Luisa? Another lover?'

Jean-Pierre lifts his brow; shakes his head.

Rafael's eyes flash; his tone is cold. 'You insult my wife. Be assured you will never set foot in our home again.'

Father looks to me. To me! Does he expect me to speak for him? I turn away and retake my seat at the window.

'Luisa,' he says.

I ignore him. He won't see the tears on my cheeks; in case he thinks I mourn him. I don't. I cry because I feel nothing. I cry for the father I never had.

The Correct Procedures

I am making good progress; my target was to pace three lengths, and this is my fourth. But I should stop now because I'm lightheaded.

I crave fresh air. Sometimes I think I'd go back to my old cell for its tiny window, even if it meant foregoing the privileges of the infirmary.

Doctor Balleza returned with the prosecutor, and they read out my sentence, so I know it's real. They left me with a copy; I know it by heart.

> *BY THE AUTHORITY VESTED IN US BY THE HOLY OFFICE OF THE INQUISITION.*
> *In the Royal Palau of the Inquisition of Barcelona, on the 14th August, 1756, the Prosecutor Don Joseu de Montejo y Anieva and Inquisidor Licentiate Don Manuel de Soler y Montana being at their morning audience, and having examined the proceedings against Don Antonio Albrono as far as the accusation and answers thereto ordered, unanimously, that this person be severely reprehended, admonished, and warned, in the Hall of the Tribunal with closed doors, and he be banished perpetually from the Spanish dominions at a date to be fixed upon, and he be informed that if he fail to comply punctually with every order, he will be severely punished and proceeded against with all the rigor of justice; that this trial be suspended and the sentence submitted to the Council. In Nomine Patris, et Filii, et Spiritus Sancti,*
> *Don Joseph de Vallera, Sec'y.*

No mention of Don Fausto.

No use looking to my friar companion for answers; my bad fortune to have been assigned one who's taken a vow of silence, although I suspect fortune has nothing to do with it. How I miss Juan.

Banishment will be no loss, as I once said to Catalina: *It won't be a bad thing to live outside.* I wonder when I shall receive my reprimand and leave this place. I suppose I should be grateful I have had this time to gain strength. Again, I think of Catalina. I suspect she will never leave me.

Doctor Balleza arrives with his medical bag; he pulls up his chair by my cot and bids me lay down. I sit.

'You seem well today, Don Albrono.'

'Thanks to my amigo here.' I nod towards the silent monk, encouraging him with a smile. Nothing.

Balleza flicks his fingers, signalling for me to hold out my left hand. I obey. He begins to unravel the bandages encircling my wrist, winding the fabric into a neat coil as he does so: *unwind, wind.* 'Have you been sleeping?'

'Perhaps too much.'

'Impossible, rest as much as you are able.'

By now he is peering at my flesh. The wound has dried and scabbed, skin that once burned red and swollen is now calm, puckered around what will be a permanent scar.

'Do you feel any pain?'

'No.'

He touches the skin next to the wound. 'Now?'

'A little.'

'Move your fingers.'

My third and fourth fingers twitch but otherwise refuse to obey. He frowns and removes a pin from his bag.

'Do you feel this?' He jabs it into my fingertip.

'Yes, a little.'

'Good, when feeling returns, movement will follow. Flex your fingers every chance you get.'

'Sí.'

'I will leave the bandage off.'

He repeats the process with the other wrist. As he's examining my ankles, I'm compelled to ask: 'Did you intervene?'

He flicks a glance at my face. 'What do you mean?'

'El potro. You said I was unfit to proceed. Was I?'

'Move your toes.'

I comply. 'Why is Don Fausto's name omitted from the sentence?'

'Can you feel this?' He jabs my toe. Hard.

'Ow! Sí.'

'Bien. The other foot.'

'Doctor Balleza.'

He ignores me. This time I withhold my question until after he has put his infernal pin back in its case.

Now I'm on my back as he listens to my breathing – a cold brass horn is pressed against my chest.

'Why did Fausto not sign the sentence, Doctor Balleza?'

'A deep breath, Don Albrono.'

I inhale and hold it. He doesn't tell when me to release, so I exhale anyway.

'Again.'

We repeat. Next, he shifts the horn over my heart.

'Doctor Balleza –'

He raises one finger. 'I am counting.'

'Doctor Balleza, you are avoiding my questions.'

He sits back in his seat. 'What do you wish to know, Don Albrono?'

And with that simple question, all of my own evaporate. There is only one that matters.

'When will I be released?'

'Mañana.'

Did I hear correctly? My heart leaps into my mouth and my first thought is: *Thank God I will breathe clean air again.*

'What date is it?'

'Once de septiembre.'

The eleventh. A month since my last audience. A month since they strapped me onto el potro. I cannot believe how many days have slipped by. 'Why the delay?'

'Procedure required a meeting of Council to ratify the decision.'

I absorb this.

'What about my reprimand?'

'That was done in the course of your audiences.'

This seems pragmatic; never a word I believed I'd use in relation to the Inquisition.

'You will be released at dawn.'

Of course. I remember Catalina's exile. I wonder if I too will be escorted by two soldiers of the garrison. I examine my clothes: second-hand rags found for me by my silent friar. They are clean but still… a shameful exit. I am nobody. *Anónimo.*

'Doctor Balleza, why did you intervene for me, and not for Catalina Margueles?'

His looks at me sharply. 'You mentioned her before. How do you know of her case?'

'I was one of the guards tasked with escorting her out of the city.'

'But you are not Spanish.'

I shrug. 'We were short of men. Why did you allow it?'

'Allow what, Don Albrono?'

'Her torture. And then her release when she was so unfit to face the world.'

'The correct procedures were followed.'

I recoil but his face remains impassive, blank. He seems incapable even of understanding why his words would shock me. I gather myself. 'But you intervened with me.'

'Again, the correct procedures were followed. Or perhaps I should say, *in*correct procedures were being followed, so I put it right.'

'*Procedures*.' I shake my head.

I gulp water to quench the heat of rage building, watching his cursed, emotionless face as I swallow. His very existence is a taunt. I want to provoke, to puncture his equanimity, for this cold, emotionless façade is intolerable.

'What was incorrect about Fausto's *procedures*, Doctor? Starvation? Withholding the charge? Denying me a defence? Torture? But no, those are acceptable according to your *procedures,* aren't they? Let's go back further. Was he in breach of *procedures* when he committed fraud? What about when he sent three bandoleros to assassinate me on the Road to Bellvís?'

It's no use. I'm winding myself into a rage while all he does is watch: implacable, unmoved. Does this man even have a soul? I lower my voice, slow my words. I want to shake him.

'Doctor Balleza. Shall I tell you why I sold that spell to your spy, Joaquim?'

He blinks twice in rapid succession. 'I am not permitted to confirm the names of our deponents.'

'Nevertheless, shall I tell you what I used the money for?'

He's silent, watching, I may as well be talking to the rat once more.

'I took his silver dollar and gave it to Catalina. I wanted to give her a chance to survive.'

Still nothing. Any remaining wisdom deserts me as I lean forward and speak through teeth I cannot seem to unclamp. 'I'm here because I wanted to save a victim of your *procedures*.'

A flicker. I grip the edge of my cot and press the point.

'I suspect your *procedures* will call that an insult to the Holy Office of the Inquisition.' I hold my wrists out – damn, they shake – but I set my face, resolute, so he knows. 'Do your *procedures* not require you to arrest me once more?'

I must have lost my mind but I mean every word.

He shifts his gaze to my outstretched hands, then back to me, his expression smooth and untroubled – perhaps a little perplexed; the fine line between his eyebrows the only sign.

Then he rises and snaps his bag closed. 'Don Albrono. We have no procedure for prosecuting a man in Barcelona for an insult to the Tribunal in Valencia. And since you're leaving Spain, there will be no occasion for you to set foot in that city again. I suggest you get some rest, because you leave this place at dawn.'

So Long Let Us Hope

Rafael sits sideways on the window-seat, half facing the window – the better to watch Papa's retreat. 'I shouldn't have left you alone with him.'

'You weren't to know,' I say.

'A good thing you came when you did,' says Marta. She has been hovering behind my seat but now crouches beside me, taking my hand.

Jean-Pierre, leaning against the window frame, folds his arms. 'So, now we know the case is being examined.'

'It would seem so,' says Rafael. 'Luisa... what this is costing you... I don't know how to protect you.'

'Get him out of there.' I bite off the words.

Jean-Pierre and Rafael exchange a look: *she's crumbling*. How can I not?

'We might be too late,' I say. 'We should have tried your "*inelegant way,*" Jean-Pierre.'

The Frenchman raises his eyebrows. Rafael shakes his head – and that tells me they discussed it. A moot point now.

I'm not so naïve I didn't know what Jean-Pierre meant, and I feel no guilt for wishing harm upon the man who called himself my uncle – for the things he's done; the hurt he's caused. 'Did he really do it for money?' I say, 'Don Fausto, I mean.'

'People do terrible things for money,' Rafael says.

'But Luisa is right,' says Jean-Pierre. His lips are pursed again – that expression that always makes me impatient for his next words. 'It is odd.'

'By your standards, that's an underwhelming insight,' I say, and am rewarded with a grin – there have been too few of those lately.

'Would your friend Shakespeare not have something to say?' Marta asks.

At this, Rafael bursts into laughter, deep and real, and I cannot help but follow suit. Like a cool breeze on a stifling day – it's a respite that makes the next wave of close heat tolerable.

'*What does Fausto value above everything else?*' That's what Jean-Pierre asked me that day – it must have been a month ago now.

'Marta, what does Fausto value above everything else?' I ask.

She shrugs. 'Power,' she says. As if it's obvious.

Which it is, of course: power, authority. I've always known it.

A clamour of footsteps on the stairs rips me from my thoughts. Marta leaps up, the door flies open, and in bursts Enzo, shining with joy.

'He's to be released at dawn.'

The words hovered.

If I misheard, I will come undone.

'Antonio?' asks Marta.

'Who else?' says Enzo.

'How do you know this?'

'Matheo – his old sargento – has arranged it so he will provide the escorts.'

'How?'

'Connections, I suppose.' He shrugs – as if we're missing the point; and we are.

'Where is he to be escorted?'

'He has been sentenced to exile. He will be placed under house arrest at a designated address before he sails.'

'What address?'

Enzo chuckles. 'This address.'

Silence. The air pulses. How has Enzo accomplished such a thing? But then I realised he was a marvel when he produced my grandfather's will – ransacking my father's office while my parents were at my wedding – with Marta's help of course.

'Mi scusi, Signore.' Enzo addresses Rafael. 'I hope I was not presumptuous.'

His ridiculous question shatters the ice, and Jean-Pierre strides over, lifting him off his feet in a hug that has me worrying for the little lawyer's ribs. Then, Marta goes to him. They kiss – *on the lips* – and I realise there has been more to Enzo's absences than research. How did I not see it?

I haven't moved; I *cannot* move.

Rafael takes my hand. His so warm I must have turned to ice. 'Luisa?'

I can barely say it.

'I'm afraid.'

The Confessor's Final Act

Lorenzo takes his leave of Antonio for the last time. His final meeting has not brought the closure he hoped, and he cannot understand why. The right outcome has been accomplished: the prisoner will walk away with his life, and Spain will have one less heretic. But why does he now think of the prisoner as Antonio? His training does not allow such familiarity, such *personalisation*. Something has shifted, and it does not sit well. His life had a certain order, and he intends to return to it: Valencia and its routines.

His wooden trunk waits like a hungry mouth, half-packed with his folded confessor's gown, the smart shoes he brought for the trial, a linen-wrapped shaving set, comb and pomade – for those long nights in the office. Alongside them, he tucks his journals, prayer book, rosary – too little used of late. He will attend mass before he leaves, and confess of course.

All that remains is to assemble his case files to hand over to the Barcelona Tribunal. He slides open his desk drawer and removes a sheaf of documents. The depositions still carry the clean, sharp tang of ink, as if Montez penned them only yesterday. Yet their edges have begun to brown. He leafs through, checking their order.

The first is that of Joaquim Gil, reliable spy. That sloppy signature, a scrivener too! He stood before him in the Tribunal Hall, eager to spill his colourful story. No doubt Antonio's nobility made him a mark – after all, it had caught his attention. He'd sent Joaquim away with two silver dollars: one for payment, the other for entrapment. And Antonio gave the latter to Catalina. How strangely the world turns.

Here are the witness statements: a young alguacil named Sanchez, who had apparently been too drunk to join the conversation at the meson, but not too drunk to observe it. A traveling woman and her maid – apparently Antonio had been making eyes at the maid all evening, then abruptly left. Lorenzo had wondered at the time if that had offended her more than the heresy.

And here is the statement from the landlord – Señor Matheu – affronted that such a conversation took place in his establishment on Palm Sunday. Quite right.

Matheu had given him two other names. Odd that the older alguacil, Alba, and the daughter, Teresa, seemed to have suffered memory loss. No, not odd at all. There were always reluctant witnesses. He would have pressed them harder if there had been insufficient willing ones. He hadn't bothered to follow up with the soldiers; such men never deposed against their own.

He stacks the documents on his desk, placing his case notebook on top, and – for good measure – an iron paperweight. Let Gregor handle the archiving.

Before he can leave, there is the matter of Don Fausto's charges. He must hand over the files to Señor Boxo – recently promoted to Confessor of the Barcelona Tribunal – and he will be glad to. He turns his attention to the cabinet in the corner, retrieves the box and sets it on his desk.

It watches him, solid and unyielding, its brass keyhole glinting an invitation, mocking his reluctance. He pulls the key from his pocket; it sits cold against his palm. He clicks open the box.

There lie the papers that led to the arrest of the Primer Inquisidor of Barcelona. He performed well that day: held steady where others would shrink; showed masterful command. Pride might be a sin, but God takes no offence at fact.

Yet another unshakeable fact – a reality that has cost him his sleep – is that the Inquisition erred. Worse still, had it not been for the persistence of the Delmaus, he would have erred with it.

There is a scratching tap at the door. Gregor of course, because only he has such a timid knock.

'Sí,' he calls, without lifting his eyes from the notes.

A few seconds pass before he realises Gregor hovers, so silently did he enter. The novice's arms stretch around a box, fingertips white against its vertical edges, spine curved backwards against its weight.

'What have you got there, Gregor?'

'Don Fausto's confiscated possessions.' Gregor tries to nod down at the box, but the strain of carrying it stiffens his neck.

Lorenzo steps forward to help. 'Why have you brought it here? It belongs with Inventory.'

'Discúlpeme, Doctor. I thought you might want to go through it first.'

'It is a matter for Doctor Boxo now.'

He helps Gregor manoeuvre it onto a chair – one normally reserved for visitors, the place Don Rafael Delmau sat.

He's made his delivery, yet Gregor waits, shuffling from one foot to the other. Lorenzo knows him well enough by now to understand there is something he wishes to share. He sits behind his desk and steeples his fingers. 'What is it?'

'The matter you asked me to investigate.'

Lorenzo scrambles; he'd forgotten tasking the novice. What does it matter now? Still, he might as well hear him out. He nods.

'Don Fausto… his career.'

'I did not expect it to take a month.'

'Discúlpeme –'

'Stop apologising. Go on.' Lorenzo does not need this conversation, but Gregor, it seems, has something to say, and – what with the poor boy's recent loss – Lorenzo doesn't have the heart to stop him.

'I could find nothing in the records until the year seventeen hundred and twenty-one.'

Despite himself, Lorenzo is intrigued; the date is familiar. Was it not around the time of the first Albrono claim? He would have to check.

'That was when he was called to serve as Vicar General.'

Lorenzo dropped his hands onto the desk. 'He would have been young for such a position, no?'

'Sí, in his late twenties.'

Goodness. A priest wouldn't be ordained before twenty-five; such a rapid elevation after… that was rare. But not impossible if a young priest had a powerful mentor. 'How do you suppose he accomplished that, Gregor?' His voice feels disconnected – words forming of their own accord.

Gregor hesitates, but there is a flicker beneath – the relish of the reveal. 'He was sponsored by the Archbishop of Tarragona, Luca Spinelli.'

That name. *Spinelli.* Again.

Lorenzo knows now – Gregor understood more about his assignment than he pretended. He studies the novice, Juan's brother. Gregor scratches the back of his left hand, but holds his gaze, he does not even blink.

For the second time since becoming entangled in this damnable case, knowledge – unwanted – lands in his lap. Two ambitious young men, a secretary and a cleric, perform an enormous service for the powerful Spinelli family. One is rewarded with the Protectorate and a wife. The other with financial assets. This he already knew. But he had known only half of the truth. Fausto's reward had been far greater. Power and status. Promotion to Vicar General.

But what a risk they took, those two young men. Did they really choose to spend their lives peering over their shoulders, hoping truth did not find them? What a relief it must have been when the Marqués died a few months later. As for Archbishop Spinelli…

'Gregor. What happened to Archbishop Spinelli? Did you discover that in your research?'

'Sí. It was a terrible thing. He was waylaid by bandoleros on the road to Bellvís. They killed him.'

Now he understands. The walls close in; the floor tilts. He plants his hands flat on the desk, and hears Antonio's voice – so clear he might be standing beside Gregor.

'*… he sent three bandoleros to assassinate me on the Road to Bellvís.*'

He could ask the year of Luca Spinelli's death, but he already knows the answer. The same year the Marqués died. Two men promoted. Two witnesses removed. A case sealed shut. Little wonder he hated Antonio for opening it again.

A groan, disembodied; a sound of its own.

And now Gregor speaks high and fast. 'Doctor, are you well? Here. Water.'

'*And yet you put me on trial,*' says Antonio.

'Leave me, Gregor,' he says.

'But, Doctor….'

'Leave me. Please.'

Alone, he goes to his window, opens it, breathes sweet fresh air. Below, in the square, people go about their business. A young couple ride side by side on a calesa, a maid perched on the seat behind them – their chaperone. A courting couple, enjoying the air, ignorant of the decisions and deeds that take place all around them.

He turns back to his office. The box is on the chair, silent but insistent. Oh, how he wants to ignore it. But it draws him in. He lifts its wooden lid and peers inside.

A thing gleams on top of a pile of folded vestments, heavy enough to leave a sharp-edged indent. He lifts it, tilting it against the light. A masterpiece of intricate gold and silver filigree, studded with rubies as crimson as Christ's wounds.

He runs a finger along the edges of the crucifix, feels cold metal, weighs it across his palm, turns it over. There is something engraved on the back. He looks closer, squints, reading the letters engraved in ornate cursive. A name.

Luca Spinelli.

He drops the accursed thing back into the box, and slams the lid, pressing his weight against it, as though it might fight its way out.

He has no idea how long he stands there, hands on the box, waiting for his breath to steady. Eventually it does. His mind empties, *gracias a Dios*. He does not feel peace, so much as a strange sense of space – no, of absence.

His feet move to the desk; his legs lower him onto the seat; his hands lay a blank sheet of paper onto the writing slope, then select a quill. He watches himself testing its tip against his thumb, and dipping it into the inkwell. A bead of ink clings to the nib, dark and glistening. It transfixes him, that dark sphere. He follows its pull towards the pristine surface before him; watches letters and words appearing.

Royal Palace of the Inquisition of Barcelona
11 de septiembre del año 1756

For the Notice of Don Ignacio Ortes de la Peña,
Primer Inquisidor Licenciate, Tribunal of Valencia
Your Most Illustrious Lordship,
I write with utmost respect to tender my resignation, effective immediately, from my position within the Secret Prison of the Holy Office of the Inquisition.
It has been my profound honour to serve, discharging the sacred duties of Confessor, and latterly Physician, to the best of my ability. Whilst I have learned much, and will forever be grateful for the trust placed in me, I feel called towards a secular vocation, namely the practice of medicine, with a view to offering my skills and learning to the New World.
With utmost loyalty to the Tribunal of Valencia, I offer the view that the position of Confessor would be better served by one who

could devote themselves to that role alone. For indeed it is a position of the highest gravity, and worthy of a better servant than myself.
I entrust my resignation unto your understanding, and remain, as ever, your most obedient servant.
May God guard Your Reverence.
Doctor Lorenzo Balleza

He sprinkles pounce, admiring the way the chalky powder swallows the gleam of wet ink. Tilting the page, he taps the excess into the corner of his writing slope. For a long moment, he stares, unable to believe the words before him, written as if by a guiding spirit.

The powder catches his sinuses, and he sneezes. Writer's powder has always affected him this way. He covers his nose and mouth with the crook of his elbow until the fit subsides. He's alert now, fully aware of his actions.

With deliberate care, he lifts the page, folding it into thirds with two hard, precise creases. Reaching for the wax and candle, he watches the drops pooling a bloodstain onto the edge of the letter. With a practiced hand, he presses his signet ring into the warm wax. His Confessor's seal. The last time he will use it.

One Step, Then Another

I stand behind the iron-banded doors and I'm terrified. Beyond lies a world I categorised as dream, not memory. A realm where I will make my own decisions in the space between thoughts. Incredible to think I used to have the capacity to navigate life without permission. I buried that skill somewhere deep, and I fear I've forgotten where.

The first thing is the light. I screw my eyes shut then squint. The light is yellow; piercing yet hazy with dawn. And despite what it does to my eye-sockets – they might be radiating cracks like dropped bowls – it's glorious. Ahead, the grey wall of the cathedral blocks my vision, but above is sky: cloudless, blue, infinite. If God exists, He's there, not in these stone monuments to hypocrisy.

And the smells: damp flagstones, straw, horse manure, and over it all, the fresh, sweet smell of clean, moving air carrying with it the city: herbs, citrus, baking bread, leather, and wood. I might be intoxicated, and I've only taken one step. Away from the looming shadow of the prison, I'll surely be overwhelmed.

Three soldiers lean against the wall to my left. Three? Do they think me a threat? A man who may not even be able to walk beyond the length of the prison wall. I brace myself for the worst. But as I step forward, one of them springs upright, his voice familiar.

'Antonio.'

'Sargento?'

Matheo takes my shoulders, his hands huge against my bones. Over his shoulder is Ramirez, and next to him, my Milanese *amico*, Gianni.

Matheo holds me at arm's length. I know what he sees: a ragged, cadaverous man with matted hair and an unkempt beard. A man who touched death and will always be haunted by it. Barely a man at all. I shrink from his stare, and concentrate on the ground. I'm happy to see them, and I want to tell them, but perhaps it's duty that brought them here.

I'm supposed to walk the length of this alley. *Va bene.* I've trained for this. Except the most I managed yesterday was ten lengths of my cell, and by my reckoning, that's half the distance I have to cover now. God help me. We set off. And I manage it.

By the time we reach the cart – a canvas-covered contraption hitched to a dappled mare – my breath is ragged, my knees shriek. Ramirez bounds onto the driver's seat with mocking agility while I eye the step into the cart and wonder if it would be too humiliating to crawl aboard like an infant. They see, Gianni and Matheo.

'Every man needs a little help now and again,' Gianni says.

They haul me up, no hesitation, gripping my arms and setting me down on a wooden box too fast for mortification to catch up.

'Where are we going?'

'Enzo has found an address for you. You'll stay there until you make passage,' says Matheo.

Enzo. Of course.

I almost fall sideways as the cart lurches off; Gianni swings an arm around my shoulders.

'Amico mio.' He dips his head level with mine. 'You have no idea how good it is to see you.'

'We feared the worst,' says Matheo.

I fix my eyes on the rough planks between my feet.

'Antonio.' Matheo watches from his crate opposite mine. 'You will get past this. We will deliver you to Enzo; all you need to do is let him take care of you until you are strong again.'

I allow my gaze to travel up: the scuffed square toes of his boots; the buttons glinting at the hem of his breeches – one is snapped in half; I wonder if he knows. His tan chaleco, darkened behind the toggles, blue jacket, red cuffs… every inch the professional soldier going about his duties.

My fingers find the frayed cuff of my shirt, and I tug it down over the scars on my wrist. I cannot meet his eyes; I speak to a space just below his chin.

'I don't remember how to exist.'

He lowers his head, finding my eyes. 'Place one foot in front of the other. As long as a man can manage a step, he can manage the next.'

'Like marching,' says Gianni. 'One, two. One, two… and the destination finds you.'

Gianni the unmoveable, the thick-skinned – how bad must my plight be that he studies me with moist eyes? I won't have it.

'Profound.' I elbow him in the ribs.

He makes a point of looking me up and down. 'I think you are within your rights to make a complaint about that mesón you have been staying at.'

I raise my hand to my beard, combing my fingers through it. 'Food was terrible.'

Matheo lifts one corner of his mouth.

'How is the sección?' I direct the question at him.

'Same duties, different city,' says Matheo. 'Your camaradas all wanted to come today.'

The sense of unworthiness sweeps over me once again, and I cannot bear him to see. I look at my hands; every tendon and vein bulges, poised to burst through my skin. 'How did you swing it to be my escort? How did you even know I was to be released? I didn't know myself until yesterday.'

'Made it my business to get a contact in the Palau guard,' says Matheo, as if it would have been a simple matter.

The cart tips right. I've barely steadied myself when it tips right again. Nausea stirs. When did I become so fragile? I brace a hand against the cart's side and focus on drawing air deeper, but my ribs protest.

'¡So!' Ramirez's call reaches us from outside the canvas, and we sway to a halt.

Gianni climbs down first, then Matheo, who turns and stretches out a hand to help me. The pavement looms and ebbs beneath – too far, unreachable. I grip the side of the cart and lower my right foot into the vast chasm before me. My left knee sets about trembling, and soon my whole body joins it, shaking, sweating with the effort. '*Fanculo*,' I mutter through gritted teeth. It's coming. My fall. Too funny to survive the Inquisition and dash my brains out falling from the back of a cart.

My standing leg crumples. I pitch forward, and Matheo catches me as easily as if I were a sack of wool, propping me against his chest. I'm beyond humiliated.

Ramirez watches with his hands laced against the nape of his neck, and the memory surfaces, raw and tormenting. 'Like Catalina, eh?' I say, my voice wheezy to my own ears.

Matheo lowers me onto the edge of the cart and sits beside me. 'Take your time, Antonio. When you're ready.'

I do. I breathe slowly until my trembling subsides; Gianni squeezes his fists into balls. Ramirez hands me his skin of water; I gulp, tip it onto my face, rub my eyes.

I look at the house, this place, this address. *House arrest.* The weight of privilege crushes me from within. I hand the pouch back to Ramirez. 'Not like Catalina at all, is it?'

He lifts his brow and shifts his eyes to Matheo – a signal. I shut my mouth; some things our sargento would rather not know.

I can't keep my camaradas here all morning. I stand, this time without help.

'This is where we leave you, amico mio.' Gianni stretches out a hand. I grab it with both of mine and submit to his embrace. I fear I may break down. 'Grazie, Gianni. You've been a good friend.'

'Arrivederci, Antonio,' he says. 'I'm coming to visit you when you're settled.'

'I don't recall inviting you.' I hug him again, thumping his back so he doesn't think I've gone soft.

Ramirez steps in, and I fear his arms might crush me. 'Adiós, amigo,' he says, 'you taught me much.'

My eyes are hot; I cannot break down here. I kiss his cheek hard.

Matheo holds my arm and walks me to the door.

My pulse hammers in my throat. 'Are you sure this is the address?'

'Sí,' he says, 'our friend Enzo is never wrong.'

Our friend? I swallow. 'Where is he then?'

Matheo knocks, and fear surges. What manner of lodging is this? Not a tavern. I suppose I wouldn't be allowed in a public place. But how would Enzo find the means for such a house? I want to bolt, to run and hide, but where would I go?

It's a good thing the door opens before my thoughts spiral.

A man with yellow hair stands before us. He looks straight at me. 'Antonio.' As if he knows me.

I nod.

'Bienvenue.' He opens the door. A man dressed in the uniform of a mayordomo approaches, and the blonde fellow grins at him. 'Too slow again, Señor Alves.'

Matheo steps inside with me; faces me, holding both my shoulders, giving me that same hard squint I've seen a thousand times – piercing and assessing. He nods once. Firm. Steady.

Then his face crumples.

I catch only a glimpse before he pulls me into an embrace, trapping my arms in his. He exhales hard, his breath against my ear, then pulls away, searching my face. 'Antonio.' He swallows; clears his throat. 'Arrivederci.' He loosens his grip, but he's not done, and squeezes again – a tiny shake of my shoulders, all the while working his mouth.

I blink, both at his Italian and his tenderness.

He's already turned away. I have to thank him. To tell him I know what he did for me.

'Sargento?' It's all I can manage.

He turns back, face set, stern once again. A sharp nod at the people behind me, then back to me. 'One foot in front of another, *Cabo*.'

Time to face the unknown.

I stand before strangers – a blonde man, a dark-haired man, a lined man in a pale blue silk uniform with ribbons at his knees. Their mouths form words, but none come. I wandered in off the street. I'm in the wrong place. At any moment they'll call a constable. I would.

An arrangement of roses on a pedestal – because a world exists where they build pedestals for vases – flings a petal in a bold attempt to break the impasse. It sways, holds the air, quivering, then falls defeated beside a browned and curled companion. It tried. I watch for another performance. I'm well aware the men watch me, because their gazes itch.

Enzo. Ridiculous, beautiful Enzo: face like a walnut, no wig today – he's tidied his hair behind his ears; it's gone grey at the temples. His embrace digs sharp-edged buttons into my chest, but he's warm, clean, familiar, and my breath loosens. I hold him, cling to him more like, because he's the only thing between me and drowning: death by goodwill. I bury my face against his neck, it's as good a place as any to hide.

'What did you do, Enzo?'

'It's over, amico.' Warm breath against my ear.

Easy to say.

I take his shoulders and ease back. His eyes are moist. Christ, not Enzo, too. I tighten my grip and give him a small shake.

They're clustered behind, those men, and I can read them as though they're holding up signs: blonde curiosity, dark-eyed hesitancy, silk-clad bewilderment. Behind them all that ugly spectre – cruelty dressed as benevolence – pity. The moment stretches but won't break. I taste acid and swallow it back.

Enzo speaks again, but now it's just sound; it makes no sense. I let him go and step past him – because I need to show some initiative. But my legs start to shake. I lock my knees.

The dark-haired man touches my arm, and I square my shoulders, with one thought, and one alone – to shrug him off and stand like a man. His eyes are wide and warm. He means well. I don't know how to tell him I know it. I want to find clever words, or crack a joke, so they'll know I'm not broken and stop tiptoeing around me. Half-ideas form: What of this new cologne? How do you like my fashion? Shoes are over-prized; they only fall apart anyway… I laugh, not at my wit but at my utter lack thereof. They look at each other, and I know I've only made it worse.

The uniformed man – Alves – says something about a physician, and for a wild moment the blonde man's features shift. Balleza. Then he speaks, and it cannot be the confessor, because his voice is draped in French.

Movement now: touch, and voices, skittering like wind-blown leaves, and I'm swept into the current. My heart says flee, but my feet won't follow. Just a hallway. Just people. But I can't feel my hands or my feet; I'm vanishing from the outside in. Sweat slides down my spine. What am I doing here? What was Enzo thinking? I need quiet. A cell. A corner. I need to be unseen. *Anónimo.*

'Antonio.'

She watches from the top of the stairs, her hand resting on the banister. The world narrows. I wrap fingers over my wrist to cover the worst of the scars.

She moves, step following step until she stands before me. Her skin, her hair, vanilla and salt, so familiar as to be part of me. Her face: the way light catches her skin, the way her lashes rest on her cheek when she looks down.

Too late, I pull away, but she catches my hands. Her touch is gentle; her fingers cool. Her brow furrows, and how I want to smooth that line away with my thumb. I want to bury my face in her hair.

But she's not mine.

She examines the worst scar – deep and ugly, shameful – and though I try to pull away, she lifts the damaged skin to her mouth and brushes it with her lips, gentle as a feather.

She lifts her head, and I'm lost in her eyes. There's no revulsion, only curiosity and frank, honest love. I could hold this moment forever, imprint it on my soul, because I know I'll reach for it a thousand times.

'Say my name again, Luisa.' I whisper it. I need it.

A flicker. A small smile. Each syllable a separate breath. No more than air shaped by her mouth.

'Antonio.'

Epilogue

September 1757

Here they come.

'Signore e Signori, ecco a voi gli… the newlyweds!'

Along with everyone else, we applaud Enzo and Marta. She's radiant, and he proud. As he should be; he's married a fine woman – confidante, dear friend. I'm going to cry, and my jaw hurts from my smile that won't stop.

'Here.' Rafael hands me his handkerchief, although I think he may need it himself.

The reception is at the Palazzo Mocenigo in Venice – thanks to Jean-Pierre and his incredible list of friends and contacts. He's been in his element since we arrived here last year. He talked so much about the people we would meet, and the experiences we would share, that I'd assumed nostalgia had softened his memories. But no, it's been a joyful whirlwind. Between setting up our home – neighbouring apartments on the top floors of a palazzo in the Dorsoduro district – hosting and visiting Jean-Pierre's intellectual friends, and organizing a wedding worthy of Enzo and Marta, I've hardly had a moment's rest.

In Venice, people are loath to pry and slow to judge – or perhaps it's the people with whom we mix. We have privacy: we talk into the early hours within our new circles, then retire to our suites with their adjoining private doors that allow us to live in a way that is our own.

Across the floor, I look for Antonio. There he is, laughing at something our new friend Francesco is saying. Jean-Pierre gestures, and Antonio watches his hands before replying with a retort that earns him a light punch on the arm. He looks my way and sends me his smile.

How different he is to the man who stood in the hallway of the house on Carrer Ample. Me too; I'm not that woman, scared of a staircase. Back then, a hundred fears had stolen my sleep: Would he forgive me? Might he reject me? How would I reach him? Worst of all, what had Fausto's inquisition left of him?

So, I stayed in my room when the wagon clattered outside. When the men went to greet him, I stayed upstairs. I waited on the landing, even after I heard the door close and voices murmuring. I hid until I couldn't anymore.

I noticed his hair first. So short, perhaps three fingers, curling around his ears. It was just a detail, a distraction, to ease me in a degree at a time because the whole was too big. The man. Caved-in. Scraped out. All angles and hollows, bruises and scars. And his body – what they'd done to it – wasn't the worst. Antonio hunched in on himself, wounded, shrinking into his own skin. Wary as a creature in a snare. Even Rafael and Jean-Pierre, normally so assured, didn't seem to know how to act. It was in panic that I called him. I needed to know who this man was, so I called the name of the man I wanted him to be.

And when I did, he looked up, and there he was. *'Antonio.'*

'Say my name again.'

That night his room was dark and cool; the windows wide open, drapes rippling. I stood in the doorway waiting for my eyes to adjust, and I realised, with a sickening lurch, that the counterpane lay undisturbed. I thought he'd gone.

'Luisa.'

I thought he'd gone, but there he sat, a miracle, silhouetted against the night, in a tall chair, one leg crossed over the other, just a man taking the air. Except as I drew close, pulling up a seat, I caught edges and sharp lines, stark now his beard was gone, as if his face had been carved by an inexperienced sculptor who'd taken a few hacks too many.

I reached for him, but he pulled away, though he tried to make it appear casual, fiddling with the cuff of his shirt.

'I thought I'd never see the sky again,' he said.

'It's a beautiful night; it's been fine for weeks…' Banal. I cringed.

He watched the night. I watched him.

'I was thinking about Juan,' he said. 'He was the only human in that place.' He'd taken the news hard that afternoon.

Stay with the pain. I swallowed back my reply – which would have been as vacuous as my weather observation.

'Once in Valencia, I had to escort a prisoner into exile,' he said. 'Not house arrest, like this –' He flicked a hand. 'Catalina.' His face tightened as if it stung to say her name.

It might have been the most he'd spoken all day, so I kept my peace and waited.

'A *woman*, Luisa. They crushed her, body and soul. I did what I could, Enzo too, and one of my comrades. But we didn't have the means. A hayloft, scraps, and a few coins. A silver dollar.'

'What became of her?'

He closed his eyes. 'She died.' He swallowed. 'I found out in prison.'

Jesu.

'Catalina. Juan. A woman and a boy.' He turned his face back to the window, to the rooftops outside. 'And here I am.'

'What are you saying?'

He didn't answer at first; his eyes tracked a night creature – a bat, perhaps. Then, in a voice so low I strained to hear, he said, 'Hardly fair, is it?'

The gap between what he needed and what I knew how to give was huge. I leaned forward. But he drew back.

'Why do you do that?' I asked.

He studied the backs of his hands, then turned them over and stared into his palms, his lashes casting shadows over his cheeks. 'It's the prison. It's all over me.'

'You must have used all the water in Carrer Ample bathing this morning.' My levity fell flat.

'Look at me.' His voice carried an edge I didn't recognise. 'I've got nothing for you.'

I *was* looking at him. So what if he had a few more lines and corners? He remained as familiar as my own reflection. I wanted to touch his cheek, to pass my thumb over his lips. To connect. But I curled my fingers into my lap, because I knew if I did, he'd retreat, and that would break my heart.

'Would you abandon me?' I asked.

'Pity then.' He shook his head. 'That I can do without.'

'*Pity*? I don't pity you; I *want* you.'

He blinked, then narrowed his eyes as if trying to read me in the dark. 'You're another man's wife.'

That stung. As he knew it would.

'I've explained how it is with Rafael.'

He said nothing. Instead, he returned to watching the sky, as if he'd been tasked with counting the stars.

He understood. And we both knew it. Furthermore, I wasn't about to let him make an excuse out of the small matter of my marriage – very well, not small, but not big enough to hide behind.

'You've every right to be angry,' I said. 'I would be.'

'You'd be angry? If I married another woman? A good thing we're drawing lines now.'

'I thought you'd stopped writing.'

'You *did* stop writing.'

'Not straight away.'

'Well, thank you for that!'

We glared like combatants between rounds. And my heart soared. It was Antonio.

'Your letters were beautiful. I know them by heart,' I said. 'I was set to grow old reading them over and over.' I gave a small laugh. 'Now here you are. And here we are, arguing.'

'Enzo told me how hard you fought. I don't mean to be ungrateful. Forgive me.' And there he was gone again. All stiff neck and chopped up formality.

'We all fought. I feel nothing but guilt. I should have known you better.'

'I want your guilt even less than your pity,' he snapped.

Now I knew what he was doing. This I recognised. Building a wall between us brick by brick. Often, when faith is torn away, one would sooner live with the wreckage than risk it happening again.

'Don't do it this way,' I said. 'If you don't want me, own up to it.'

His eyes glinted, a sliver of moon trapped in each. A good few seconds passed then he spoke. 'You don't understand.'

'So help me.'

He exhaled.

'I've nothing for you,' he said again.

He'd never been more wrong; I understood just fine. 'Tell me you don't love me,' I said.

His eyes widened. 'That's not fair.'

'I've been told I fight dirty,' I said. 'It's served me well. Tell me then.'

He rubbed his forehead as if the action would catch his thoughts. Finally, he answered. 'You know I can't.'

'Then they haven't taken you from me. Nor will they.'

He frowned.

I returned his gaze.

He chewed the inside of his cheek.

I smiled.

'Fiend,' he said.

One of his hands draped loose over his armrest, I trailed a finger over the back of it. This time he didn't pull back.

'I'm to leave Spain,' he said.

'Me too. There's nothing here.'

Surprise flickered on his face, followed by what I thought might be hope. 'But your family –'

'A new start. Jean-Pierre wants to show us Venice.' My heart hammered; the next words were everything. 'Come with us.'

He laced his fingers inside mine. 'Let me think on it.'

I did.

Three weeks later we set sail, all six of us.

He's never told me everything that happened, and mostly he is himself. But days come around when he says he can smell the prison. Though he knows bathing won't help, bathe he does until he shivers in the chilled water. Those days are fewer. Each day, he steps further from darkness.

Except the day a letter from Mother put a knife to his heart.

Barcelona, January 1757

My dearest Luisa,

Look at your address! I can scarce believe it; did you know the Marqués de la Mina once had apartments in the Dorsoduro district? I should not be surprised if you are living in the exact same Palazzo. I have heard tell of the beauty of the Grand Canal; to think you wake up there every day! I knew Rafael would be perfect for you.

I hope you have finally begun to dress as befits your status. You are a married woman now. I hear the wig-makers in Venice put our local peluqueros to shame. So, no excuses; I want to hear all about your latest creation in your very next letter.

Alas, though I thank you for your invitation, I cannot see my way to visiting you. Tu padre will not permit it. He won't even speak your name. It breaks my heart. What passed between you? He tells me nothing, only that you were the cause of Don Fausto resigning his position as Primer Inquisidor. I cannot imagine how he arrived at such a notion. The idea a woman could possibly influence the Holy Office is laughable. But he always was stubborn.

As for Don Fausto, at first, he was livid. I thought he would bring the walls of your father's study down. Never have I heard such a carrying on! I can guess as to the cause, for your Aunt Isabel tells me he was directed to repay my family the full value of El Marqués, along with every maravedí he earned from it. He had to sell his country house, and your father made him a loan; secured, of all things, against his cocoa business.

But that was months ago. Now he is pleased with himself once more. You know how he gets when he catches the scent of advancement. He certainly made the most of devoting all his time to being Vicar General. The rumour is he has cultivated friends in high places and has cast his hat – or should I say his zucchetto (haha!) – at an Archbishopric. They say his chances are good…

There was more, mostly fashion news – ruffles are quite the thing, apparently. I crumpled the parchment. I suppose the affair had been too embarrassing for the Inquisition to make public: a quiet resignation, no disgrace, move on. Had I expected justice?

I'd no idea how long he'd been there, standing in the doorway.

'Luisa? Bad news?

'In a way. I –' This was too big to hide; I gave him the letter.

He smiled, chuckled – no doubt at the notion of me in a grand wig, then the colour leached from his skin.

He walked out.

He wasn't home by nightfall. Nor next morning.

Marta and I paced through the night while the men scoured the alleys and – *God protect him* – the canals. Rafael and Enzo returned alone at lunchtime, only to eat, they said. But Marta insisted they rest. *'He's capable of taking care of himself.'* She'd never seen him at his lowest. I slipped out.

I walked in widening circles, through damp alleys, beneath laundry strung like bunting. I'd all but given up, turned for home, when something – laughter, I think – pulled me toward a tavern.

There they were, Antonio and Jean-Pierre, hunched over mugs of Merlot, a near-empty bottle of grappa on the table between them. Heads together, dark against blond, their queues had long since given up and hair spilled over their shoulders. When Antonio went to pour, he missed his mug, and Jean-Pierre had to steady his hand.

Perhaps I blocked the light from the doorway, because something made Antonio turn. 'A vision!' He went to set his foot on the rung below his seat and missed.

He would have hit his chin on the table had Jean-Pierre not caught his arm. 'Ma chère. Join us.'

I gave them both my sternest look. 'We've been searching for you all night.'

Antonio frowned. 'All night?'

Jean-Pierre blinked. 'That cannot be.'

'We were toasting our mutual friend's career!' Antonio raised his mug, slurring. 'Archbishop Fausto!'

I'd never seen him this way before – drunk and bitter. Drunk and merry, perhaps. Drunk and loving, certainly. But Antonio is a man who will meet pain, reckon with it, and discard it. Not seek to numb it.

'To our Holy Mother Church,' Jean-Pierre added dryly, lifting his own cup. 'Will you drink with us?'

I did. A cup of Merlot. A shot of grappa that burned my throat. A second shot that set my head spinning. Antonio pulled me close, so hard I almost toppled sideways from my stool, saved by his solid warmth. He pressed his face into my neck, his stubble sharp against my skin. 'You always smell so good.'

He pressed a soft kiss against my jaw, then took another gulp of wine, swirling it in his mouth, swallowing with a wince. 'Jean-Pierre has it right. Let them fester in their own swamp.'

I looked at the Frenchman; he widened his eyes and took a swig of his own wine.

I searched Antonio's face. 'Can you live with that?'

His fingers circled the deeper of the scars on his wrists. I doubted he knew he'd done it.

Jean-Pierre placed a hand on Antonio's back. 'History will judge the Church, mon ami, even if we never read those pages.'

Antonio studied the contents of his mug, tipping the wine against the light. 'Jean-Pierre. Do you never tire of being the cleverest bastard in the room?'

Jean-Pierre took a sip of his own drink. 'It's all relative when you associate with mules.'

Silence, save for the creak of the tavern's beams. It bubbled from my chest, unstoppable, my giggle. Hard to tell who broke next, Antonio, I think. One more round of drinks and we swayed home.

This is my family now. This is my life.

Jean-Pierre is writing a book. Rafael buys and sells real estate. Enzo has set up his own legal practice. Marta has just signed the deed for a coffeehouse. As for Antonio and me – we have new business prospects through my connections in Barcelona: silk and chocolate to start. Oh, and Antonio's family in Genoa suddenly wants him back in the fold, now he's a man of means. How convenient.

How did that come about?

Uncle Alejo died; God rest him. With his passing, Ambrogio inherited, and finally settled the Albrono debt. He bestowed El Marqués – its buildings, land, past profits and revenue – upon Antonio. Through a non-heretical proxy, of course. The ever-faithful Enzo, with whom Antonio split the endowment. So, in a way, Fausto has made reparations. As he should.

Now, a year since we left Spain, as Antonio smiles at me from across the room, Rafael's lips touch my ear.

'We should discuss that annulment.'

I turn, startled. 'Why now?'

His eyes flick towards Antonio. 'Is this how you want to live? Stolen glances, secret smiles?'

A relief. For a moment I thought he knew. 'It's how *you* live.'

'But are you happy?' asks Rafael.

Antonio joins us, his fingertips brush my elbow. I press my hand beneath my ribs; feel the fluttering there.

Yes, I'm happy. So happy I could cry.

I assumed I'd been tired from arranging the wedding, sick from all those cake-tastings – thought that was why my breasts strained against my stays. It was Marta who pointed out the obvious.

This is going to be complicated. But we've been through too much together to falter in the face of such a gift.

'Sí. I'm happy.'

To withhold the truth is to lie.

How I've changed. I'll keep my secret for another day.

THE END

Afterword

This novel is a work of fiction, woven around the transcript of a Spanish Inquisition trial from 1756. When I first discovered the case over a decade ago, I was struck by its grotesque absurdity; a nobleman using a simple trick with dyed water to catch a thief, only to find himself on trial for heresy. My fascination deepened when I discovered the defendant belonged to a noble Genoan family. How did he come to be a penniless infantry soldier in Spain? And what was the 'debt' he'd come to Spain to seek?

Those are the elements around which I have constructed a story. The trial itself remains faithful to the historical record, though simplified for artistic purposes (the real case involved additional, similar charges). Everything else is fiction. For that reason, and so I might give free rein to my imagination, I have changed the names of the people involved.

Though infamous in popular culture, the Spanish Inquisition was, in reality, often mundane. It was more procedural than gothic, but in many ways that made it all the more monstrous. I have tried to reflect that in my story. The lack of defendant's rights, the traps hidden within the Articles of Faith, the brutal judgements (erring on the side of guilty to 'save souls') all challenge modern-day sensibilities. Lives were destroyed by intolerance, fear, opportunism, grudges and abused power.

The case and the novel are set in the middle of the eighteenth century, at the dawn of what we now call the 'Age of Reason.' This period, championed by great philosophers and scientists like

Voltaire and Newton, began to sweep away the intolerance and superstition that had held sway over citizen's lives for centuries. It gave rise to revolutionary ideas grounded in science, equality, and democracy while igniting fascinating tensions between tradition and progress, dogma and reason. Such arguments echo today. I found it impossible to weave this tale without touching on some of these tensions, though I have tried not to weigh the novel down with them.

The transcript of the trial was published, among others, in 1828 in the book *Records of the Spanish Inquisition, Translated from the Original Manuscripts*, by Samuel G. Goodrich in Boston. The history of how this record came to light is as fascinating as the case itself.

In 1820, a mob stormed the Palace of the Inquisition in Barcelona. Citizens broke into the Holy Office, freed prisoners, and looted property. Many documents were burned or scattered in the streets. But some, including this one, were preserved and smuggled out of Spain by reformists. The riot was part of a general uprising in Spain that sought to dismantle absolutism and led to the Liberal Triennium. Although its reforms were short-lived – Ferdinand VII regained absolute power in 1823 – the Inquisition never fully recovered, and was permanently abolished in 1834.

After its abolition, the records of the Inquisition were transferred to state archives and gradually became available to scholars. Release of documents has been sporadic, limited by the sheer volume of material and political hesitancy. For me, that makes the records that have been released all the more precious, and I hope my work of fiction affords proper respect to those people – largely forgotten – that were caught in the teeth of the machine.

www.ingramcontent.com/pod-product-compliance
Lightning Source LLC
Chambersburg PA
CBHW030516190726
48283CB00006B/1656
* 9 7 8 1 9 1 9 3 5 5 8 0 1 *